Lindsay Pedersen

ADVANCE PRAISE

I found myself nodding in agreement on page after page. Your business will benefit from the ideas in each chapter. Comprehensive and fun to read and use.

DAVID AAKER, THE "FATHER OF MODERN BRANDING," PROFESSOR OF MARKETING STRATEGY AT UC BERKELEY'S HAAS SCHOOL OF BUSINESS, AND AUTHOR OF 16 BOOKS ON BRANDING

If, as stated in this splendid book, "a brand strategy provides a unifying song sheet for business-wide harmony," then Lindsay is the ultimate music teacher. And like all the best teachers, she both educates and motivates. She'll have you humming the brand tune by chapter 6 and composing your own symphony by chapter 14. Open this book and feel the brand beat.

PAMELA DRESSLER, CEO OF CYPRESS GROVE CHEESE

I've had the pleasure of working with and learning from Lindsay Pedersen on numerous brand strategy projects. She possesses an encyclopedic knowledge of brand. What's more, she turns her seasoned, pedigreed expertise into something accessible and jargon-free for all of us. This book provides inspiration and a replicable method for any business, and is mandatory reading for leaders.

JEREMY KORST, CMO OF AVALARA

A savvy, pragmatic analysis of a topic usually convoluted with fancy creative speak or made inaccessible by theory. Leaders, read this book.

SUZANNE SENGLEMANN, FORMER CMO OF
ANGIE'S BOOMCHICKAPOP SNACKS

For anyone in a leadership role or even those newly entering the field of marketing, Forging an Ironclad Brand Strategy is a practical guide to the tried-and-true, proven brand and marketing strategies for long-term business success. Whether this book serves as a reminder or as first on-ramp, readers will find a brief and compelling compilation of clear frameworks, case studies and personal experiences to accelerate their knowledge and find success in their daily pursuits as a leader.

BRADY BREWER, SENIOR VICE PRESIDENT,
STARBUCKS COFFEE COMPANY

Rather than complicate brand, Pedersen provides an unintimidating approach to this essential tool. Marketers and leaders—do yourself a favor. Read this book and put it to use today.

MATT OPPENHEIMER, CEO OF REMITLY

Lindsay Pedersen's approach is as disruptive to conventional notions of brand as the design thinking revolution has been for companies who used to develop entire product lines without bothering to let people evaluate them early and often. Both startups and big companies can clarify their mission and purpose from the process she outlines. You will quickly have "reasons to believe" an ironclad brand is not some nice-to-have—but is central to your company's soul.

MATT SHOBE, CO-FOUNDER AND CHIEF
UX OFFICER AT MIGHTY AI

An authentic and insightful read that offers new, inspirational ideas for unleashing the elusive yet mystical power of brand. A MUST read for any modern-day business builder seeking to transcend the transactional to the deeply personal. This book should be at the top of any list!

JONATHAN ZABUSKY, FORMER CEO OF SEAMLESS

Lindsay is the best at what she does. And in this book, she shows us all how. The practical guidance in this book will yield immeasurable results for your business. Read it now!

CLAYTON LEWIS, CEO OF ARIVALE

The mystery of building a great brand is mysterious no more: Lindsay Pedersen will shine light on why brand matters, excite you about its power and lead you step-by-step to uncovering and cultivating your unique brand strategy. Leaders of all disciplines need to read this book.

ROBERT NEER, DIRECTOR OF PRODUCT
MANAGEMENT OF BEST BUY

Regardless of how good at branding you think you are, this book will help you focus on what matters most: the thing you uniquely bring. In the process, this makes your teams feel more meaning and investors see better returns. Substantive and practical, this will become the brand bible you'll refer to again and again. Smart brand strategists should buy one for EVERYONE on their team.

JONATHAN SPOSATO, SERIAL CEO, ANGEL INVESTOR
AND AUTHOR OF *BETTER TOGETHER*

If you are looking for a practical and insightful guide for defining your brand and bringing it to life, you should buy a copy of this book. Or buy several and give them to everyone on your team.

TIM CALKINS, PROFESSOR OF MARKETING AT THE KELLOGG
SCHOOL OF MANAGEMENT, CO-AUTHOR OF *KELLOGG ON
BRANDING* AND AUTHOR OF *HOW TO WASH A CHICKEN*

Lindsay's analytical approach is grounded in a general manager's experience, and it was invaluable for our business. This book is true Lindsay—smart, practical, awesome. Part manifesto on the power of brand and part operating manual, it's the only book on brand worth reading, and you will be so glad you did.

LEIGH MCMILLAN, GENERAL MANAGER
CONSUMER BUSINESS AT WHITE PAGES

If you think brand is fluffy, then you haven't met Lindsay Pedersen. Lindsay shows how solid brand strategy IS solid business strategy. If you're looking for how to increase the value of your organization, you've found your playbook.

STEWART MEYER, CMO OF KUOW

Forging an Ironclad Brand decodes the relationship between customers and products, enabling leaders to set a product vision beyond the functional. A must-read.

AARON WOODMAN, GENERAL MANAGER OF
MICROSOFT WINDOWS MARKETING

Forging an Ironclad Brand is a book you will turn to again and again, whether you are a business leader trying to grasp brand or a marketer building one every day. A great tool for helping people and organizations really understand the power and nature of everything that comprises a great brand.

HALLE HUTCHESON, VP OF MARKETING FOR ROVER

If you find yourself wondering what "brand" means, and if you think it's about fonts, photography and logos, please do your shareholders and career a favor and read this book. Lindsay masterfully breaks down what a brand means, how you can build a great one and how it is central, not peripheral, to the success of your business.

HEIDI DOROSIN, CMO OF MADISON REED

Lindsay Pedersen is a true "brand whisperer." In the Ironclad Method, she's created an actionable course on brand strategy at its most hard hitting. This book is a must-read for startup founders and corporate leaders alike.

KIRBY WINFIELD, SERIAL CEO AND ANGEL INVESTOR

With the rapid pace of change in the world of marketing, just keep calm and read Forging an Ironclad Brand. Lindsay makes the complex simple to such a degree that practitioners and non-practitioners can align on the business's most valuable asset—its brand.

MATT CRUM, VP MARKETING & SALES FOR MEYENBERG
AND REDWOOD HILL FARM & CREAMERY

In today's world of commerce where just about everyone is bombarded daily with a pitch for this and a pitch for that, the question is, how do you make your offering stand out as something truly different and unique?

And now in Forging an Ironclad Brand we have the definitive answer, given to us by Lindsay Pedersen, a seasoned practitioner and deeply immersed student of the concept and strategy of branding.

She takes us way beyond the usual basics and tells us not only how brand works at a psychological level but also why it is so critical to business success today.

Using countless examples and providing numerous practical tools and frameworks—all conveyed in a writing style that exudes both clarity and engagement—Pedersen walks the reader through the underlying logic of branding and how to implement this tool for your own organization.

In short, Pedersen has crafted the one and only guidebook you will need to understand and leverage the concept and power of a brand. The book is a joy to read, and it deserves a commanding spot on your bookshelf.

PAUL TIFFANY, PROFESSOR OF STRATEGY AT UC
BERKELEY HAAS SCHOOL OF BUSINESS

FORGING AN IRONCLAD BRAND

FORGING AN IRONCLAD BRAND

A LEADER'S GUIDE

LINDSAY PEDERSEN

LIONCREST
PUBLISHING

FORGING AN IRONCLAD BRAND: A LEADER'S GUIDE

ISBN   978-1-5445-1386-7 *Hardcover*
       978-1-5445-1384-3 *Ebook*

For Luke and Kate

You have taught me more than I could ever teach you.
I love you to the moon and back.

CONTENTS

FOREWORD

I've been involved in marketing for thirty-seven years and have seen a lot of change during my career. And one of the most striking changes is that our access to information has exploded. It has never been easier to communicate with buyers and consumers than it is right now. Everyone has a blog, a Facebook, an Instagram, a Twitter account, a YouTube channel—and on top of all these new marketing vehicles (and there are hundreds of them), we still make use of the old classics like print and broadcast.

In other words, we marketers are *communicating* like champs. But here's the bigger question: are we *persuading*? When all is said and done, we have to reach the customer in a way that makes him or her say, "Yes, I see why I should buy this brand out of all the others. This is the brand that will solve my problem."

The famous expression by Edward Hallett Carr comes to mind: *Change is certain. Progress is not.* All the new marketing vehicles that have risen up over the past few decades have created an incredible number of options for sending messages to customers. This is a blessing but also a curse. For one thing, it's easier than ever for marketers to confuse activity with progress. Also, not only are our own messages being fragmented, they have to compete with all the other fragmented messages from all our competitors for the customer's attention.

This barrage of fragmented information overwhelms our customers. So does the sheer number of choices they have to choose from. To break through this wall of noise and confusion—to make your brand "pop" in a way that gets noticed and that persuades the customer to trust your brand—is harder than it has ever been. Much harder.

Even huge, well-established brands are feeling the pressure. They know that they have to evolve alongside their customers. People talk about the death of big traditional brands, but I believe this is an exaggerated fear. We can continue to reinvent these brands. As long as the fundamentals are in place, they still resonate with people.

Clorox Company, where I served as CEO and worked with this book's author, Lindsay Pedersen, a few years back, is a good example. Clorox bleach has been around 105 years. It had a 65 percent share of the market ten years ago, and it has a 65 percent share today. But it's now using probably 40 percent of its marketing budget on digital. That didn't even exist ten years ago.

But how you reach people, determining the right mix of media, is only part of the story. You must be able to get outside yourself and continually think about how to persuade today's customer. That means constantly gaining insights into how people are now, how they live, what they know, and how they look at problems.

One thing I saw when I was with Clorox was that Millennials

were just not aware of all the things bleach does. Their mothers and grandmothers are aware of the disinfecting properties of bleach—of its use outside of the laundry room—but Millennials were not. So, we created a new advertising campaign with lots of humor in it; ads that featured small children being potty trained or a toddler sneezing all over a bystander's sleeve. You see, the problems Clorox solves haven't really changed. What *has* changed is how we communicate with a whole new audience to convince them it's the right product to solve these problems.

Navigating all these factors—choosing the best marketing mix among endless choices, staying on top of changes in consumer behavior, understanding what persuades today's audiences—to create and sustain a great brand over time is no easy task. It requires the right balance of creativity and discipline—concepts which on the surface may seem like opposites but are actually intertwined and mutually dependent on each other.

That's what I think is so powerful about this book, *Forging an Ironclad Brand*. Lindsay has provided a "one stop shop" for all brand builders that beautifully illustrates how creativity and discipline work together. And here is the other crucial point that is inherent in her message: marketing is a team sport.

Once in a marketing meeting at Clorox I said, "You know, marketing is too important to be left to the marketers." I truly believed it then, and I believe it now. And I think Lindsay's book supports this point of view. When she talks about the three big moments of truth with a target customer—**desire, decide,** and **delight**—she alludes to all the different roles that go into creating a brand, from the product itself, to the packaging, to the price, to the advertising, to the person-to-person interaction with the clerk in the retail store.

Take "decide" for instance. The marketing department doesn't own "decide." After all, before a consumer can decide on your products, you've got to get the right assortment to the store, the right prices, the right shelf position, the right promotions. The marketing department sitting at headquarters doesn't make these things happen. The sales organization does.

In other words, we need to make sure everyone truly understands the fundamentals of marketing. This book can help that happen. Leaders in every department should read and absorb its principles: the salespeople, the R&D people, the finance people—anyone and everyone who touches the ability of a brand to resonate with consumers. When the whole company is aligned and working toward the same marketing goals it's far more likely to create demand for its brand.

Marketing is a complex job. It's an important job. And when you approach it in a disciplined way, it's a richly rewarding job. And here's the main point I've been trying to get to—it's everybody's job. The more people who understand this, the better. When leaders and employees at every level take responsibility for the role of marketing, your organization will thrive.

Don Knauss
Former CEO of The Clorox Company, and Board Director at McKesson Corporation
Sugar Land, Texas
November 2018

WHY READ THIS BOOK?

Ask yourself these questions:

- Do you lead a business?
- Do you yearn to create something truly different and truly enduring?
- Do you ever say that your customer is "everybody"?
- Do you have trouble galvanizing employees to a common purpose?
- Do you believe that you have the best product, but getting others to discover it is the problem?
- Do you want to create value not just today, but to still be creating value in the years and decades to come?
- Do you get caught up in chasing flavor-of-the-day ideas?
- Do you assume that "brand" belongs in marketing?
- Do you recognize that brand positioning is important, but feel overwhelmed or intimidated or turned off by its fuzziness?

- Do you sometimes feel the efforts of your leadership team and employees are spread thin?
- Do you feel drawn to storytellers?

If you answered "yes" to even one of these questions, then this book is for you.

CHAPTER 1

WHAT THE HECK IS BRAND?

The word "brand" is used broadly, disparately, and confusingly. Let's reclaim it.

What the heck is brand?

Good question.

During my years as a classically-trained consumer packaged goods marketer at Clorox, I assumed everyone understood the answer as I do. I know brand to be the crux of commerce itself, the value your business brings that gives it the right to exist. Brand formulates the most direct route for a business to create, sustain, and scale value. Good brand is good business.

It turns out, though, that my reverence of brand is unusual, even among formidably savvy business leaders. The disconnect stems from the mistaken belief that brand is squishy, elusive, and superficial. And if there is a person who dislikes squishy, it is a business leader.

So, brand gets dismissed. It is handed to a talented graphic designer, or outsourced wholesale to a capable agency, or tucked tidily away inside a marketing department.

But listen up: underappreciating brand leads to your business suffering. It results in lost investment, revenue, employee engagement, focus, scalability, and purpose. Brand establishes the conditions to thrive. Dismissing brand results in a barren business, inhospitable for your customers, your employees, and all of us who benefit from knowing and experiencing the value you bring.

So, that's the question behind the question of what is brand: what does brand do for my business? You can employ brand as your most important leadership tool by understanding the depth and breadth of brand's layers—each of which I will explore in this chapter:

- Brand Is What You Stand For
- Brand Is a Relationship
- Brand Is Your Promise and Your Fulfilment of That Promise
- Brand Is a Filter
- Brand Strategy Is the Deliberate Articulation of Your Business's Meaning
- Brand Fuels Differentiation
- Brand Is Your North Star

When I was a Clorox brand manager, I was responsible for the P&L. I was the CEO of my individual businesses, from Clorox Bleach to Armor All to Hidden Valley Ranch. I was on the hook for growing a healthy business—period. I managed relationships with manufacturers and retailers. I fine-tuned our sourcing and supply chain. I built a diverse, robust innovation pipeline. I drove demand through advertising and promotional tactics. My North Star for all of this leadership was our uncommon value to the customer, articulated unambiguously in our brand strategy. This brand-strategy-as-North-Star was my most essential tool for growing a thriving business.

The view of brand as a business leader's North Star is so fundamental in the world of consumer packaged goods that I was puzzled when I left that realm and learned that this definition of brand was far from universally understood. What's more: brand is equally as vital for companies outside consumer packaged goods.

Using my Clorox training, my MBA, and my fascination with leadership and behavioral economics, I founded a brand strategy consulting business. I left the Bay Area for Seattle—a tech hub, rather than a consumer packaged goods town. My career in brand building led people to wildly differing conceptions. When I shared that I was a brand strategist, I heard, "Oh, so you do logos!" I adore design, but believe me, I'm the last person you'd want to create your logo. "No," I would reply. "I most certainly don't do logos. I do brand strategy."

It didn't stop there. "Brand—oh yeah, TV advertising is fun," or "Yup, we've got a brand—it's the name of our company." In more recent years, I've heard, "Oh, so like personal branding on social media!" and "We don't do brand because we market with SEO." It was bewildering. Some professionals I came across did make full use of brand. At larger consumer companies like Starbucks and T-Mobile, leaders—who often had also begun their careers in consumer packaged goods—used brand as the North Star. But I personally yearned to help leaders and entrepreneurs who most needed the focus a brand strategy provides, and these were the very people most likely to misunderstand—and underestimate—brand.

Ultimately, I understood the reality, which is that the word brand takes people to different places. There are reams of interpretations of this word.

The tricky thing is that everyone is correct—to a degree. All of those definitions are part of brand. Logo is part of brand. TV and social media are parts of brand. Naming is part of brand. So are your product, your customer experience, and your SEO tactics. So are your font, your tagline, your business's personality, and the color of your employee uniforms. But none of those are, by themselves, brand.

Brand is the interconnected web of what our business means and how we deliver that meaning, all made possible by our special position in our customer's universe.

Once, I heard Malcolm Gladwell share on Debbie Millman's Design Matters podcast that the word brand reminded him of the word Africa. I yelled at my phone, "Yes!" If you are discussing the townships near Johannesburg, or the Maasai tribe outside Nairobi, or the camels in Morocco, or the fighting in Qatar, or the beaches of Mauritius, or even the geological land mass of the African continent—you are pointing out aspects of Africa but not Africa. When one person says "Africa," this person might mean Egypt when the listener might be picturing Ghana. What a confusing conversation that would be.

The subject of brand evokes this same misinterpretation and resulting confusion. We all use this one word as though everyone else's understanding of it is the same as ours, but chances are it's not. And most of us do not consider brand in its entirety and, therefore, lose its potency. Someone says, "brand is dying," because they define brand as traditional TV advertising, which indeed is declining. The listener is thinking of brand as the character and soul of a business, and they think, "Brand is certainly not dying. What a strange thing to say."

Here's why this matters: there are massive consequences to dismissing brand. To conflate brand with one of its many manifestations is to miss its power.

Brand reflects and taps into the human experience. It connects the business to the customer in a human-to-human way. Using brand gives your business a doorway into your customer's world. Done well, it forms your scalable and enduring competitive advantage.

So, do not confuse brand with one of its aspects and conclude that brand is squishy, elusive, or superficial and therefore not worthwhile. By not using brand, you forego the most elemental tool for guiding your business. You make it more difficult for your customer to engage with you and less likely that your business will thrive.

Good brand really is just good business.

What is a "good brand"? A good brand is one that unleashes your competitive advantage. I call this an "ironclad brand." To define your ironclad brand, I formulated a method that harnesses classic marketing frameworks and then hones them into steps to an optimal brand.

At the end of this process, you have an ironclad brand strategy to serve as your North Star. I wrote this book to share with you this method and the ways the resulting ironclad brand strategy can create value for your business.

In writing this book, I interviewed business leaders and brand experts to shed light on the importance of brand from a variety of perspectives. Regardless of your industry, brand can be your tool for creating value. The rest of this book will show you how.

Now let's examine brand from the different angles I mentioned earlier, so you can fully grasp what it is and how it fuels your business.

BRAND IS WHAT YOU STAND FOR

A brand is what you mean to your customer. It is the place you occupy in your customer's mind.

Everything you do as a business either reinforces your meaning, solidifying and growing its place in your customer's mind—or it weakens that meaning, blurring its place in your customer's mind. If your business sells shoes that enable customers to run fast, then everything you do either reinforces or blurs your meaning of fast shoes. If your business is hospital software that streamlines patient check-in, then everything you do either reinforces or blurs your meaning of streamlined check-in. When your brand is clear, solid, and unambiguous, your customer better understands your exclusive value and meaning.

Why is it important to mean something? We humans are meaning-seeking machines. We crave it, we want it, we need it, on all levels, from practical to existential. From customers to employees to stakeholders, we are all looking for meaning throughout our experiences. "She winked at me; what does that mean?" "My direct report left for another job; what does that mean?" Discerning meaning is part of what makes us human. It's why we have religion and philosophy. It is why some political leaders resonate more than others. It's why we do volunteer work or write books or create art. When a person or a business boldly stands for a chosen meaning, the rest of us are more likely to see and embrace that meaning.

Kellogg School Marketing Professor and co-author of the classic *Kellogg On Branding*, Tim Calkins, agreed with me in a recent conversation. He shared, "A brand is your distinct meaning, and it brings with it all sorts of different connotations. So, ask yourself as a leader, 'How are we going to end up with the brand that we really want to have?'"

BRAND IS A RELATIONSHIP

Brand is the relationship between your business and your customer.

Whether you are a deep-pocketed business or one with zero budget, whether your audience is mass or niche, whether you sell to businesses or consumers—all of us have a relationship with our customer. We humans are a hyper-social species, hardwired to have relationships with the people, animals, businesses, and things with which we interact. (Some people even name their cars.) And today, most businesses are serving customers who have access to a growing voice and a growing set of alternative dance partners.

Brands have always been in this relationship, this dance. Millennia ago, before the appearance of today's brand regalia, businesses had relationships with their customers. For example, the pre-industrial-age, small-town butcher made a promise and faithfully fulfilled that promise time and time again, which made his relationship with his customer ever more meaningful for both.

Today, with the web and social media and the countless ways customers can communicate with a business, it is even more important that businesses deliver value to customers. There was a time when the business with the most spending power had the loudest megaphone and, therefore, the most powerful brand. Now, the customer has a megaphone, too. and once again carries clout in the relationship. The feedback loop demands a mutually-fulfilling relationship. Businesses must carefully make distinctive promises and deliver on them faithfully.

Compounding this rebalancing of clout between business and customer, the web's platforms have democratized the megaphone so that businesses with small budgets can initiate and fuel conversations as well. Dollar Shave Club produced its launch promo video on a shoestring ($4,500), posted it on YouTube, and created a business so valuable that monolithic Unilever purchased it in 2016 for $1 billion. All businesses now can access the megaphone with their particular audiences, so all businesses now can say what they stand for, and thus relate directly to their customer. It increasingly behooves all of us to have clarity on our own distinctive meaning as a business so that we can activate that meaning with vigor and message it with laser focus.

BRAND IS YOUR PROMISE AND YOUR FULFILMENT OF THAT PROMISE

When a brand has integrity, its promise is true. The business makes a promise and delivers on that promise. It is not merely what you say you do—it is what you actually do, how you do it, and why.

Don Knauss, a brand-building giant who was previously CEO of Clorox and head of North American operations for Coke, told me:

"A brand is a promise of performance. Any transaction between two parties requires a promise of performance. To sustain your business over time, you've got to, first, be very focused on defining your promise of performance and, second, be diligent about delivering consistently. If you can't do these two things, you are not a sustainable business."

These are your foremost decisions as a leader, so approach them with care. What do you promise? Do you promise to deliver a scrumptious-tasting dinner? Do you promise to make a company's internal communication more fun? Do you promise to eliminate a software system's downtime? Do you promise to bring a busy single parent an afternoon of rejuvenation? Do you promise to help an outdoorsy family find a safe hike? Do you promise to make a home-buying experience more enjoyable?

Brand strategy is stepping back to distill the value you promise and deliver. When you define it with precision, brand sets your meaning into sharp relief, helping customers see you and relate to you and organize you in their heads exactly the way you hope they will. As Don Knauss urges, "If you are in commerce, you need a brand strategy."

BRAND IS A FILTER

A brand captures and guides our attention. It serves as a filter for customers as they perceive your business, shaping how they see you and believe you. We humans need these filters. When faced with too much information, we use cognitive shortcuts as filters to tame sensory overload.

Behavioral economics has demonstrated and codified many

of these mental shortcuts in recent decades. For example, the *availability bias* is a cognitive shortcut that leads people to make decisions based on the information most easily accessible in a given moment. The availability bias explains why we fear sharks more than we fear cows or vending machines. While the media ensure we know about every shark attack, we seldom hear about deaths caused by cows or vending machines, even though both are statistically more dangerous than are sharks.

Another cognitive shortcut we use as a filter is the *confirmation bias*, in which we seek and interpret new data that confirms our existing beliefs and theories. When interviewing a job candidate whom we have pre-judged as highly capable, we privilege inputs that confirm that judgment, and ignore inputs that suggest otherwise. A reporter writing an article on a controversial issue may unconsciously elevate the perspectives of experts that support his preconceived conclusion. I promptly notice when my fiery, mischievous son teases his more serene younger sister, but I miss it altogether when she picks on him.

Humans are hardwired to simplify—even if it means erroneously oversimplifying. We see only what we deem relevant. We use these cognitive shortcuts not because we are unintelligent or bad people, but because we need them. These shortcuts conserve cognitive resources. Oversimplifying may be erroneous, but it once equipped us to survive in the wild.

A brand is a filter too, one that when authentic helps both the customer and the business. A brand can help a customer to see your business effortlessly. Brand ties your business to something already in your customer's head, making it easier for the person to engage with your business. Brand creates a similar neural pathway leading the customer to choose your business with ease.

Brand also serves as a filter for leaders and employees, bringing clarity to the choices you face as you build your business. It pulls a company together internally around the same vision. "Does this idea help me to become better at delivering my brand promise to my target customer? If no, then discard. If yes, then proceed." You, too, are prone to cognitive fallacies like the availability bias and the confirmation bias, as your mental bandwidth is scarce, too. Brand can filter so that you focus on what matters most.

BRAND STRATEGY IS THE DELIBERATE ARTICULATION OF YOUR BUSINESS'S MEANING

While brand is the meaning you stand for inside your customer's mind, your brand strategy is the deliberate articulation of that meaning. Brand strategy distills your promise so you can make choices across your business to carry out that promise. Brand strategy answers the questions: What kind of business are we, and what kind of business do we want to be? What do we want to mean to customers? Tarang Amin, CEO of e.l.f. Cosmetics, echoed my thoughts when he told me, "Brand strategy is a tool that guides the choices you make and the priorities you set to reinforce what you mean in your customer's mind."

By distilling what you stand for, you give yourself a tool to guide the choices you make to grow the business you want. Brand strategy is about getting to self-knowledge. It's about defining your business as its best possible self, so that it can become *more* of that—more of its most intentional, most purposeful self.

When you reflect on your life, you might ask, what kind of a person am I, and what kind of person do I want to be? Do I want to take risks and embrace adventure, or exercise prudence and caution? Do I take pride in being direct, or in being tactful? Do I favor alone time, or social time? Do I live a quietly expressive life, or a loud one? Do I stay within the lines most of the time, or am I someone who breaks rules? The outcomes of these choices define the way we show up, the friends we attract, and the meaning we stand for.

Defining your brand is similar. It is applying self-reflection to your business. What kind of business is this? What kind of business do you want it to be? Carolyn Feinstein, CMO of Dropbox, agreed. "Brand strategy is: what are we at our core? What is it that we want to be to the world? Why do we exist beyond the products that we build?" The act of defining who you are itself creates meaning for you in the work you do, and as significantly, for your employees who cannot read your mind, and who crave direction and purpose.

It's useful to have one single brand idea internally and externally, from employees to customers, from front-line workers to senior leadership, because then the meaning reverberates and harmonizes. All your musicians play in concert. A brand strategy provides a unifying song sheet to facilitate business-wide harmony.

One of my favorite brands is Volvo, because Volvo's articulation of "safety" is clear, bold, and unambiguous. No matter where in the world I go, when I say "Volvo," people complete the thought with "is safe." Volvo has stood for safety—has used safety as its unifying song sheet—since the company's roots in 1920s Sweden. Everything Volvo does reinforces "safety." Volvo's head of brand, Sven Desmet, told me that brand strategy "is how I tell employees and customers what I stand for."

Volvo is safe all the way to its fibers. Every product detail, every customer touchpoint, every aspect of corporate culture stems from the ideal of "safety." Volvo's engineers build everything for the sake of optimizing safety. The shape of the car is boxy, which both looks safe and is safe structurally. The car itself feels firm and safe to drivers. It does not accelerate as would a sports car. Volvo has elected not to take patents on many innovative safety features, including the three-point seatbelt that they pioneered and is now standard on all cars. Volvo dealerships are upscale but not flashy. There are play rooms for customers' kids. Salespeople dress conservatively but casually and are trained to discuss safety features. The buying experience is nurturing. When recruiting, Volvo seeks people to join the company who resonate with the safety intent.

All these things, big and small, coalesce to fortify safety. The customer's entire experience of Volvo adds up to a car that is safe to drive. It is an orchestra of musicians all performing a single song in perfect harmony.

Consider the contrast between Volvo and another excellent car brand: BMW. While Volvo stands for safety, BMW stands for driving performance—it is the "Ultimate Driving Machine." I know that not only because of what they say, but also because of what they do and how they do it.

BMW engineers craft a car with responsive acceleration that enables you to drive fast and feel like you are driving fast. The exterior is high-design beautiful: glossy and aerodynamic. The interior focuses on the driver's ability to enjoy the road. There are no coffee cup holders on the driver's side in many models. A dealer once told me as I searched in vain for a place to put my coffee cup while test-driving a BMW, "Coffee is for passengers, not drivers." There are no play rooms at the BMW dealership because BMW is focused on the driver, not on the driver's family. The customer's entire experience is the single song of driving performance, reverberating in harmony.

The power of brand strategy is this singularity, this laser-sharp deliberateness. When you make the concerted effort to define your distinctive meaning through a brand strategy, you approach the question of who you are with intention. Pinpoint your meaning, your particular reason for existing, your distinctive song, and then play it in concert. Volvo's song is safety. BMW's song is driving performance. Etsy's song is celebrating the soulful artisan. Salesforce's song is intuitive sales enablement. Slack's song is team collaboration that is both effective and fun. Nike's song is shoes that win the race. Nordstrom's song is phenomenal customer service. By approaching the development of their brand strategy with humility and empathy, these brands identify a song their audience deeply wants to hear—and that only their business can play.

BRAND FUELS DIFFERENTIATION

Consumer-packaged-goods leaders, such as those at Clorox, Proctor & Gamble, General Mills, and Nestle have been using the power of brand for decades because they have to. Consumer-packaged-goods companies are bastions of excellent brand building because the largely-undifferentiated products force brand excellence. When your products are pretty much the same as those of your competitors, you better have an outstanding brand.

Brand works in these unforgiving, product parity conditions. Take a look at the economics of the Clorox Bleach business: a bottle of Clorox Bleach contains essentially the same bleach as store-brand bleach—6% sodium hypochlorite, 94% water. But the consumer price of Clorox Bleach is often double that of store-brand bleach, and Clorox Bleach still wins 65% market share of the bleach category.

That's because the Clorox brand stands for something different from the others, something that resonates and motivates the target customer. Most bleach customers are willing to pay the price premium because they receive more value from Clorox than from the alternatives. Clorox stands for feeling like a good, competent, loving parent. The target customer values this, and Clorox can deliver this.

So, we filtered our choices on which bets to place based on this question: will this initiative / tactic / partnership / innovation enhance our ability to make our customer feel like a great parent? If yes, pursue. If not, find something else to pursue. We at Clorox needed a hard-working brand strategy to thrive in the parity product categories in which we served. Despite a parity product, our brand dominated the market in both sales and profit margin.

BRAND IS YOUR NORTH STAR

Working in the fertile brand-building environment of Clorox, I learned the value-creation power of brand. Now that I have spent over a decade building brand-driven growth strategies for businesses in numerous industries, I am continually astonished to learn that most leaders ignore brand. They use brute force to try to grow, eschewing the power of focus and empathy, foregoing insight about human nature to attract customers.

When every element of your business is aligned around a

single brand strategy, you leverage human nature to work for you, and all parts of your business work in concert. This creates a compounding loop of goodness for customers, employees, and investors. Operating this way simply makes growth easier and more gratifying.

Successful brand strategies are not squishy, elusive, or superficial. They are logical, proven, and always ready to guide you. When you create a brand strategy deliberately and carefully, you define the business's North Star that will clearly guide every decision you make and every decision your team makes. Brand forms your most durable competitive advantage. It lights your way to creating purpose, value, and scale.

In this book, I share with you the what, why, and how of an ironclad brand strategy.

- Chapters 2–4 demonstrate the "why" of brand. In these chapters, I present to you my case for making brand your essential leadership tool.
- Chapter 5 untangles the components of brand and debunks the brand myths that you no longer need to fall for.
- Chapter 6 defines the criteria for an ironclad brand strategy—the qualities that together enable your business to punch above its weight.
- Chapters 7–14 spells out my step-by-step Ironclad Method for building your ironclad brand strategy. I pull back the curtain and share how I approach building a brand for my clients.
- Chapters 15–17 explore the ways to implement and amplify your brand with everything that you do.

Now let's dig in.

CHAPTER 2

CREATE VALUE NOW

We just identified brand as the meaning your business stands for, and brand strategy as the deliberate articulation of that meaning. In this chapter, we explore the first reason why you should use brand—to create value now. In the following two chapters, we will zoom out to see brand's ability to create value in the longer term as well.

A worthy business is one that creates value for customers, employees, and owners. The value you bring your customer translates to value for the rest of your business's stakeholders. Brand is the articulation of that value. It identifies why customers should part with their hard-earned money in exchange for your offering. As Tarang Amin, the CEO of e.l.f. Cosmetics whom we met in the previous chapter, says, "the biggest driver of value creation is brand."

Brand creates near-term value for a business at every point on the P&L. By increasing customers' willingness to pay, brand elevates your pricing power, which propels margin and profit. Brand commands attention, engaging and motivating more customers to buy more of your offering. By doing so, brand increases sales revenue. Because brand enables your product and messaging to nail a precise need, your resource allocation and spending can be precise, improving your return on investment (ROI). Uncommonly delighting customers by solving their deep need fosters loyalty and accrues high customer lifetime value (CLV). Competitors cannot truly copy a distinctive brand, so brand insulates your business from downward price pressure and commoditization. Brand also enables you to attract and retain superb employees who, inspired by your purpose, will give their best.

A business's balance sheet reflects brand's effect on value creation. A recent study found that 87 percent of business value among the S&P 500 is intangible value, including brand equity. Another study valued S&P 500 companies' intangible assets at 74 percent, with brand comprising 20 percent of that.

Nestle's acquisition of Blue Bottle Coffee in 2017 reveals brand's sizable influence on valuation. At the time of purchase, Nestle valued the forty-store Oakland, California, coffee company at $700 million and paid $500 million to become its majority stakeholder. Most of that jaw-dropping value Nestle purchased is intangible value; most of that value stems from brand. This monolithic international corporation does not buy a small, local chain like Blue Bottle for its hard assets, of which Nestle has plenty. By owning Blue Bottle, Nestle now owns all the feelings associated with a local joint that is perceived as hip, friendly, and caring. Nestle owns something they could not have copied—the Blue Bottle brand and its loyal customers. This is not merely sentimental value—it is dollars-and-cents value.

This chapter shows how brand creates immediate value in these ways. Brands:

- Elevate Pricing Power
- Command Attention and Make It Easy to Choose
- Create Mental File Folders to Reduce Effort
- Create a Mental File Folder in a New Category
- Enable the Optimally Distinct Sweet Spot
- Foster Loyalty
- Dig a Moat

Let's address these aspects one by one.

ELEVATE PRICING POWER

Your pricing power reflects the value that you bring to customers. It reveals how much customers want what you offer. Customers' willingness to pay gives you pricing power. If you do not offer value, your customers will tell you with their inaction that your offering lacks the right to exist—and they will be correct.

By delivering customer value, you earn pricing power, which your business needs in order to thrive. "The single most important decision in evaluating a business is pricing power," Warren Buffett has said. "If you've got the power to raise prices without losing business to a competitor, you've got a very good business. And if you have to have a prayer session before raising the price by 10 percent, then you've got a terrible business."

The customer receives value when the benefit she enjoys exceeds the price she paid. Consider this math:

Customer Value = Benefit - Price

From this equation, we see that there are two sources of high customer value: big benefit and small price. Only the first of those brings value to your customer *and* to you. When your benefit is big, your customer's willingness to pay is also big, allowing you to enjoy robust margins. While you could bring value to the customer by charging a low price, this erodes your business's value. Unless you enjoy the lowest cost structure in your category (e.g., Amazon), then you cannot sustainably bring value via low price. In order to create value, most of us must bring a sizable benefit.

For your brand to thrive, you need to help your customers thrive, which helps your business thrive. Brand is a relationship within which the support and benefit are mutually reinforcing. Customers thrive because your business's big benefit solves a big need, bringing them closer to the lives they want to live. Your business thrives because your big benefit enables you to charge enough to fuel a profitable business and grow it as you wish. A big benefit is what constitutes value for your customer and for you.

Increase your business's value by increasing its value to customers, the people you are asking to give you money. How do you know how to increase the value you bring to your customers? Listen to them and deliver to them a big benefit that no one else delivers. Zappos delivers the big benefit of on-demand shopping with stellar customer service. Lego delivers the big benefit of stimulating and fun spatial toys. Ikea offers the big benefit of affordable, cleanly designed housewares.

Define this big benefit through your brand strategy, the North Star that helps you ever increase the value you bring. It enables your business to consistently gratify your target customer so that more of them buy more of your things at a higher price.

Strong brands capture better margins than do weak brands, because preferred brands by definition confer higher customer willingness to pay. In a recent study, strong brands on average commanded a 13 percent price premium over weak brands. Look to your own purchase behavior. When you love a brand, aren't you willing to pay more for it than you would for an alternative brand?

Matt Oppenheimer, CEO of financial technology company Remitly, told me, "A unique and meaningful brand promise that you truly deliver on gets you beyond the functional reasons a customer buys from you, such as price or speed. It transcends that functional benefit to something greater, more valuable. It gets you away from a race to the bottom on price so that you can stand for this bigger, more meaningful thing. And that creates preference, and it creates loyalty."

And as venture capitalist Jason Stoffer suggests: "Go to an Apple store and then go to a Microsoft store. You will see for yourself that one has higher value per square foot. One brand is emotionally resonant, the other isn't. Go to a Nike store and then go to the shoe department at Kohl's. Tell me why Nike is selling their shoes for more."

COMMAND ATTENTION AND MAKE IT EASY TO CHOOSE

A differentiated and customer-meaningful brand strategy helps you break through to get and hold the attention of your customer, building awareness, loyalty, and meaning.

A customer can only engage with your business when she

knows that it exists. By harnessing customers' attention, brands make it easier for customers to see, want, and buy your offering.

Consider the infinite stimuli competing for your customers' attention. To break through and secure a place in their minds—and their wallets—you need to make it easy for them to notice you. The solution is not to shout the most loudly—most lack the marketing budget to shout loudly enough. The solution instead is bracing clarity. Be crystal clear about what your business is and why that matters to customers.

There is a storefront near my office that failed to get my attention. From the window photos featuring women clad in fleece tunics, combined with the exterior sign indicating a vague and new-age-y name with an equally obscure tagline, I had assumed that this business sold crystals and incense. Then one day I learned, to my surprise, that this store was a Pilates studio.

I practice Pilates. And I frequent this neighborhood. I imagine that I am smack in the middle of this business's target customer profile. But this Pilates studio failed to make their business easy for me to see, so I did not see it. They did not capture my attention by making it relevant to me. I did not become a customer because they did not make it easy for me to do so.

Brand's role is to ease and motivate potential customers to see, buy, and become loyal. This is both practical and aspirational. Sometimes business leaders are so excited about the aspirational part that they forget that before someone becomes loyal to a business, she needs to know that the business exists. The UK's Aviva produced a £9 million aspirational TV ad in 2008 featuring Bruce Willis and Elle Macpherson, and almost forgot to mention what Aviva even is—an insurance company. We can only understand what our brains will let in.

Jeremy Korst, previously CMO for B2B software company Avalara and General Manager for Microsoft Windows Marketing, told me that he thinks of brand as this pragmatic guide. "How do I understand what this thing is in the crazy world around me so that I can make quick and easy decisions, whether it's inside the company about how I'm going to prioritize limited resources, or if it's outside the company making decisions if I'm going to invest or purchase services?"

When your brand brings crystal clarity, the customer's mind has to do less work to grasp your offering. This reduces the customer's effort, leading to several happy consequences:

- You have made it easier for them to give you their prized attention.
- With this prized attention on your business, customers will more likely to understand, remember, and like what you are bringing to them.
- The next time your brand is relevant to them, they will more easily recall your offering because you have already created a familiar, likable path for them.

Attention is your key to growing. Capture the attention of your customers and your employees and you will unlock growth.

CREATE MENTAL FILE FOLDERS TO REDUCE EFFORT

Attention is selective. To conserve cognitive resources, our brains are picky about what they attend to, as "paying attention" costs us. So, our brains conserve by using attention to enhance the prominence of things that are relevant (worth the cognitive cost) and deselect things that are not relevant (not worth the cognitive cost).

Because attention is cognitively expensive to customers, it is your duty to make it less expensive to them through a clear brand. Give people a mental file folder before telling them all the stuff you will ask them to put inside that folder. The mental file folder you provide tells customers how to organize your business in their heads. It tells them which associations in their brains your business will connect to.

If you have never before seen or heard of a kumquat, but you do know other fruit, then someone saying "fruit" helps you more than someone saying "kumquat." Fruit is your easy, relevant mental file folder. You can align that kumquat in your brain to other fruits you know.

If the Pilates studio I described above had given me the mental file folder of "Pilates studio," or "place to exercise," I would have understood them and connected their business to the ideas in my brain around Pilates. They certainly would have had a better chance of winning me as a customer.

CREATE A MENTAL FILE FOLDER IN A NEW CATEGORY

What if you are in a new category that is not yet defined, where there is no existing mental file folder to leverage? The bad news is that you have to work harder to communicate your meaning, and in the most difficult cases, you have to instigate a new behavior. The good news is, rather than differentiating in an incremental way versus other things in the established category, you instead can differentiate in a big way. You can own something bigger and more customer-meaningful.

Let's take a new-ish comer to hair care—dry shampoo. Dry shampoo has been around for decades for people on camping trips who need to clean their hair but lack access to water. The mental file folder would be "hair product for when lacking water." This was, until recently, a tiny mental file folder because for most of us, camping occasions are sparse. But in the last decade, numerous beauty brands have taken the same basic dry shampoo product and given it a new mental file folder: "hair product for longer-lasting good hair day."

Now my dry shampoo comes out not one to two days a year while camping but one to two days a week when I need good hair. Needing a good hair day is a vastly larger need state and brings more value to a larger group of customers than does clean-hair-while-camping. Previously, we lacked a solution for the frequent need to extend good hair days, and now we have this solution. This leads to more value for me, the customer, and more value for the dry shampoo category, which is growing at twice the rate of the rest of the hair care category globally.

In consumer technology, the iPhone has accomplished something similar. Mobile phones had been around for decades, and even smartphones were not new when Apple launched the iPhone in 2007 (remember the Blackberry?). But iPhone's smartphone solution was immeasurably more mean-ingful to customers than were previous smartphone devices. You now have an astoundingly intuitive and delightful com-puter (and camera and watch and datebook and flashlight and GPS and a million other things) in your pocket. This is a mas-sively larger need state than the one previous smartphones had addressed: "need my phone to send an email." The iPhone has contributed to Apple becoming the most valuable brand on Earth, and the first business to achieve a $1 trillion market capitalization.

ENABLE THE OPTIMALLY DISTINCT SWEET SPOT

In order to make it easier for customers to see, understand, and buy, brands need to strike a balance between familiar enough to be understood and different enough to communicate new value.

Wharton School marketing professor Jonah Berger writes in his book *Invisible Influence* that people like a blend of similarity and difference. When it's the right blend, he refers to it as "optimally distinct." For a brand position to be compelling to customers, it should be similar enough to something a customer already knows so that the person will feel its "warm glow of familiarity," as Berger has called it—yet it should be different enough that it stirs the customer's curiosity and desire to be different themselves.

The blend of old plus new leverages the way our brains learn. In order for us to perceive, attend to, and remember something, we need to relate to that something. If the new thing piggybacks on top of something else that we already understand, we can then comprehend it. This is how we learn new things in general—we tie the new with the associations we already know. Done well, a brand makes it easier for customers to learn your offering by being both familiar and different, old and new.

If your benefit is quite novel, balance that with something else, such as a mental file folder. It helped automobiles become mainstream when they were positioned not as newfangled machines but as "horseless buggies." By referencing the old (buggies), they could anchor the new (horseless).

A more recent innovation is Airbnb. It's a dramatically new-to-the-world idea to use the internet to find non-hotel beds to sleep on when you are traveling. So Airbnb leaned into what was familiar about the concept. They called themselves Airbnb (referencing the familiar B&B idea). Their character emphasized belonging and safety and psychological comfort—old, reassuring ideas. Airbnb achieved "optimally distinct" by leaning into the *familiar*.

The Pilates studio with the vague name I discussed above was overly different. It failed to root its new in something old. This business might have made it easier for me to learn of it by balancing their different-ness by adding the familiar mental file folder of "Pilates."

The more successful examples of dry shampoo and the iPhone embraced the intersection of old and new. Dry shampoo retained the familiar term "shampoo" to counterbalance the novel benefit of longer-lasting good hair. Apple called its revolutionary device "iPhone"—something extremely familiar—to balance its radically new experience. If either had concocted completely new terms, they might have been overly different, which would have made it harder for the customer to grasp and buy. Happily for these categories, they created an optimally distinct positioning, which brought customers along with them to grow.

We will dive deeper into the notion of "optimally distinct" in Chapter 6 when we explore the criteria of an ironclad brand strategy.

FOSTER LOYALTY

As we have discussed, good brand is good business. For a brand to be good, it needs to make a meaningful, differentiated, easy-to-learn, easy-to-understand promise and then deliver on that promise every time. A brand that does not make such a promise does not earn customers. A brand that does make such a promise but fails to fulfill it consistently does not *keep* customers.

Brand sets the groundwork for loyalty. The math for a lasting and vibrant business only works if a business has not just customers, but loyal customers with a high willingness to pay and an inclination to recommend to others. Businesses with low customer churn turn better profits than do their peers. To get to that profitable math, pinpoint the thing you bring that both leverages your exceptional strengths and delights your customers, blending familiar with novel.

Your brand strategy enables you to focus on what matters to the target customer—on that which produces customer desire for your business. Once customers have found it easy to see you and buy you, and those customers value your big benefit, they will love your business. In this way, brands deepen and lengthen your customer relationships, increasing customer lifetime value. Brands set the conditions for loyal customers who come back again and again because you singularly bring significant value.

Rob Grady, former VP of Global Beverage for Starbucks, told me that defining your brand facilitates depth in the relationship between your business and your customer. "If you want to have a deep relationship with your customers," Grady expressed, "meaning you want to interact with them on a repeated basis, have high lifetime value to you as a business, then you accomplish that through a compelling brand." Uniquely bringing a big benefit to customers inspires their gratitude, which keeps them engaged with your business as long as you continue to deliver that needed value.

Clayton Lewis, venture capitalist and CEO of scientific wellness company Arivale, told me, "A great brand is one where consumers are willing to pay over and above the cost of goods. Starbucks does this beautifully—we gladly wait in line to spend five bucks for fifty cents' cost of goods, because we so value what we get for that five bucks." Starbucks brings a big benefit—good coffee, uplifting third-place space, human connection, consistency across locations. This fills a deep need and delivers meaningful value, which spurs loyalty. It makes somebody a customer not just once, but countless times.

DIG A MOAT

So far, we have been discussing brand as your offense. Brand encourages lots of customers to buy lots of your offering for lots of money, over and over again with ease and loyalty. This offense helps your business to thrive.

Now consider another angle: brand is good defense. Brand protects what you have, helping you to survive and defend, as well as thrive and grow. Brand strategist and author Denise Lee Yohn told me, "Brand can be a way of defending what you have. I like to talk about it as a way of growing and guiding growth, but another way to think of it is as a way of safeguarding your asset."

As we will discuss more in this book: position or be positioned. If you do not position yourself actively, you will be positioned by the market passively. Your customers and your competitors will pick your position. As Ethan Lowry, co-founder of Crowd Cow, a service for connecting consumers with craft meat from small family farms, told me: "If you don't understand what you stand for, your customers will decide what you stand for based on their limited information. And what they come up with and what you want may not be the same thing. In absentia, if you're not providing a clear message, then your customers will actually infer what they think you must stand for. That muddiness is unhelpful to you as a business. You have to pick what you're going to stand for."

If you have built a powerful brand, your competitors cannot credibly copy it, and this un-copy-ability protects your business's long-term value. Pretty much everything else can be copied, given enough time. Patents expire; features obsolesce. But it is hard to copy an emotional territory that your brand occupies in the mind of your customer.

Instead of trying to outdo your competitors, use brand to change the game so that you are the only player. Disney is about having magical experiences. Not about movie production, or theme parks, or cruises, but the emotional benefit you get from any of those experiences. Many theme parks and production companies have come and gone, but Disney has been around since 1923. Disney's moat is the Disney brand.

"Brand strategy is how you safeguard and grow the value of your business. The brand is the company. Without the brand, what else do we have? We have recipes. We have products. Others could do that," Pamela Dressler, CEO of Cypress Grove. "The brand is the whole business."

Your differentiated brand prevents you from becoming a copied and commoditized price play. If you are a price play, you cannot command favorable margins, efficiency, or loyalty, and therefore, you will struggle to survive. Carolyn Feinstein, CMO of Dropbox who we met in Chapter 1, shared with me, "If you're not seen as different from your competitors, then it just becomes a game of who has more money to spend. If we aren't different from our competitors, and they have the money to outspend us to oblivion, they win. But if we are truly different and perceived as different, then [a competitor] outspending us is no longer a threat."

As Pamela Dressler summed it up: "A brand is who you are, what you bring to the world, and how you do it. If you can't articulate that for yourself, how could you tell your customers and the world? You can't," she said. "And if you aren't going to go through the trouble to define it, how can you expect customers to take the trouble to see you and care about you?"

Your business's right to exist is the value it creates for customers. Your brand defines your value by articulating your large and distinctive benefit. This serves as your North Star for continuously building value across all that you do. You can expand that value and make it ever more delightful to your target customer. It starts with distilling: What is in it for the customer? What is the reward the customer enjoys as a result of choosing to engage with this brand? How can we make it easy for them to grasp? When you thoughtfully, intentionally, and honestly answer these questions, those answers become your secret weapon for creating value for your business.

This chapter explained how brand strategy enables you to create value in the near term. In the next chapter, we zoom out to see how brand strategy enables you to scale for enduring value over a larger time horizon.

CHAPTER 3

SCALE FOR ENDURING VALUE

In the previous chapter, we discussed something immediate: how to use brand to create value in the near term. In this chapter, we zoom out to view how your brand parlays creating value today into scaling and thriving for years.

Focusing on the thing you uniquely bring to customers multiplies your business's value. Your chosen brand strategy empowers you to magnify your investments and use of resources.

Your chosen brand strategy empowers you to magnify the meaning and value of your business. Made explicit, your brand strategy allows your employees and partners to make aligned decisions and, therefore, help you grow your business with integrity. Your clarity becomes your competitive advantage, enabling you to punch above your weight, scale, and endure.

For the sake of long-term scale and enduring value, brands enable you to:

- Apply a Force Multiplier
- Magnify Your Investment and Allocation of Resources
- Push Decision-Making Down and Out

APPLY A FORCE MULTIPLIER

Brand helps you create scale for the long term by pinpointing and shining a spotlight on what makes you special. By selecting a position that answers a deep customer need and that leverages your individual strength, you build a business around something meaningful that only you can do. This focus enables you to double down on the very heart of your value. Your clarity makes it easier for customers to buy you, be delighted by your offering, and help you grow. With a focused brand, more people come, more people stay, and more people are willing to pay more.

In this way, brand strategy is a force multiplier for value creation. As with any force multiplier, brand strategy makes everything else more effective.

Consider another force multiplier in which I happen to believe zealously: sleep. When you sleep well, your waking life is easier and more successful. When, at a cellular level, your brain has regenerated and your body has repaired, you don't have to use as much brute force to operate and prosper during your day. Your moment-to-moment interactions, whether with family, friends, or colleagues, will be more effective, more relationship-enriching.

The problem with brute force is that it's finite. Even with only moderate sleep loss, you will falter. The same happens in business without focus. Too much trial and error, even with the occasional win, will enervate you and your employees. If you have to dig a well every time you need water, life is going to feel very hard very fast.

Instead, develop a brand strategy that identifies a well that is both deep and self-filling. As a body performs better with ample sleep, a business performs better with intentional focus. Brand's clarity fuels your growth with a continuously bountiful well. It makes the most of your resources, extending every dollar and every hour you spend growing your business. It enables you to expand brand affinity with ease, efficiency, and consistency. This is the force multiplier effect.

Serial CEO and investor Kirby Winfield is the person who, years ago, first articulated to me that brand is a "force multiplier." When I asked him recently to share more about that, he told me, "A lot of people do it backwards. They are creating a Google ad, or doing a web page, or doing a direct mail piece, or doing an email newsletter. Then they think, oh, what do I say? Which forces me to think about my value proposition, which forces me to think about differentiation, which forces me to think about my customer, which forces me to think about brand. But that's backwards. Do [brand] first, then build your business according to that, so that it benefits the whole experience rather than just the advertising tactic. Then it is your force multiplier."

When the light is bright, you can see things better. Your brand strategy provides this light, this North Star, showing which ideas to pursue and which not to, separating the high-leverage activities from the distracting ones.

What should our message be? Who do we talk to? Toward what end should we innovate? With brand as North Star, you can think breakthrough right from the start. When weighing multiple options, you can choose the option that most advances your ability to deliver on your promise. Brand can guide your decisions and actions, from the mundane to the monumental. The clarity becomes the force multiplier for you as you create value for your business.

MAGNIFY YOUR INVESTMENT AND ALLOCATION OF RESOURCES

Your ironclad brand strategy pinpoints the thing you bring that most matters to customers so that you can optimize for that. You can do more with less, making every dollar and every hour work hard to grow the business. "Brand is a really pragmatic tool," former Clorox CEO Don Knauss shared with me. "It enables you to allocate your resources so that you can win."

Focus magnifies the output of your scarce resources. David Aaker said in "Aaker on Branding," "It is possible or even likely that a $5 million budget behind a brilliant idea will be superior to a $20 million budget behind a mediocre idea." Because brand strategy brings focus, it concentrates your spending. A small but hyper-focused budget enables you to compete with businesses with larger, but less focused budgets.

Kristen Hamilton is CEO of Koru, a B2B startup bringing predictive analytics to hiring. She shared, "Brand is the principles you live by for your people—your customers, your employees, your partners. It's your relationships. It's your culture. Brand is what enables us to punch above our weight because of the strength of our customer relationships, because we are in service of something bigger than self-interest. It flows through everything. The thing that's cool about brand is if you do it right, you spend *less* money. Because it doesn't cost money to be really clear on what you stand for."

It is not only promotion where you will spend money more efficiently. Your investments in R&D, supplier choice, strategic partnerships, and distribution channels will also gain more for your business when it is laser-focused on your particular strength.

Crowd Cow is a startup that makes craft meat accessible by curating small ranches and selling their craft meat to foodies across the globe. Although they launched by selling only craft beef, they are now expanding to chicken, pork, and seafood. CEO Ethan Lowry told me that because of the deliberate brand promise of "craft meat discovery," Crowd Cow can grow and innovate without shooting darts. "When you know your brand you know your mission, and that can inform decisions, not just in marketing but throughout everything you do...

"For example, recently I was talking to a fisherman [whose salmon we were considering offering to our customers]. I was like, 'OK, tell me what makes Copper River Salmon different, what makes [your] sockeye different, and what makes your particular boat different?' And the fisherman just nailed it. Because of our brand strategy, I knew that she had nailed it. I could evaluate and right away say yes."

PUSH DECISION-MAKING DOWN AND OUT

When you scale, you must empower others to make decisions, because as a leader, you cannot be everywhere. The more you scale, the more you rely on others to help you build. By enabling you to push decision making outward and downward, brand replicates you as a leader, so the business scales even in your absence.

Brand provides a North Star to guide employees to grow the business you want to build, and to do so with autonomy and cohesion. They are using the same song sheet as you are, so they can make decisions that are on-brand just as you can. In addition to extending you as a leader, brand strategy gives your employees more meaning in the work they do for you every day.

As venture capitalist Dan Levitan shared with me, "unless you stand for something clearly articulated, you can't scale your team." Levitan, who co-founded venture capital firm Maveron with Howard Schultz in 1998, has funded and advised illustrious startups including Zulily, Allbirds, Cranium, Drugstore.com, Pinkberry, and Everlane.

Andrew Sherrard served as CMO of T-Mobile. He told me, "We are trying to grow and scale our company. And the way we do that is by pushing more decision making out to the edges while still ensuring they're grounded in the common principles. Getting the attention of employees and partners can be just as hard as sustaining the attention of customers, so they need shorthand too. Our shorthand at T-Mobile is we're here to change wireless for the better. So, employees can make their decisions accordingly without senior leaders needing to weigh in every time. It ends up creating the ability for us to act much more quickly than if we didn't have a brand that was unified and thought through."

To scale, you need everyone focused on what matters. For them to know and internalize the thing that matters, they need a visible North Star. Your brand strategy is that North Star.

Within your organization, brand should not be tucked away tidily inside marketing. Just as a strong P&L is not only the concern of the finance department, and a compelling culture is not owned solely by HR, your brand should not be solely a marketing responsibility. Use brand company-wide as your beacon to guide decision making everywhere, including innovation, pricing, sales, promotion, and partnering. When brand is owned by everyone in the company, it amplifies all efforts throughout your business.

People are hungry for clarity and will shine when you provide it. At Patagonia in 2016, teammates were brainstorming ideas for a marketing splash for Black Friday, the biggest sales day of the year. It was a junior employee who suggested the audacious idea that the company donate 100% of Black Friday sales to the environment. He had so internalized the Patagonia brand that he could make a bold, deeply on-brand suggestion despite his short tenure and junior status. Patagonia CEO Rose Marcario reportedly approved his idea within minutes.

For startups, frequently there is a brand strategy that has not yet been made explicit. Tarang Amin of e.l.f. Cosmetics, shared with me, "Often founders have a brand idea in their heads even if they've never articulated it. But articulating it is a tool that will make it more powerful. It's quite helpful to get everyone on the same page with your brand strategy, particularly as you scale."

The brand living in the founder's head can work for a time. But at some point, the founder either is going to want to work less or is going to want to scale. This is when it is a gift to make explicit the implicit.

Suzanne Senglemann was CMO of Angie's BOOMCHICK-APOP Snacks when she shared with me that her founder did just that. "With Angie's, there was a brand strategy, it just lived in our founder's brain. She knew what she wanted to do and what she didn't want to do. She knew the feeling she wanted to convey...Then there came a point when not having it overtly articulated prevented scale, actually created a bottleneck to scale. At that point, we articulated it on paper in a framework, and that was freeing."

Jeremy Korst, previously General Manager for Microsoft Windows Marketing, agrees. He even credits brand with one of Microsoft's most successful product launches. He told me, "Where brand really gets powerful for me is as an internal prioritization tool. These internal teams are craving clarity and singular purpose." He saw this when his team was developing Windows 10 and used the Windows brand strategy. "They had this tool to clarify choices—it was a decision-making tool for everyone. This helped make Windows 10 the most quickly adopted version of Windows in its entire thirty-year history. It's because clarity is so empowering."

Seamless, which merged with GrubHub in 2013 and went public in 2014 as a combined entity, uses the principles of brand across the company. Jonathan Zabusky, who was CEO of Seamless, shared with me that brand guided his decisions when building Seamless Web on everything from company culture to marketing, from partnering and hiring to exiting people. "Brand is all-encompassing for all of our stakeholders," he said. "It permeates every part of the company, internally and externally. I think that's the dimension that people lose—they associate brand simply with marketing. But it's everything. It's the way that we make difficult trade-offs, from business strategy, to which sectors to go after, which geographies and market segments, to who we hire and who we ask to leave."

If you want to scale your business, and if you hope that it endures beyond you, then dig deep and identify your focus through the lens of brand strategy. This will fuel you to capture value today (as we discussed in the previous chapter) and scale beyond your current state (this chapter).

Without focusing, the wind is in your face. Without a clear understanding of why you are here, it is hard to convince customers and employees that you have a reason for being here. As Dan Levitan put it, "I don't think anything differentiated or anything extraordinary or anything enduring can come without a definition of what you stand for."

Any business with longevity endures because it brings something truly different and needed. A brand strategy brings that uncommon thing to center stage, so everyone readily sees it and uses it and reinforces it and lives it.

In this chapter, we saw how brand enables you not only to create value in the near term, as Chapter 2 explored, but also in the longer term. Brand empowers your business to scale and endure. The next chapter zooms out even further to show how brand enables the non-monetary goal of achieving purpose with soul.

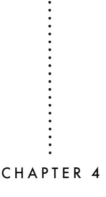

CHAPTER 4

KNOW YOUR PURPOSE

Until now, we have been talking about surviving, thriving, scaling, and enduring. This chapter transcends that to the question: why does the business you're building deserve to exist at all?

Brand strategy serves as an overt articulation of your purpose. By defining your brand strategy now, you position your business proactively, staying in a forward-leaning stance, preventing others from positioning you in a way that's not favorable to your business. This enables you to harness what makes your business one-of-a-kind—which invites the customers who most need what you uniquely bring to engage with you and stay with you. And, brand galvanizes your employees. When employees internalize purpose, they are better equipped to create value for customers, and this in itself extends your purpose. Your explicit and clear purpose even enables employees themselves to find and express their own meaning.

To unlock the beyond-money value of your business, you need to know your purpose. To do so, remember these things:

- Be Intentional
- Position or Be Positioned
- Do Not Wait
- Engage Employees
- Muster Your Leadership Courage

BE INTENTIONAL

An ironclad brand strategy is not small or incidental. It is big and intentional.

All businesses have a brand, whether they've been intentional about it or not. You could lollygag your way to a position, but it's pretty unlikely that it will be a good one. Instead, consciously craft an ironclad brand strategy, pinpointing your most right positioning, and then bring it to life with everything you do. As venture capitalist Dan Levitan told me, "Every business will have a brand. The question is: do you do it intentionally or subconsciously? Every good business should be intentional in how it shapes its brand."

T-Mobile CMO Andrew Sherrard compared brand intentionality to culture intentionality. "Brand is in this sense like your culture. Whether you deliberately craft it or not, you have culture, whether intentional or not. Same with brand."

So, be intentional. When you approach your brand choice with intention, you brighten your North Star. When you don't, you not only cede this power to competitors (who might be using brand to their advantage), you also miss a chance to contribute in a way only your business can. By taking charge of what your business will stand for in a forward-leaning stance, you give it backbone and empower your vision.

POSITION OR BE POSITIONED

As we touched on in the last chapter and will continue to explore throughout this book, not all positions are created equal. Not all positions are equally attractive for you as a business, or for your customers as they are becoming aware of your business. If you don't intentionally claim your business's best position, then the market will position you, and it likely won't be the most favorable.

Do not be an accidental brand. It's too important. A business's brand can either unleash your competitive advantage or it can thwart it. "Without a brand strategy, you're haphazard," Pamela Dressler of Cypress Grove Cheese shared with me. "With a brand strategy, you dramatically up your odds for success. Wouldn't you rather have that than rely on dumb luck? It's key to be intentional about it and do the work upfront."

As Kirby Winfield shared with me, "You could hope that people get what you want without you investing time, energy, and trying to control it. Unless you're really lucky, it's pretty unlikely that without having thought about it, or invested in it beyond a logo, that you've actually unpacked the things that a brand strategy will unpack for you…

"And that matters," Winfield went on. By not deliberately positioning your brand, "you're making your job harder and you're making it less likely that you'll be successful. Certainly, you're making it take more time to achieve the outcome that you want. And that's the *best* case. In the worst case, you're communicating something that has actually nothing to do with—and potentially is completely against—what your customer wants and needs. At which point, you can tank the whole thing."

DO NOT WAIT

Ironclad brand strategy is not just for established businesses with traction. It is also for startups. A startup business is one with few resources and, therefore, has a particular need for focus. "A lot of times entrepreneurs will wait too long to get crisp on brand," shared Erika Shaffer, Director of Strategic Communications for Madrona Venture Group. "It's good to get traction on product, but brand resonance makes the product easier to sell. So, it's a mistake to be too passive about brand. If you do, like a ball of string, it kind of unravels down the hill."

There is no chicken versus egg in this matter. The sooner you have a brand strategy, the sooner you'll have both your North Star and your rudder. With the overwhelmingly numerous possibilities for your business right now, your brand strategy shines the spotlight on the ones worth your while so that you can ace those.

Startup leaders often forego brand strategy because they prefer to wait and do it "right." Don't let the perfect be the enemy of the good. The right way to develop a brand strategy early in the business may be to do so in a quick-and-dirty way, to be revisited later. But do know your purpose now. Your brand positioning can evolve as your product gains market fit and momentum. As with any business, you will refine your direction as you learn more about your customer, the competitive space, and your own strengths as a business.

ENGAGE EMPLOYEES

The purpose that your brand strategy codifies builds human capital. Work without clear purpose hampers and numbs employees. Work with purpose engages and enlivens employees.

Rich Barton has founded some of the most novel and successful consumer businesses of the last two decades, including Expedia, Glassdoor, and Zillow. His counsel on building effective teams is to cultivate purpose. "People want to work on something big and important, something that's meaningful," he shared on stage at the Zillow Premier Agent Forum 2017. "When you work on meaningful stuff and you can communicate to other people why that is, you can get them excited about working with you."

Employees who care about the purpose of your business will be more motivated to help you win. Brand provides this clarity of purpose and meaning. You want your employees to care, and a brand-driven purpose invites them to care.

As Carolyn Feinstein, the CMO of Dropbox who we heard from in Chapters 1 and 2, related to me, "Great brands stand for something. They have a point of view. Being able to articulate your beliefs doesn't just help you externally—it's the secret sauce of a successful, focused internal culture. A clearly defined brand story and purpose allows you to hire and retain the best talent, whose beliefs are aligned with yours, while giving meaning to the team's work and validating why they're all here. When we first shared our new brand story, it was like a light went off. It not only centered our teams, it created tremendous pride and inspiration—now everyone wants a Dropbox tattoo on their bicep."

With brand, employees go from working for a business that makes crayons to one that helps parents and teachers raise inspired, creative children. From a business that sells wireless phone plans to one that enriches interpersonal relationships. From a business that sells coffee to a business that nurtures the human spirit through daily connection. From a business that sells outdoor gear to one that champions the planet.

"Having a higher-order purpose also makes employees feel more engaged. Would you rather work for a company that is trying to sell people more stuff?" Robert Neer, Director of Best Buy's Technology Development Center, asked me. "Or would you rather work for a company that is helping people explore their passions? When employees feel more connected to that purpose, they in turn help build value in the product that in turn makes the end reward that much bigger for the customer." Brand helps employees tap into what inherently inspires them.

The inverse is also true: employees who feel purposeless do not perform as well as those who feel purpose. Absence of purpose leads to disengagement. And disengagement among US workers is appallingly high. A 2015 Gallup poll found that a staggering 51 percent of US workers describe themselves as "not engaged" at work, and another 17.5 percent report that they are "actively disengaged." What a waste.

Here is an interesting distinction: a sense of employee purpose is different from passion. UC Berkeley Professor Morten Hansen surveyed 5,000 employees and managers to uncover the markings of the high performers. Hansen observed that while purpose is the sense that you are contributing to something larger and therefore your work has meaning, passion is excitement toward the work itself. The data was conclusive—employees with a high sense of purpose were high performers regardless of their level of passion. And passion was only correlated with high performance if it was coupled by a sense of purpose.

Purpose *dramatically* outperforms passion. And, while you cannot use your will to create an employee's passion, which is individual, you can organizationally cultivate purpose, which is collective.

An explicit purpose can also attract future employees who resonate with this purpose. Woven into your culture, "brand can even become a criterion for recruiting employees and an asset for retaining them," Jonathan Zabusky, CEO of Seamless, shared with me. It is a North Star not only for attracting your right customers, but for attracting your right employees.

Volvo, too, uses brand as an employee engagement tool. Volvo head of brand Sven Desmet, who we heard from in the previous chapter, shared with me, "If you like the brand, then it is more likely that you will buy its product and services, and it is more likely it will become an employer of choice. How do people gravitate to your product and service, and why would people want to work for you and not for somebody else?"

When your employees grasp and internalize your purpose, they will find more meaning in their work, giving more to your business and to your customers. It will become a virtuous cycle of employees feeling fulfilment in the work, making it ever more valuable for your customers to stick around.

Brand as North Star not only attracts customers willing to pay more, it attracts employees willing to give more, to contribute with gusto. Think of how much more your business could achieve if you could engage your disengaged employees. Think of how much meaning you could be creating for them. These are the individuals who ultimately create your value. Don't you owe it to them, as a human? Don't you owe it to your business, as a leader?

As with any choice of strategy, brand strategy includes closing doors. It necessitates choosing what you are not going to focus on. By choosing what falls inside your brand purpose, you are also choosing what falls outside of it. This is the focus that empowers success. Focus is how you win.

Denny Post is CEO of Red Robin Gourmet Burgers and Brews. While sharing with me her views of brand, she said, "Ultimately, what a customer is buying is your promise, and your brand is your promise. Defining what your customer is buying is the toughest strategic work you will do, and the most important decision you will make as a leader."

Do muster the effort to undertake this heavy-lifting strategic work. Do choose to stand for something—one thing. As we have discussed, your brand is what you stand for. Your brand strategy is the choosing of what you stand for. It is your choice of purpose. In choosing your "yes," you necessarily choose many "no's." Shining the light on one thing darkens what lies outside that beam.

Tarang Amin explained, "Strategy in general is about the choices you'll make as a leader, what you'll prioritize. What are you going to do, and what are you not going to do?" Brand strategy is "the choices of what you'll stand for and not stand for. It encompasses the benefits you'll prioritize, and the character that will bring it to life. Again, these are choices. When you choose to be one thing, you are choosing not to be something else. When you choose to prioritize a given benefit, you are deprioritizing others. Otherwise it is not a strategy."

Now, let's acknowledge something here. Choosing focus may make you nervous, because your fear tells you to keep doors open, not closed. But as Clayton Christenson wrote, "Focus is scary—until you realize that it only means turning your back on markets you could never have anyway." The thing that makes brand strategy scary—choosing focus—is also the very heart of its power. The more you hedge, the more power you relinquish.

Compounding the fear of choosing might be the knowledge that once you do choose your focus and make it explicit for others, there is nowhere to hide. You have turned on the North Star so bright that your equivocating is more visible. This clarity, though, is of course brand's very power. After all, if you were a customer or employee, wouldn't you more likely connect with a business that goes to the trouble to get clear on why it exists?

So, how do you spark your leadership courage?

First, you choose to stop hedging. You internalize that you owe it to your business, customers, and employees to choose. You grasp that you cannot be all things to all people, and that it's also a choice not to make a choice. You acknowledge that the act of choosing alone unleashes power.

Second, you get highly empathetic to your customer. You listen to your customer intently to learn the true nature of the problem your business is solving and what it is like to be your customer facing that problem. You develop the ability to channel your customer while making decisions that affect the customer experience.

Third, you define your brand strategy, which articulates your business's purpose explicitly, so that everyone can amplify and advance this purpose. Part 2 of this book gives you a method for doing so.

Ultimately, defining brand strategy is an exercise in building self-awareness. It is an exercise of looking in the mirror unflinchingly, identifying the specific and customer-meaningful thing you bring, and then defining it so that you can remember it and use it as your filter for every decision you make. By knowing your purpose and embracing it, you contribute the meaning that is why you are here.

In these last three chapters, we have discussed how brand strategy is worth your while for creating value in the short-term, long-term, and forever term. Next, we will deconstruct what brand is and is not, so that you can master the application of brand.

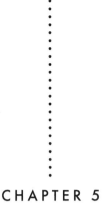

CHAPTER 5

DECONSTRUCTING BRAND

This first part of this book has taken the sky-level view of brand, discussing what brand is in the big picture—the meaning your business stands for in the mind of your customer and the relationship this confers—and also why brand is an essential leadership tool: because it is the biggest driver of value creation in the short, medium, and long term.

We are now going to deconstruct the components of brand. If we can understand the language of brand, including the myths we often tell ourselves about it, we can keep its often-conflated terms teased apart—and, therefore, better see and know it.

To make full use of brand:

- Trace the Origin of Brand
- Understand the Components of Brand
- Don't Indulge False Dichotomies

A hopeless word geek, I revel in learning the origins of words and the journeys those words made to their current form in the English language. It's especially satisfying to learn the etymology for elusive words such as "brand."

The English word brand comes from *brandr*, an Old Norse word that means "to burn." Cattle ranchers burn symbols indicating their ranch names into the haunches of their animals. Artisans carve their names into pottery to show that they created the piece. I put my kids' names into their jackets and gloves before a new school year begins to indicate that the items belong to us, in the hopes that they return home.

Thus, the original meaning of the word brand, which has been used for centuries, is about ownership. Later, another reason for denoting ownership emerged. Brand came to signify worth. People started branding things they made to elevate the items' value so that they could encourage another to buy it and pay more for it. Signals of ownership became a way not only to facilitate keeping property but also to facilitate trade of that property.

One of the oldest known examples of this is Pompeii bread. From loaves preserved by the volcano's eruption, we know that bakers branded their products. This marked ownership and generated demand. It acknowledged that the customer had many choices and could have elected to purchase from another bakery. Bread marked with the baker's name indicated, "This bread was made by me, and I stand by its quality. It is worth lots. You should want it."

Brand today continues to serve as an economic tool that benefits both the business and the customer. For the business, brand creates demand (and therefore revenue) by showing the customer that the business has skin in the game, thereby making the proposition more compelling to the customer. For the customer, brand improves the likelihood that the purchase will be a successful one and reduces the risk of money poorly spent.

Consider a modern example reminiscent of the stamped bread of the ancient Roman empire. Advil presents a distinctive orange coating and flavor, in addition to the Advil logo stamped onto each pill. If it is mixed in with other pills in my medicine cabinet, I can tell it apart from others (ownership). If I ingest that Advil and it successfully relieves my headache, I will know that it worked (worth). Advil's brand first signifies ownership so that I see it, and then delivers on its worthy promise again and again. I am more likely to purchase it (value for the business), and less likely to be disappointed by it (increased benefit and reduced risk for the customer).

UNDERSTAND THE COMPONENTS OF BRAND

Brand is the meaning you stand for in the heart and mind of your target customer. Not yours, theirs. Brand strategy is the deliberate articulation of that meaning, so that you can make decisions to make that meaning ever more true and compelling. Although every business will have a brand, only the businesses that are deliberate about brand will have a brand strategy.

In creating your brand strategy, you identify how you are meaningful and different to your audience. Then you claim ownership of that differentiator. Then you tell the world about that and deliver that distinct meaning in everything you do. Your brand strategy is your way to capture the power of brand in a forward-leaning way, rather than in a haphazard or defensive manner. Defining brand intentionally magnifies your leadership, your spending, your innovations, your people, and your very meaning.

Let's dive into the components of brand strategy. Following is a primer for all the terms we will use in Part 2 as I explain the steps in building an ironclad brand strategy. Not only will these definitions set you up for that process, but they will also clear up some confusion, as some of these terms are bandied out loosely and inconsistently.

BRAND POSITIONING

Brand positioning is the place your business occupies in your customer's mind in the context of the customer's alternative options. Done well, you've placed it in a way that makes it easier for your customer to see you, consider you, and buy you. Indeed, as Geoffrey Moore discussed in *Crossing the Chasm*, a book instructing how to bring new technology to mainstream customers, the very purpose of positioning is to make it easy for your customer to buy you. When you define your brand positioning, you are identifying the doorway into the customer's world. This makes your offering compelling compared to the alternatives, and easier for him to see you and choose you.

Said another way, "positioning is not what you do to a product. Positioning is what you do to the mind of the prospect," as positioning pioneers Al Ries and Jack Trout elegantly wrote in 1980. Rather than creating something new and different, you are taking what's already in the customer's mind and retying your offering to the associations already present. Positioning is latching your business into a particular place in the customer's mind.

As we discussed in Chapter 3, positioning happens, whether actively or passively. Position, or be positioned. If you don't intentionally position your business, the market will do so for you. Not all positions are created equal, and if you don't take an active role in claiming yours, you'll likely wind up with one that's not optimal.

BRAND PROMISE

A brand promise is the benefit you pledge to your customers and fulfill when your customers choose to engage with your offering. Your brand promise is the crux of your brand strategy. By creating a promise that is meaningful to your customer and distinctive to your business, and then by delivering on that promise consistently and robustly, you earn loyal customers with high willingness to pay and high customer lifetime value.

Outside the context of brand strategy, your brand promise is synonymous with your value proposition—literally (from the Latin roots), what is the thing of worth (*val*) that you are putting forth (*proponere*). In various contexts, your brand promise might also be called your core benefit, your raison d'être, your "special sauce," or your "biggest yes."

BRAND CHARACTER

While your brand promise is what you singularly bring to your customer, your brand character is how you show up to deliver that promise. It is the way you talk, look, and act. It is the way your business would manifest if it were a person.

When you imbue your business with personality, you make it easier for customers to like you and bond with you. Brand character facilitates customer relationship building, because we humans are a highly social species with an affinity for story and human-like characters. A customer likes a business because of the way he feels having interacted with that business, just as a person likes a person because of the way their interactions feel. A customer is more likely to bond with a playful, anthropomorphic bear called Charmin than with a plain, old roll of toilet paper.

Brand character also enables you to show up in an inherently differentiated way, as no other business can credibly copy your brand character. In this way, brand character is itself a source of differentiation—and, therefore, competitive advantage—for your business.

REASONS TO BELIEVE

Your brand promise is how your business benefits customers. But to take root in your customer's mind, your promise must be credible by providing reasons to believe. Also called proof points, pillars, or support, these reasons enable your customers to trust your promise. They are your offering's specific attributes that enable it to deliver on that promise. While a promise is the benefit a customer experiences, a reason to believe is the attribute that makes that experience possible.

If your brand promise were a car with a smooth driving experience, your reason to believe might be its four-wheel suspension. If your brand promise were soap that softens skin, your reason to believe might be that it contains ¼ moisturizing cream. The role of these reasons to believe is to support the promise. Customers do not care about your four-wheel suspension for its own sake. They care about the smooth drive that this feature enables. Customers do not care about your soap's ingredient per se. They care about the soft skin they experience as a result of that ingredient. The reason to believe helps them to integrate your promise into their minds.

END REWARD

The end reward is the ultimate benefit the customer enjoys because they experienced your brand promise. It's the "So what?" or the "Why should I care?" Just as the reason to believe enables the brand promise, the brand promise enables the end reward. Think of the structure like this:

- Experience [brand promise] SO THAT you can [end reward].
- Experience lightweight shoes SO THAT you can win the race.
- Experience clean water SO THAT you can enjoy the healthy benefits of hydration.
- Experience speed dial on your phone SO THAT your friend feels nearby.
- Experience fast skis SO THAT you can feel like a bird.

The end reward is the way your brand brings deep, abiding value to the customer. It represents something that the customer likely would not overtly articulate as a need, but that the customer nonetheless wants at a subtle but profound level. The brand promise serves as a doorway in, meeting the customers where they have a conscious need. The end reward delights those customers, making them feel bigger and closer to the life they wish to live. This delight builds a relationship with your customer marked by loyalty beyond reason.

Frame of reference is the set of alternatives your customer would be using if your product or service did not exist. It's what they would be using or buying instead of your offering. It is the true competitive set—the things your brand competes against for your customer's heart and mind. This might be a direct competitor, a substitute, a workaround behavior, or even "doing nothing" to solve the problem.

A useful frame of reference is customer-centric, not you-centric. It is not merely your direct competitors in your industry as you see them, but the actual competing solution—however satisfying or unsatisfying. It is common for a business to equate frame of reference with direct competitors, when actually customers are not using or considering competitors. Pinpoint the true frame of reference for your customer, rather than merely concluding you compete against your direct competitor. Why? To differentiate your brand promise, you need first to know what you are differentiating from.

For example, if you sell soda, your customers' frame of reference might be another soda brand (direct competitor), or it might be water or chewing gum (substitute), or it might be distracting oneself from thirst by reaching for the phone (work-around behavior).

When developing the brand strategy for this soda business, you must identify the most salient of these frames of reference so that you know which emphasis to select. If the main frame of reference were another soda brand, then this might lead you to emphasize your distinctive flavor. If the main frame of reference were tap water, then you might lean into an emphasis of a fun bubbly drink. If the main frame of reference were distracting yourself from the discomfort of your thirst, then you might lean into the immediate satisfaction of quenching thirst at its source.

BRANDING

Where brand is the relationship between business and customer, branding is all the activities you engage in to make that relationship vibrant.

By embodying your brand through your product offering, messages, and purchase experience, you enrich that relationship with meaningful associations so that your audience is attracted to—and remains attracted to—your business. Branding is "relationship-ing." It is all the things that you are doing—or not doing—to deepen and expand the relationship between your business and your target customer.

As Carter Cast, entrepreneur, venture capitalist and former CEO of Walmart.com told me, "All the leadership decisions you make are either brand accretive or brand diminishing." By branding according to a deliberate brand strategy, you're more likely to make decisions that are brand accretive.

Branding is verbal (your name and messaging), visual (your imagery and colors), and experiential (what it's like to use your product). It is the big things you do (your big events and advertising) and the small things you do (your email signature). It is the things that feel quite obviously like marketing (social media, ad copy, website), and it is the things that don't clearly fall into marketing (the way you answer your phone, the quickness of your product fulfilment). The bad news is that branding is everything—you can't relegate it to the marketing team. The good news is that branding is everything—it can be the unifying song sheet for your whole organization to create value in concert.

The person evaluating whether to engage with your brand considers all the ways they see you, all your branding, all the ways your brand manifests. Effective branding provides multiple cues across multiple touchpoints, consistently and authentically. These cues communicate your brand positioning every time in the same cohesive voice.

For example, Starbucks' brand positioning is a warm, consistent, premium coffee drinking and social experience—a "third place" to reconnect and recharge. All of these are manifestations of that brand positioning:

- Logo
- Ad copy
- Instagram caption
- Exterior signage
- In-store signage
- Store layout
- Green aprons
- Menu legibility
- Smiles on baristas' faces
- Accessible food
- Delicious, fresh coffee and seasonal beverages
- Money-back guarantee, and the messaging of this guarantee
- Aroma of coffee and sounds of the espresso grinder and ambient music
- Clean bathrooms and recently wiped tables
- Sense that you are invited to linger and enjoy

DON'T INDULGE FALSE DICHOTOMIES

Brand is so large and overarching that we can easily mistake it as being useful in only one of its roles. Doing so causes us to lose out on the complete scope of its power. A common way that business leaders dismiss brand, and therefore relegate it to a weaker place in business, is by believing these brand myths:

- Brand is only a business's name.
- Brand is only a logo.
- Brand is only advertising.
- Brand is only for businesses with large media budgets.
- Brand is irrelevant for businesses that use performance marketing tactics.
- Brand is spin.
- Brand is only for businesses in certain industries.
- Brand is only for B2C companies, not B2B companies.
- Brand is not for product companies.

I'll demystify each one so that you don't have to fall for these myths and miss out on the power that brand strategy brings to a business.

NAME AND LOGO ARE EXPRESSIONS OF BRAND

Many equate brand with name and logo only. This is understandable, because name and logo are the most visible and concrete expressions of brand. The business name identifies the brand with words. The business logo does so with image and color, offering a useful visual cue for the customer about what your business is like. While both are overt expressions of brand, they are not brand in its entirety, just as my name and signature are not me in my entirety.

ADVERTISING IS A TACTIC TO EXPRESS BRAND

Often leaders conflate brand with advertising, or "brand marketing," a la Mad Men. Since advertising is shouting your business's message and what you stand for, advertising is quite literally an expression of brand. But advertising alone is not brand, any more than a texted announcement from me to my friends is all that I am. Kirby Winfield quipped, "Equating brand strategy with advertising is like saying the only reason I would work out at the gym is if I was going to be a model, or if I was going to the beach. The purpose of working out is the benefits that accrue internally to you, throughout your life, in a way that has nothing to do with whether you're taking glamour shots." Brand influences everything, not merely a single, temporary tactic.

MARKETING BUDGET AND BRAND STRATEGY HAVE LITTLE TO DO WITH ONE ANOTHER

Since traditional advertising is expensive, most businesses wisely do little or none of this tactic. Because brand is often conflated with this typically expensive tactic, some leaders use this as further reason to dismiss brand as something that they cannot afford. In reality, an intentional brand strategy can make expensive advertising less necessary. Brand gives you resonance regardless of the volume at which you can afford to shout.

For example, brand can help you attain earned media through PR outreach, which is typically free or inexpensive. The reason is that successful PR requires a compelling story, a compelling brand idea. As PR expert and head of communications for Madrona Venture Group, Erika Shaffer, related, "Most businesses want more media attention to get the word out about their brand. And what leads to media attention is brand resonance. You can't get media attention without an emotional connection, a story." That emotional connection, that story, stems from brand.

BRAND STRENGTHENS ALL MARKETING TACTICS, INCLUDING PERFORMANCE MARKETING TACTICS

Businesses may eschew traditional advertising not only because it is expensive but because the ROI is tricky to measure. These businesses often elect instead to generate demand through performance marketing tactics such as SEO, SEM, email marketing, and digital retargeting. Brand, if linked with advertising, becomes collateral damage. But performance marketing tactics indicate to customers what you stand for—and so those too are expressions of brand. Brand should *inform* this tactic as it should inform all tactics. When brand informs the performance marketing, these tactics can not only amass clicks and sales in the near term but can accrue brand affinity and enduring growth in the long term.

BRAND PREVENTS THE NEED FOR SPIN

Another cause for brand dismissal is the belief that brand is merely spin, as in "that's just brand," accompanied by an eyeroll. Of course, some brands are nothing but a hollow shell of lies, but that is not because they are brands. That is because they developed thoughtlessly and likely in the absence of customer empathy and integrity. They force themselves into a corner where they have to shellac themselves in shiny spin. By committing yourself to building your brand with authenticity, you inherently eschew spin. An ironclad brand doesn't *have* to use spin because it finds the intersection between what truly serves the customer and what truly serves the business, and then transparently communicates and builds toward that. As we learned earlier, brand lives in the hearts and minds of customers. Spin cannot change this.

BRAND WORKS FOR BUSINESSES IN ALL CATEGORIES AND OF ALL SIZES

Another reason people mistakenly dismiss brand is related to its confusion with advertising we touched on earlier. Because the biggest advertisers tend to be consumer packaged goods companies and behemoth technology and telecommunications brands, many consider brand to be exclusive to those industries specifically.

Kristen Hamilton, CEO of Koru who we met in the last chapter, told me, "I used to think that brand was either a consumer packaged goods brand, like a Proctor & Gamble soap, or a big company like Microsoft. I used to think that brand equals advertising, and since we didn't advertise, brand strategy wasn't for us. [But] if you have customers, then you have a brand and need a brand strategy. Brand does not equal advertising. Brand is your soul. It's - who are you? What matters?"

In other words, the businesses that most need a brand strategy are the ones that cannot afford expensive advertising. A brand strategy allows you naturally and sustainably to earn your customers' attention without your having to purchase their involuntary attention through advertising.

BRAND IS FOR BUSINESSES THAT HAVE RELATIONSHIPS WITH HUMAN BEINGS, WHETHER B2B OR B2C

Some believe that brand is only for businesses that sell to consumers (B2C), and not for those that sell to businesses (B2B). This likely stems from the fact that consumer businesses like Clorox, Nestle, Proctor & Gamble, and Unilever were the ones in the twentieth century that used the power of brand to great and visible success. But this is another false dichotomy. Both B2C and B2B serve human beings, so brand is relevant to both. Whether buying as a representative of a household or of a corporation, a human being is in a relationship with your business, and brand facilitates and reinforces that relationship.

Consider the phenomenal success of B2B brand Salesforce. Mark Benioff, founder and CEO of Salesforce, said "Brand is not just a logo. It's your most important asset."

BRAND AND PRODUCT WORK TOGETHER, NOT SEPARATELY

I have heard leaders argue that their business is a "product" company, and therefore, they dismiss brand. This altogether misses the meaning of brand.

Product is an essential *part* of brand. In fact, product is such an integral brand expression that I consider it the least forgiving of brand's many expressions. No amount of excellent messaging or promotion or sweet-talking will compensate for a poor product. (Remember, spin does not work, ultimately.) Aaron Woodman of Microsoft told me, "I can't market my way out of a bad product or one that's inconsistent with people's emotion."

Product is vitally important, but product is the means, not the end. Customers don't care about your neato product. They care about what they get as a result of your product. They care what's in it for them. You should care most about that, too. Building an ironclad brand strategy puts what customers care about into sharp relief for everyone.

Additionally, all companies are product companies, at least loosely described (a service is an intangible product). That product is the mechanism through which customers experience your brand promise. So, all companies have a product and all companies have a brand. The leaders who recognize the role of both the product and the brand set the conditions to prosper.

Brand is the meaning you stand for. Brand strategy is the deliberate articulation of that meaning. Brand position is the thing you own in the context of your customer's alternatives. Brand promise is the benefit you bring to customers. Brand character is how you come across. Reasons to believe are the proof that customers can believe your promise. End reward is how the customer's life is ultimately better because of your promise. Frame of reference is what the customer would buy if not your offering. Branding is everything you do to bring to life your brand.

In this chapter, we have teased apart the components of brand so that their precision serves your businesses. We have also unraveled the myths that surround brand to see brand's universality.

The next chapter is the final chapter of Part 1, "The What and Why of Brand." This next chapter defines the criteria marking the most value-creating brands. In Part 2 of this book, you will learn the step-by-step method to crafting an ironclad brand strategy that meets those criteria.

CHAPTER 6

THE NINE CRITERIA FOR AN IRONCLAD BRAND STRATEGY

An ironclad brand differentiates your business in an enduring way. Product can be copied. Patents expire. Features obsolesce. What cannot be copied is a relationship. What does not expire is the trust you earn by particularly and consistently solving a customer need. What never gets old is delight. Loyal customers will not only stay with you—they will follow you as you evolve. They will love you—and encourage others to engage with you, too.

Focusing on the thing you uniquely bring to customers multiplies your business's value. Your chosen brand strategy empowers you to magnify your investments and use of resources.

Ironclad brands occupy the single best position in the hearts and minds of their customers. Precisely identifying this optimal position enables you to create value, maximize scale, and lead with purpose. The most value-creating brand strategies are the ones that meet the nine criteria we cover in this chapter:

1. Big
2. Narrow
3. Asymmetrical
4. Empathetic
5. Optimally Distinct
6. Functional *and* Emotional
7. Sharp-Edged
8. Has Teeth
9. Delivers

In the chapters that follow this one, you will learn a step-by-step method for crafting your optimal brand positioning. With every step, pressure-test your brand strategy against each of these nine criteria. Your brand strategy is ironclad when it has survived this crucible.

BIG

Your brand positioning is the space you own in your customer's head. Make it a big space. Represent a big promise, a big benefit. By mattering to your customer, you create a business that matters.

Recall this equation from Chapter 2:

Customer Value = Benefit – Price

The customer receives value when the benefit she enjoys exceeds the price she paid. There are two levers for creating customer value: big benefit and small price. As we saw in Chapter 2 while looking at how brand immediately creates value, only one of those levers brings value both to your customer and to you. When your benefit is big, your customer's willingness to pay is also big, allowing you to bolster margins. Customers thrive because your benefit brings them closer to the lives they want to live. Your business thrives because your big benefit enables you to command the robust economics you need to be profitable and grow. Big is important for customer value, and it is commensurately important for *your value.*

Stewart Butterfield, CEO of Slack, said, "In the long run, the measure of our success will be how much value we created for customers." To provide big value, provide a big benefit. And to provide a big benefit, start by listening to your customer to understand with nuance the big problem you could solve. The more attuned, curious, and open you are as you listen, the bigger the problem you will unearth. At this point, you are problem finding, not problem solving. By empathizing, you can then develop a big benefit solution for those customers, opening the way to big business value for you. Here are some brands that bring large benefits:

- Tylenol makes you "feel better." That is a big benefit. Less big might have been "lessen headache" or "easy-to-swallow." With its big benefit, Tylenol enjoys a market capitalization at an estimated $2 billion.
- Salesforce enables you to grow your business faster. This is a large and resonant promise for Salesforce's target customer. A less big alternative might have been "track customer communication carefully" or "largest storage capacity among

CRM solutions." With its big promise, Salesforce is a revered brand with an $87 billion market capitalization.

- Dropbox brings customers the feeling of freedom by being able to access your stuff from anywhere. This is a big, bold promise. A less big promise might have been "cheap document storage" or "rapid uploading." With this large benefit, Dropbox has a market capitalization of $8 billion.
- Slack provides users with simple team communication—a big benefit. A less big one might have been "communicate faster" or "better archive search capability." With Slack's big promise, the company's market capitalization is $5 billion.

The first criterion of an ironclad brand strategy is that it brings something big. Test yourself as you evaluate the directions you could take your brand—is this big enough to matter? Or am I letting myself off the hook with something small?

NARROW

As much as your brand idea must be big enough to matter, it also must be narrow enough to own. Choose a position you can dominate, one where you are not just better or different, but where you are only. As activist Jonathan Kozol suggests, "Pick battles big enough to matter, small enough to win."

Be narrow enough that you are the only one who could own your position, who could serve that particular customer with that particular promise. "Only" is far superior to "best." Peter Thiel advises in *Zero to One* to be the only player in a space by thinking vertically rather than horizontally: focusing on depth rather than breadth. Be so good that others are irrelevant. Be narrow enough that no other player comes close in delivering the specific promise you own. If you are not the only, you have not yet narrowed enough.

To narrow your big, use these four levers of positioning:

· Target customer
· Frame of reference or category
· Specific promise
· Character with which you show up to deliver that promise

For example, imagine you are an entrepreneur wishing to open a brand of spa that will rejuvenate guests. Not a bad start—rejuvenation is a big benefit. But rejuvenation is table stakes for a spa. All spas rejuvenate. That is not narrow enough to own. To narrow to the ownable portion of that big benefit, your spa might provide rejuvenation to a target customer, perhaps an audience traditionally underserved by spas (narrowing by target customer). Or you might narrow your frame of reference so that you are providing rejuvenation in the spas of five-star hotels (narrowing by category). Or you might narrow your promise to making clients not only feel younger but look younger (narrowing by promise). Or you might narrow your character to be a spa with a rebellious edge (narrowing by character often entails pushing against category stereotype).

Here are some examples of how real brands have narrowed. Notice how each one stays big enough to matter, but one lever of positioning narrows so that the brand owns that position.

NARROWED TARGET CUSTOMER

- Steelcase Furniture is office furniture for architecture firms.
- Edmodo is a social media platform built for K–12 teachers.
- FreshBooks is accounting software for small business owners.

NARROWED FRAME OF REFERENCE

- Enterprise Rental is a rental car agency with locations not only near airports but also near car repair shops.
- Arc'teryx is an outdoor equipment brand for alpine sports and climates.
- PBTeen is décor for teen bedrooms.

NARROWED PROMISE

- Everlane is the apparel brand that brings radical pricing transparency.
- Rick Steves Travel is a travel guide that enables you to feel like a temporary local.
- OXO Good Grips is premium cooking tools that are ergonomic.

NARROWED CHARACTER

- Geico is the insurance company with a clever character.
- Dollar Shave Club is the shaving brand with a rebellious attitude.
- Slack is the team collaboration platform that is fun.

Once you have chosen a narrowed position, you have all kinds of room to grow. Direct your efforts within that position, going deeper within your focus. For example, clothing pioneer Everlane owns its brand position via the narrow promise of radical transparency: the company shares with its customers sourcing information and production costs. Upholding this promise, the company would not diversify to fast fashion, but it *could* move far beyond cashmere sweaters and loafers. Everlane might expand to any category in which radical transparency would be compelling to customers, such as cosmetics, skin care, even home furnishings.

Or consider Dollar Shave Club, which narrowed character to a rebellious voice in the stodgy shaving category. The brand has broadened to serve women as well as men, and to bring personal hygiene products beyond razors. What remains narrow is Dollar Shave Club's irreverent voice.

By narrowing, you eschew vanilla and broad in favor of specific and deep. You eschew the illusion of a safe idea in favor of something bold and real. Narrow foregoes the fool's errand of trying to be liked by everyone, and instead doubles down on the thing that will make you loved by the ones who matter.

ASYMMETRICAL

In his book *Good to Great*, Jim Collins shares how we can think of competitive advantage through a Greek parable about foxes and hedgehogs. Collins believes that companies, like characters in the parable, are either foxes or hedgehogs. The fox companies develop numerous complex and cunning strategies to achieve their many goals. Foxes seem to know a lot about a lot. Hedgehogs, in contrast, know about only one thing: rolling into a ball.

But knowing how to roll into a ball is all the hedgehog needs to know. None of the fox's tactics can beat a spikey sphere. The hedgehog's goal is to survive a fox attack, and she achieves this goal because she focuses on her asymmetric strength. Not by being medium-good at a lot of things, but by being excellent at one thing.

At its most basic, strategy is how you compete, how you shape your future. Whether it is evolutionary strategy, military strategy, political strategy, corporate strategy, or brand strategy, effective strategy identifies an asymmetric advantage and then uses that advantage to achieve the goal. In the same way that hedgehogs embrace their asymmetric strength, world-class brands identify the thing that will gain them disproportionately large strides toward their desired end. As leader, you eat, sleep, and breathe increasing your business's value. You do this by embracing and nurturing and harnessing your asymmetric strength.

Harnessing this strength will be at the expense of other strengths not unique to you. If all your peers have a given strength, you need to identify and grow a strength where you can dominate. This helps you avoid petty one-upmanship in favor of big, meaningful strides. If you are a tennis player with great groundstrokes, super. But it's not enough to have only great groundstrokes when all your peers do as well. You need to dominate with your serve-and-volley game. Or on grass courts. Or in doubles.

So, what is your asymmetric, lopsided, disproportionate strength that far exceeds the rest of the market? Where do those strengths overlap with a significant unmet need among customers? Where do you shine? Now, where do you *alone* shine? Consider your strengths and then evaluate where you asymmetrically own that strength, where you are not only great but phenomenal. Where you not only beat your competitor but are in a different league altogether. Where there is substantial variance. As venture capitalist Jason Stoffer counsels, "Make sure you are ten times better than the customer's other option; otherwise, why should the customer care about you?"

EMPATHETIC

Ironclad brand strategies reflect the emotional life of their target customer. They honor that through everything they deliver. They are empathetic before, during, and after a person becomes a customer. They are fascinated by and curious about their customers and the problem the brand solves for those customers.

Listen to your customers. What essentially matters to them? How might your strengths deeply help them to thrive? Developing empathy starts with listening and being fascinated with the customer and the problem she faces.

In *Power of Moments*, Chip Heath and Dan Heath share the research findings of social psychologist Harry Reis, who sought to distill relationship science to the single idea of responsiveness: relationships are stronger when we perceive the other to be responsive to us. This is a hallmark of an ironclad brand. Ironclad brands seek to understand their customer rather than first seeking to be understood. They genuinely care about their customers. They view customers as the human beings they are in the business of serving. They care, and in return, the customers care, too.

Empathy requires you to reach outside your brand's walls. It stretches you, helping you tap into a greater source of creativity and meaning. It reinvigorates you, and it also fosters an outside-in, customer-centric perspective. Get outside your conference room. Get attuned to the people your product is devoted to. It is hard not to feel empathy when you regularly talk to your target customer.

Find depth in the mundane. Empathy needs not be dramatic. For example, wiping counters might seem mundane at first—that's okay—find depth in it. My experience helping develop Clorox Anywhere Hard Surface Cleaner showed me that kitchen counter cleaning is a proxy for nurturing. When your counters are clean, you feel like a good caregiver.

Harvey-Davidson provides huge meaning to its customers. The feeling of freedom and breaking through boundaries fills the souls of Harley riders. Part of this brand's success in creating and delivering on such an empathetic promise is that the company actively seeks customers to become employees. It is not a stretch to understand those who share the Harley-Davidson values. One reflexively feels empathy toward one's own people.

And consider OXO Good Grips. OXO was created by a husband for his wife. Company founder Sam Farber knew intimately his wife Betsey's difficulty working small mechanisms because of her arthritis. As he watched her struggle with a vegetable peeler, he wondered why such every day, even simple, tools had to hurt to use. Sam empathized with his wife and other arthritis sufferers, thereby tapping into an insight that enabled him to create an empathetic brand.

Empathetic is being fascinated by your customers' needs (clean counters, transportation, sore wrists) despite their mundane cloak. To the customer, that need represents something bigger. Be open and humble enough to see your customers' needs as a doorway into something profound.

OPTIMALLY DISTINCT

An ironclad brand strategy strikes a balance between old and new, familiar and novel. Giving a customer something completely familiar will not break through the clutter and generate appeal. Giving a customer something completely novel and unrooted in the familiar will be confusing and thus also fail to draw her in. Your brand must be optimally distinct, rather than radically different.

In Chapter 2, we discussed the way that brands help command attention, making themselves easier for customers to see, understand, and buy, and how Wharton School professor Jonah Berger explores this concept of "optimally distinct" in his excellent book *Invisible Influence*. The reason for this is that our brains work in associations, and they need to attach something new to something familiar and already known. One of Berger's examples is skinny jeans. They became popular over the last decade because they are similar enough to something our brains already know (jeans), our frame of reference, but different enough (the skinny shape) to be a breakout product.

Some businesses have nailed the familiar, and so need to balance by establishing the differentiator. When I worked at Clorox, brand was the primary differentiator among near-parity household products. Getting to optimally distinct required pushing away hard from the rest of the category.

Other businesses have nailed the different, and so need to balance by establishing the familiar. Psychologists have observed something called the "mere exposure effect," noting that, among humans, familiarity breeds liking. Startups that are creating new categories and other businesses with low awareness must lean into what makes them recognizable so that the audience "lets in" the rest of what they bring that is different. By leveraging something familiar, the audience will like it better because of the mere exposure effect and will be more likely to listen to the different thing the startup brings. Do not be *too* different.

I interviewed Berger for this book, and he discussed the obligation to meet customer needs before offering them something new. "Often when I work with startups and organizations, they say, 'Oh we've got this great technology.' I say, 'That's fine, but what problem does it solve. What customer need does it address?'"

Berger used Chobani yogurt as an example. Today, Greek-style yogurt is a major category in American grocery stores. But until Chobani entered the market, Greek yogurt was a tiny niche with the sole occupant of Fage, which led a quiet existence on the shelves for ten years before Chobani appeared. Why did Fage not succeed for a decade at what Chobani did relatively quickly? "Because Fage was *very* different," Berger explained. "Not only was it Greek yogurt but it was in large family size containers and only plain flavors." Americans were not used to any of that. All of Fage's attributes were different, and none were familiar. "For Chobani to be successful, what they did is they took that difference and they cloaked it in a skin of familiarity," Berger explained. "They made a few more features feel familiar. They used single size servings. They used fruit on the bottom like Americans were used to. So they took something new but they made it feel more familiar."

Make your brand idea similar enough that it will feel familiar, and their brain will latch, feeling "the warm glow of familiarity." And make your brand idea new enough that it brings the newness we crave alongside familiarity.

SUCCESSFUL DISRUPTIVE BRANDS EMBRACE
THE FAMILIAR WHILE CREATING DIFFERENCE

Let's examine how optimally distinct can look by imagining the brand positioning framework for two major companies: Netflix and Amazon. Here is the classic brand positioning structure, which you will learn more about in Chapter 10. We will complete this structure for both Netflix and Amazon Kindle Fire.

To [the target customer], [our brand] is the one [frame of reference] that [brand promise]. That's because only [our brand] brings [reasons to believe] so that [the target customer] can [end reward].

Netflix: The Limitless Video Rental Store

When Netflix launched, the familiar frame of reference was brick-and-mortar video rental stores, epitomized by Blockbuster. Netflix used that and then pushed away from it with its breakthrough differentiator of no late fees. Here's a positioning statement they might have used:

To film renters, Netflix is the one video rental service that has no late fees. That's because Netflix charges you a simple monthly rate for DVDs you send back when you're finished watching so that you can catch movies whenever without limitations.

If Netflix had not embraced the familiar category of video rental service, they would have nothing familiar to anchor their idea. Instead, they made it easy to understand by noting the familiar before pushing away from that to the different.

Amazon Kindle Fire: The Affordable Tablet

Amazon Kindle Fire came out with a positioning around value.

It is the tablet that is affordable. By showcasing that it's familiar (by playing in an established category, tablets), it could then push off of that with its differentiator, which is low price. Their positioning statement might have been:

To Amazon customers, Kindle Fire is the one tablet that is low-priced. That's because only Kindle Fire is less than one hundred dollars so that Amazon customers can enjoy the freedom of a tablet at an accessible price.

The source of familiarity is the frame of reference (tablets), and the source of differentiation is its astonishingly low price (my Apple iPad was $700, by comparison). If Kindle were to push away too far from the familiar category of tablets, its benefit of being super affordable would be less compelling because there would no longer be a relative and familiar frame. Kindle has a superb brand positioning in part because it embraces the familiar.

BOTH FUNCTIONAL *AND* EMOTIONAL

Your brand must benefit customers both functionally and emotionally. Functional benefits bring credibility and a foot in the door, while emotional benefits lead to competitive differentiation and ultimately a more attractive P&L. Own a benefit that brings customers enormous functional, rational value—and ensure it enables an emotional, inspirational reward that over time you can come to own as well.

Your emotional benefit must be firmly rooted in a functional one. Similarly, your functional benefit should give rise to an emotional reward. They are mutually reinforcing. Together, they make a whole benefit, serving the whole customer. Give your customer the functional benefit she readily needs, and then that can become a foothold to provide her a higher-order emotional benefit.

Here are some brands that provide a whole benefit—substantial functional benefit yielding an emotional reward.

- Target's functional benefit of superb design enables the emotional benefit of feeling triumphant for getting high design for low price.
- Brooks's functional benefit of precise fit enables the emotional benefit of joy in running.
- Amazon Prime's functional benefit of fast delivery enables the emotional benefit of instant gratification.
- Survey Monkey's functional benefit of a turnkey survey enables the emotional benefit of feeling in control.
- 24 Hour Fitness's functional benefit of always being open enables the emotional benefit of feeling authority over your workout schedule.

I find that most leaders know functional benefits are important but need more convincing that emotional benefits are worthwhile. So, let's pause for a second to look at this. While functional benefits provide heft and credibility, emotional benefits bring healthy margins, enduring competitive insulation, and more customer motivation.

- **Emotional benefits drive financial premiums.** When you bring an emotional benefit, you will command higher prices. Look at Lululemon: their flattering athleisure apparel makes customers feel hip and fit. Lululemon yoga pants are ninety-eight dollars and usually sell out; similar pants at Old Navy are nineteen dollars, but the cut isn't as flattering and, therefore, doesn't make the wearer feel as attractive—and those pants do not sell out.

- **Emotional benefits are longer-lasting and thus provide more competitive insulation into the future.** Even the most distinctive functional benefits can be duplicated by competitors or fall out of favor as the market evolves. In the case of 24 Hour Fitness, at any moment Gold's Gym could expand its hours to match those of 24 Hour Fitness. Whereas Adidas could come after any functional benefit of a Brooks shoe, Brooks still owns the emotional benefit—and hard-earned market share—of joyful running.

- **Emotional benefits motivate by making use of our neurology.** Humans are emotional beings. We make decisions on a gut level more often than we realize, or sometimes would like to admit. Behavioral economics is showing that we make decisions with our reptilian or "old" brain. This is the part of our brain that we rely on for survival, and it functions very quickly, below our consciousness. Then we use our neocortex or "thinking" brain to (much more slowly) rationalize the decision our old brain has already made. Emotional benefits appeal to the quick, instinctive, reptilian brain, while functional benefits appeal to the slower, rational neocortex.

An ironclad brand strategy meets the customer where she is and then enables her to rise above where she was. Functional benefits provide the foundation, and emotional benefits help her to become more of what she wants to be.

SHARP-EDGED

Think of brands you admire and synthesize their essence in a word or phrase. Now ask a friend or colleague what word comes to mind with each of those brands. Because these are strong brands, I bet you both thought of the same or similar words. We can even try it here. If I say Patagonia, what words come to mind? Ethical, durable, high-performance. If I say Trader Joe's, there's fun, tasty, quirky. Those brands draw a sharp line around what they promise to their customers. They do not hedge. Their edges are not blurry.

Ironclad brand strategy is spare, simple, sharp-edged. Murky edges, or a vague positioning, make it hard for the customer to see you and bond with you, which makes it less likely they will grasp you, remember you, buy from you, and tell others about you.

Sharpness brings more clarity because it brings contrast. Just like one's eye can see objects better when there is high contrast around that object, customers can see a brand more clearly when there is high contrast between that brand and others in its space. You must choose what falls inside and what falls outside your brand to sharpen the edge. In choosing to be fun and quirky, Trader Joe's trades off reliability and ubiquity, and even ease. Their parking lots are a bit of a pain. There is no home delivery. And I am no longer surprised when they are out of Joe's Os.

But because of these sharp edges, it is easy to "place" Trader Joe's in one's mind. While I cannot distinguish Safeway from Kroger, Trader Joe's is crystal clear to me, and I seek them out. Sharp-edged brand positioning facilitates customers seeing you—and therefore remembering and buying from you.

Sometimes the best way to sharpen your edges is to remove things, to simplify. John Maeda said in *The Laws of Simplicity:*

Design, Technology, Business, Life: "Simplicity is about subtracting the obvious and adding the meaningful." Removing unremarkable things concentrates the remarkable thing about your business, sharpening the edge around your position.

Think of some car brands whose position you instantly could articulate. When I think of Prius, I think "eco-friendly." In owning the position of eco-friendly, Prius is not a sexy sports car, or the safest car, or a big car for transporting large families. Volvo owns "safety." Volvo does not have an eco-friendly car, or a sexy sports car, or a utility truck.

Do the hard work to make your brand easier for customers to see, grasp, and bond with. Clayton Lewis, who we heard from in Chapter 2, told me, "During brand strategy creation, you are doing the heavy lifting of distilling the primary value you bring so that the consumer does not have to do that heavy lifting for you."

Being clear about who you are and who you are not breeds trust. Blurriness breeds mistrust. It weakens conviction among customers and employees, muddying your position and eroding your brand. When your brand position is sharp-edged, you have set the conditions to build a lasting relationship.

Not only do sharp edges provide clarity for your customer, but sharp edges also provide clarity for you as you lead. The sharper the edges of your brand, the brighter the North Star for you to reference as you grow and expand the value of your business. As you make decisions big and small, when your edges are sharp, your brand makes your decisions clear and fueling, rather than fuzzy and draining. A sharp-edged brand positioning makes it clearer what to choose to add to your brand's value.

HAS TEETH

Your brand strategy not only needs to be true, it needs to be *demonstrably* true. It must have the power to make people believe it, trust it, and follow it because it offers compelling proof that it will live up to its promise. An ironclad brand strategy has teeth. Those teeth can be an attribute, a feature, a fact, a guarantee, an ingredient—any special thing the brand offers and follows through with that proves its promise, its reason for existence. The less debatable, the better.

I recently saw an ordinary computer mouse package with the tagline "Enjoy what you do." This is a big claim for a computer mouse that appeared no different from any other computer mouse. Nothing I could discern demonstrated that this mouse could deliver on such a lofty promise. Whether or not this mouse could indeed enable enjoyment, I did not believe it. There were no teeth to show me the promise was true.

Contrast that to Zappos, a brand that represents best-in-class customer service. That is no squishy promise, because specifics back it up. For example, while most retailers bury their 1-800 customer service phone number in small print on their websites, Zappos' 1-800 number is displayed "proudly" (in CEO Tony Hsieh's words) on every page of Zappos's site. And when you call it, a live person—not a computerized switchboard—answers. There are no scripts and no time limits for these calls. The humans who pick up the phone and speak with you seem genuinely glad that you called. The Zappos promise of customer service has teeth.

Starbucks VIA Instant Coffee is Starbucks Coffee taste made in an instant. That is a big, hard-to-believe promise because instant coffee is typically low-quality coffee, not Starbucks caliber.

Starbucks VIA follows up its promise with this reason to believe: VIA is made from the same Starbucks beans, micro-ground to be part of Starbucks VIA. They even name the VIA blends the same as the blends it serves in its cafés. Starbucks VIA's promise of "Starbucks Coffee in an instant" has teeth.

Some more brands that have teeth:

- Zildjian Cymbals is the gold standard of cymbals. That is an audacious promise. Zildjian Cymbals was founded in Constantinople in 1623. Wow, that was centuries ago, and made in the land where cymbals originated. Now I believe that promise.
- Dove soap softens skin. That is hard to believe, because soap is known to dry skin, not soften it. Dove backs up that promise by telling us that it contains ¼ moisturizing cream in each bar. Now I believe that promise.
- Original Pantry Cafe is always open. Really? Always open? All day every day no matter the time or holiday? That is a daring promise, and I don't quite believe it. Original Pantry Cafe backs it up by saying that since they first opened in 1924, they have never had locks on the doors. Wow, no locks. You can only have no locks if you are always open. Now I believe that they truly never close.

As you are defining the teeth for your promise, make them as granular, as specific, as you can. High granularity increases believability. A University of Michigan study asked participants to estimate the battery life of two GPS devices, with one device claiming a battery life of "up to two hours" and the other "up to 120 minutes." Participants estimated the first to have a battery life of 89 minutes and the second 106 minutes. People associate the finer granularity of one proof point with more credibility than the more general proof point.

DELIVERS

Your brand needs to be something you deliver on every time. In choosing your brand strategy, you need to be extremely honest with yourself about your capabilities before you establish your promise. As brand strategist and NYU marketing professor Scott Galloway wrote in *The Four*, "Brands are two things: promise and performance." Your promise must be something you always fulfill.

Don't you know this to be true of any relationship? Keep your promises to customers just like you would keep promises in any relationship that you value. Inconsistency breeds mistrust and consistency breeds trust. "The better and more consistently you deliver on your unique promise, the more customers will trust you and want to hang out with you in the future," Andrew Sherrard, CMO of T-Mobile, told me.

Many brands fail to perform, fail to fulfill their promise. On one hand, this has made customers slow to trust. On the other hand, your business can stand out all the more powerfully by performing according to your promise. Not just the letter of the promise, but also the spirit of it. Not just with the big things, but the little things. Not just for new customers, but for loyal customers. Not just where it's visible, but also where it's less visible.

As Marc Benioff, CEO of Salesforce, wrote, "A delivery service that promises to meticulously care about your packages cannot have dirty trucks. A bank that says it cares about its customers can't have twenty people waiting in line with only two tellers on duty. Brands cannot break the promises they make. Broken promises destroy customers' trust. That ruins everything." A treasured brand consistently delivers on its promise, consistently aligns what it says (messaging) with what it does (product):

- Dove actually does make skin soft.
- Netflix actually is the feeling of limitless entertainment.
- Brooks Shoes actually do fit so well that running is joyful.
- Survey Monkey actually is a turnkey experience.
- Harley Davidson actually does help you touch freedom.
- Driving my Volvo, I actually am safer.
- Thanks to Rick Steves, I actually do feel like a temporary local while traveling in Europe.
- With Slack, our team actually does communicate better and with more fun.
- On Dropbox, I actually can access all my files from anywhere and with any device.

After sharing these nine criteria, I want to acknowledge something you might be thinking, a realization mounting through this chapter. These are stringent, exacting, tough criteria—a true crucible. For a brand to meet these criteria, leaders must make difficult choices and trade-offs. It can feel scary to decide so boldly and shine a spotlight on what you have selected.

This choosing demands leadership courage, and as Peter Thiel wrote in *Zero to One*, "Courage is in even shorter supply than genius." Choosing is what separates good leaders from great leaders, what separates flash-in-the-pan businesses from the ones that endure for generations.

The purpose of an ironclad brand strategy is to create enduring value. How much do you want this? Is it enough to spark the courage to make difficult choices? Choosing might scare you. But the idea that it is safe not to choose is an illusion of safety.

This is high-leverage work you are doing. As entrepreneur and venture capitalist, Andy Rachleff said, "Delight is the greatest form of virality." Seek to be loved, not liked. If you were your customer, wouldn't you only connect with a business that stands for something bold? If you were your employee, wouldn't you only give your all to a company that is clear and unwavering on who they are?

We have now unraveled the meaning of brand, and brand's ability to create enduring value. We have deconstructed brand so that you can apply its power with precision. And we have identified the nine criteria for an ironclad brand strategy.

Now you will roll up your sleeves and build your ironclad brand strategy, using the eight-step Ironclad Method that Part 2 illustrates.

IRONCLAD METHOD

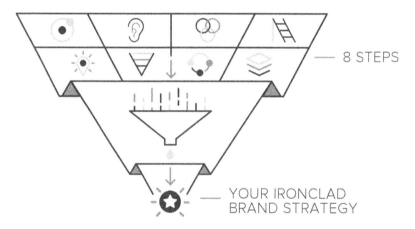

8 STEPS

YOUR IRONCLAD
BRAND STRATEGY

PART 2

THE HOW OF BRAND

With a deep understanding of what brand is and why it matters, you are now poised to craft a robust strategy that will bolster, nourish, and grow your business durably.

Part 2 of this book gives you a method for doing so. The Ironclad Method is the eight-step process for crafting a brand strategy that I developed and use for businesses of all shapes and sizes, from solo-owned to publicly traded; from B2B to B2C; from stodgy, old-economy categories to disruptive, new-to-the-world innovations.

I'm sharing the Ironclad Method with you so that building your brand strategy can be a natural, energizing, fortifying discovery for your business. Brand is the crystallization and delivery of your business's value to customers. If you lead a business, you can and must gain this clarity.

AN OVERVIEW OF THE IRONCLAD METHOD

The Ironclad Method begins by establishing context. In the first step of creating your brand strategy, you **orient** to your target customer and your competitive frame of reference.

In the second step of the method, you **listen** to your customers to identify the insights from which your brand strategy will spring. By getting into a listening mindset, and preparing for and conducting customer research, you set up the richest building blocks for your brand strategy.

In step three, you **examine** the insights you have collected and synthesize them into the Uncommon Denominator framework. This reveals your potential positioning themes that strike the overlap of being both relevant to the customer and ownable by your business.

Now you establish the linchpin of your brand strategy. In step four, you develop a **ladder** of benefits and reasons to believe that specify the promise your business makes, how you prove that promise, and what your customer ultimately enjoys as a result of experiencing that promise.

With your benefit ladder complete, the method's fifth step shifts you to **characterize** your business. By pinpointing your character archetype and defining the personality and tonality of your business, you enable yourself and others to embody your brand consistently and genuinely.

In the sixth step, you will define each **stage** of your customer's journey with your brand. Explicitly describing the stages enables you later to tailor your messages for a given customer in a given piece of communication, progressing those customers along in their journeys.

The seventh step shows how to **activate creative** once you are executing a specific creative tactic. This step establishes the strategic directive, stripping out the extraneous and subjective before beginning the creative development process, setting the conditions for effective communication.

For the final step of the Ironclad Method, and our lead-in to the book's third and final part, you **zoom out** to begin seeing brand in everything. We will discuss two classic frameworks that help leaders use brand as a complete strategic platform for growing with purpose.

By the end of Part 2, you will have a "how" for brand: the eight-step Ironclad Method for building a brand strategy that sets the stage for your business to flourish.

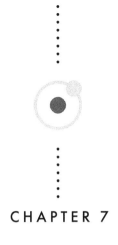

CHAPTER 7

STEP 1: ORIENT

We begin with setting the starting point: who do you serve, and what are their current alternatives for the problem you solve?

The first step in building a value-unlocking brand strategy is to establish the context of your business. Your context consists of who you're speaking to—your target customer—and what they're comparing you to—their frame of reference. By identifying your target customer and frame of reference, you define the most fertile place to lay your roots. The rest of your brand strategy will spring from these choices.

When you orient, you identify the place where your roots can grow down, so that your promise can spring from that solidity. While you likely have a general sense of your target customer and frame of reference, during this step you will come to understand them with specificity. These choices are deceptively subtle. Don't rush to a superficial, obvious answer. The more granular your orienting choices, the more powerful the brand strategy that grows out of them, and thus, the more energetically you can attract and retain customers.

This chapter explores the critical elements of orienting your brand:

- Choose Your Target Customer
- Define Your Frame of Reference

CHOOSE YOUR TARGET CUSTOMER

In this first part of orienting, you make the most essential decision of your brand strategy by defining your target customer.

These are the people you want to attract more of: the ones who bring you the most value, and to whom you bring the most value. They are the people you are most able to delight because of your distinctive strengths. By defining who these people are, you set yourself up to establish a brand promise that will connect and resonate with them, inspiring them to enter into a relationship with your business. What you contribute to the relationship will be so meaningful and compelling to them that they will want to buy from you.

The key to defining your target customer is to characterize them not in a superficial way as most businesses do, inventorying demographic data describing little of their inner world. Instead, characterize your target customer as a subtle and empathetic picture of how they view themselves.

When defining your target customer, get customer-centric, rather than you-centric, and be as specific as you can. Identify the patterns, the common themes, the threads of similarity that unite your ideal customers. At the superficial level, they may appear dissimilar. You may be tempted to throw up your hands, exclaiming, "I serve anyone who needs my product." But themes await when you dig beneath the surface. And you need those themes to make your brand reverberate.

THE BULLSEYE CUSTOMER

If you worry that you'll be ignoring cherished customers who don't fall into your description of a target customer, remember that identifying your target does not eliminate your larger addressable market.

Picture your customers as sprinkled across a dartboard. The full dartboard is your addressable market. You sell to the whole dartboard. The bullseye is your target, the customers you must aim to please the most. The target customers in the middle will ideally influence the customers on the outer circles of the dartboard.

Selecting your target customer is simply identifying that bullseye—it is not a decision *not* to service customers who are outside that bullseye. It is a humble choice of who you best serve; who your strengths, passion, and purpose will most delight; and who will bring the most value to you.

In the game of darts, hitting the bullseye garners the most points—that is, the most value. But just as importantly, simply *trying* to hit the bullseye serves your whole game—or helps you serve your whole addressable market. Aiming for the target maximizes your probability of both earning high points and landing your dart on the board at all.

Regardless of your business's size or budget, answer this question: "who is the customer I want more of?"

Your ten best (or thousand best or hundred thousand best) customers—the ones you make most happy, and the ones who make *you* most happy—may appear to be a hodgepodge group. Your job is to find their common link, because the strength of your positioning depends on the specificity of your target customer. Here are four ways to pinpoint the commonalities that define your target.

- **Identify a uniting theme among your customers.** What do they all have in common? What are they like? What do they value? What do they do? How would they characterize themselves? What keeps them up at night? What brings them joy? What do they find satisfying? What do they do with their free time? What might your offering help them accomplish? What problem does it help them solve? Be less curious about your offering and more curious about the person, the problem it solves, and the context in which that problem emerges.
- **Explore who you most benefit.** To whom do you bring disproportionate value? Who do you most delight? Who would most miss your offering if it went away?
- **Determine who brings your business the most value.** Who are the people who bring disproportionate value to you? Often, those are the people who buy frequently, who buy the most high-priced option, or who repeat with the most loyalty. They clearly value what you bring them. Since they bring you disproportionate financial gains, you should be disproportionately serving them.

- **Span out even farther and consider your mission.** Why are you in business? Who is the person that you have created your business to serve? Who do you have the most heart for serving? Be specific and nuanced.

Consider how REI might approach this definition of target customer. As a co-op that sells outdoor apparel and gear online and in retail stores, the company strives to get more people enjoying and nurturing the great outdoors. To that multipronged end, REI's ideal customers—the ones who bring REI the most value and to whom REI brings the most value—are outdoor enthusiasts. These customers spend the most money with REI, and by embracing the outdoors, they also help the company with its mission to cultivate environmental stewardship.

In superficial ways, REI's customers vary: all genders, all ages, all incomes. Yet there is a uniting theme: this group's passion for communing with nature. In one sense, these customers are diverse, but what REI rightly focuses on is the common value that makes these individuals resonate with REI's promise.

Because your target customer brings you disproportionate value, you optimize your brand and everything about your offering for this person. Not all customers are equally valuable to you. In most categories, growth strategist Eddie Yoon has explained, roughly 10 percent of customers account for roughly 50 percent of profit. By focusing on the customers who bring you the most value, you can make decisions according to what will most delight these people, and this delight then radiates outward to the rest of your customers.

As a consumer, I fall along one of the outer circles of REI's dartboard. I am within the company's addressable market, but

I am not the target customer. I camp about twice a year, and at least one of those two times is in the backyard with my kids. I am not an outdoor enthusiast. In contrast, my friend Jacqueline rock climbs, backpacks, and thinks nothing of camping in the snow. As an outdoor enthusiast, Jacqueline is REI's target customer—and she is indeed an avid REI customer.

But get this: because I trust Jacqueline's discernment, when I choose a tent and sleeping bags, I buy where she buys her tents and sleeping bags. REI did not lose me by delighting Jacqueline. By optimizing for the outdoor enthusiast, REI attracts that person, which in turn can help attract their entire addressable market.

This bears repeating: selecting your target customer does *not* exclude other customers. It's choosing with honesty the customers you have the highest ability to serve, and whose delight will in turn attract the outer circles of your addressable market.

In fact, often the customer a business is targeting at the center of the bullseye is aspirational for the rest of the market *because* they are "more so." Whether as an outdoor enthusiast (REI), fashionista (Nordstrom), or music-lover (Sonos).

Consider Walmart, a business that may not appear to have a target customer because the company's offering is so large and diffuse. According to a 2017 NPD report, 95 percent of Americans spent money at Walmart the previous year. That is a large addressable market, thus a large dartboard. But guess what— even the largest dartboard has a bullseye.

I would wager that Walmart's bullseye target customer is cost-conscious and reserved. That does not mean that Walmart would turn away people with higher discretionary spending power, and the company does not turn away people who are outgoing. But by defining a target customer, Walmart could optimize the offering—

the product assortment, the store layout and design, the pricing schematic, the messaging, the music and broader shopping experience—to ensure the shopping experience is particularly compelling to the target customer in particular.

This holds true for any business. If I were running a fast-fashion business, I might select as my target customer the millennial who likes the latest style for cheap. If I were managing a line of disinfecting sprays for homes, I might define as my target customer the parent with small kids who is worried about cold and flu contagion. If I were selling an elite running club membership, I might select runners who want guidance and accountability from a trained coach.

Now, if a Gen X couple wanted to try out a refreshed wardrobe, or if a college student wanted to buy disinfecting spray for her first apartment, or if a non-runner wanted to try running, I would still happily sell them my offering. They are in my addressable market, and they are on my dartboard. But I am not going to optimize my fashion business for a Gen X couple, my disinfecting spray for a college kid, or my elite running club for nonrunners.

I will always choose to optimize for the center.

DEFINE YOUR FRAME OF REFERENCE

Now that you have defined your target customer, it's time to define your competitive frame of reference. To position your brand, you need to understand what you are positioning your brand *against*. This involves more than simply naming your obvious competitors. A truly accurate frame of reference digs deeper than that. If a customer is evaluating your offering, she is deciding whether to choose yours instead of...what, exactly? What is your target customer comparing you *to*? This is what you need to differentiate your business *from*.

Defining this frame of reference is vital to brand strategy for two reasons. First, by putting your offering in the most relevant context in your target customer's mind, you facilitate your customer learning about you and bonding with you—and, ultimately, buying and loving your offering. Second, selecting a precise frame of reference enables you to differentiate from the other options your customers are considering. Since differentiation fuels your competitive advantage, it is imperative to differentiate with precision.

As with defining your target customer, the trick here is to be customer-centric, rather than you-centric—to think outside in, rather than inside out. Instead of merely noting the obvious direct competitors you perceive from your vantage point, notice the context in which your target customer considers you.

When your customer is considering your offering, she's trying to solve a problem. What are the various other ways she could accomplish this? In some cases, the target customer does weigh you against an obvious direct competitor. In others, she weighs you against a substitute or an indirect competitor or a workaround. Your true frame of reference is what your customer considers your frame of reference.

For example, let's say you are a handyman. From your standpoint, you might quickly conclude that you compete primarily with other handymen. But when you get to know your customers, understanding their problem and their other ways of solving that problem, you might learn that they choose to work with you rather than doing the work themselves. Your frame of reference in this case would be "homeowners doing their own handiwork." If you

THE CHOICE IS ALWAYS YOURS

Some of you may feel resistant to making these choices. You might imagine all the customers who appear from unexpected directions and feel that in choosing a focus, you are not leaving room for those surprise customers.

That is a false dilemma. By choosing a target customer, you do not exclude everyone else from buying your product. Rather, you strengthen your brand promise for the people who matter most to your brand. The door remains open for anyone to walk through and enter into a relationship with you.

You may also resist the idea of selecting your primary frame of reference since you draw from many. But not choosing—precisely—your primary target customer and frame of reference results in a timid, ineffectual brand. If you don't decide, the market will decide for you.

So, do not be vague because of the faulty sense that in choosing you are closing doors. In choosing, you establish your meaning, and with this clarity you become more attractive to more customers.

had positioned yourself against other handyman services, your brand strategy would be oriented incorrectly and thus would lead you to make ineffective choices about how to market and sell your services. At best, it would have been a waste of energy and money. At worst, it would have been confusing and counterproductive, undermining your ability to grow your business.

Remember the last time you learned about a new idea? To grasp its significance quickly, you might have thought, "Oh, it's kind of like __, except __."

When doing so, you were using your existing vocabulary and associations—your existing "mental file folders" that we first discussed in Chapter 2 while exploring brand's power to capture attention. People organize knowledge just like we organize physical things. Our minds take in stimuli, and for easy storage and retrieval, we sort it the way we might label manila file folders for monthly bills and family photos. This reduces cognitive energy for learning, storing, and recalling what we need, much as do the biases we discussed in Chapter 1.

Many years ago, at a bakery near my home, I learned about the cake pop. This was before cake pops were a trendy dessert form, but though I had previously not heard of one, I processed the cake pop readily as "a small, easy-to-eat dessert, a bite of cake on a stick." I was learning about a new offering by integrating it into the vocabulary already available to me. The cake pop was similar enough to other "little desserts" that I could put it into one of those folders without needing to come up with a whole new category.

Because the bakers called it a cake pop, they helped me learn about it by tying it to existing mental file folders (the folder for "cake" and the one for "lollipops"). That made me more likely to pay attention to the cake pop, remember it, and ultimately, try it. They made it easy for me to perceive the purpose of this product, so I invited it into my head (literally—I've now eaten an untold number of these).

When establishing the frame of reference, your goal is to use frames that are easiest for the customer. A way to approach that is to picture the customers' existing mental file folders, and to use those existing associations to discern your most relevant frame of reference.

My client Cypress Grove Cheese makes mind-bendingly delicious goat cheeses, including their signature Humboldt Fog and Truffle Tremor offerings. Cypress Grove knows that their target customer, the "mindful foodie," considers Cypress Grove to be a specialty cheese. The mindful foodie brings it out for everyday luxury, as she might bring out another fine finger food.

So, the Cypress Grove mental file folder is "specialty cheese." It is not "specialty *goat* cheese," as that would be asking customers to think of the brand in too slim a mental file folder to be useful. From the customer's standpoint, Cypress Grove is more similar to other high-end cheeses than to other goat cheeses. It also doesn't work to compare Cypress Grove to all cheeses—that's too large of a folder—mindful foodies are not choosing between Cypress Grove and Velveeta. Cypress Grove's frame of reference is other specialty cheeses.

When you are choosing a frame of reference for your brand, you make it easier for your customer by harnessing her most natural mental file folder for your offering. You want to leverage the familiar, by referencing something your target customer already knows and that is already relevant to her. This choice will help you dramatically when you define your singular promise that distinguishes your offering from your target customer's other choices (which we'll do in Step 4).

Your target customers are likely comparing you to a myriad of competitors and substitutes and workarounds, including doing nothing. Determine which comparison is *most* relevant. Here are five ways to discern the folder into which they put your business.

- **Think about your target customer's budget.** Where in her budget will she get the money to pay for your offering? How will she justify this purchase, either literally or figuratively? If your offering costs one hundred dollars, what is she not going to spend money on so that she can afford that one hundred dollars for your offering? When I bought skis for my kids, I did so with money I might have spent on other recreational gear. I delayed new tennis rackets and lacrosse sticks to make room for skis. So, my frame of reference for skis was "recreational gear."

- **Think about how your customers spend their time.** What will they not spend time on because they'll be spending time on your offering? When I started taking barre classes, I reduced the number of yoga classes I was taking. For me, barre was competing more with yoga than with other barre classes. If I represent barre's target customer, then barre's primary frame of reference is "yoga."

- **Think about your customers' consumption habits.** When it comes time to using your offering, what will they not be using as a result of using your offering? After my team launched the Clorox Bleach Pen, we learned that of our customers using the Bleach Pen, 20 percent were using it instead of regular bleach, 20 percent were using it instead of other topical stain removers, and 60 percent were using it instead of living with stains on their clothes. The Clorox Bleach Pen's primary frame of reference was "tolerating stained clothing."

- **Think about the workarounds available to your target customers.** What are the workarounds your customers currently employ because they don't have the benefit of your offering? Before Skype, a combination of phone calls and emails substituted for in-person communication. Skype competed less with other "video calling services" and more with "phone and email."

- **Think about the Google search term or the word-of-mouth phrase customers use when talking about your business.** What do people type into the Google search bar that leads them to you? If a friend referred them, what did the friend say you were? There is a museum in Seattle that my family loves called the Museum of Pop Culture. When people visit us from out of town and are looking for things to do in the city, we always suggest that. The MoPOP is competing with "things visitors should do in Seattle," not museums in general.

CONTINUALLY REVISIT YOUR FRAME OF REFERENCE

Even if your category is highly established, your frame of reference is likely evolving either subtly or drastically as the market shifts, new competitors enter, and new innovations take hold. Stay attuned to your customers' frame of reference so that you remain meaningful and relevant as the market evolves.

I observed this recently in an unlikely place. At my annual dermatology check, I noticed that the practice had renovated the private rooms with pastels, plush reclining chairs, soft music, and scented candles. It was the same footprint as my primary care physician's offices upstairs, but while those still looked like a medical space—cold, clinical, smelled like Purell—my dermatologist's office presented like a spa.

When I asked the nurse about it, she told me that half of the patients receive Botox and other cosmetic dermatology treatments. The frame of reference for these customers was less "other dermatology clinics" and more "medical spas." Previously, this dermatology clinic had been offering dermatological beauty treatments in a cold, clinical setting—which demonstrated a disconnect and presented an opportunity.

The dermatology clinic positions their business to be close enough to their true frame of reference so as to secure a place in their customer's consideration set. Then, the clinic could differentiate from the customer's alternatives to be appealing in a distinctive way. To woo cosmetic dermatology customers to come and to stay, the practice remodeled to look and feel like a spa. Because the practice was attuned to the customer's shifting frame of reference, the staff was able to retain existing customers and attract new ones.

The orientation of your brand strategy can be deceiving because, upon first blush, the choices appear obvious. You make bottled soda, so you assume your target customer is a soda lover, and you assume your frame of reference is other bottled soda brands—easy, in fact lazy, assumptions that are not likely to tap a rich need.

Using a superficial choice of target hampers your ability to cultivate customer empathy. Using a superficial choice of frame of reference makes it more challenging for your customer to learn about, remember, and want your offering. To make sharp and true choices, step into the vantage point of your customers. Who will disproportionately value what you bring? Among what other options will this person organize and consider your offering?

In the next chapter, we will use these orientation choices of target customer and frame of reference to unearth insights about both.

CHAPTER 8

STEP 2: LISTEN

Now that you've oriented your brand strategy, determining your target customer as well as your competitive frame of reference, it's time to deepen your understanding of each of those pieces. The only way to get the nuanced insights you need is to listen directly to your customers.

In the last chapter, you imagined the individuals occupying the bullseye of your addressable market and those individuals' frame of reference for your brand. In this chapter, you will glean insights about the real human beings behind the concept of "target customer." These insights will form the raw material for your brand strategy. This chapter begins with guidance on preparing yourself to listen, and then discusses concrete ways to research.

The best way to set the foundation for bonding with future customers is to unearth nuanced insights. This understanding does not arise out of nothing—you need to talk to your real-life customers. Before you do so, prepare by getting into a listening mindset and then envisioning the things you want to learn. In this chapter, we explore how to:

- Cultivate a Listening Mindset
- Design Your Research
- Compose Your Discussion Guide
- Conduct Your Research

CULTIVATE A LISTENING MINDSET

The single most important condition for rich insight gathering is having genuine curiosity. Be wide open, humble, nonjudgmental, and empathetic. Seek to understand, not to be understood. The more you adopt such a mindset during research, the truer and more nuanced your realizations will be, and therefore the more ironclad your brand can become.

Even if you elect to partner with a professional moderator to conduct the research for you, you are still the leader building your brand, and you will still be the one to lead and activate the brand strategy. Adopting a listening mindset as a default will continuously benefit your leadership.

DON'T COP OUT

I have heard business leaders say, "We don't do research because we lead the customer, rather than letting the customer lead us." This is a cop-out. Research cannot and will not replace your leadership. By listening to your customers, you gain a deep and empathetic understanding of their world, which will embolden you to take the lead. Ironclad brands both listen to target customers *and* lead them.

BEGINNER'S MIND AND GROUNDED THEORY

Productive listening begins with humility. Here's what you need to internalize: you do not know best. You are in the business of serving your target customer, which means you are now the student and your target customer is your teacher. Of course, you know massively more about your product and category than does your target customer. But you are not conducting this research to learn about your offering. You are doing it to learn about your *customer*.

From a foundation of humility, curiosity naturally arises. Genuine curiosity is not attached to outcome. Cultivate what Zen Buddhists call the "beginner's mind"—a receptive, unguarded, eager state of childlike wonder about your customer and what he is trying to accomplish. In this state, you will be vulnerable—open to learn, to be surprised, to be wrong—even though you might find that vulnerability uncomfortable. If you're not approaching your customer with vulnerability, you won't allow *him* to be vulnerable, and this will prevent meaningful insights from emerging. You will merely hear confirmation of things you already knew.

The biggest curiosity killer is thinking you have all the answers.

As the adage goes, a person who knows everything learns nothing. Ask only open-ended and expansive questions and be earnestly receptive to what you hear.

Renowned social work researcher Brené Brown uses an inductive research method called "grounded theory," which asks the researcher to listen and gather data *before* forming a hypothesis. Instead of stating a question and then seeking to prove or disprove it with data, this method systematically opens the researcher first to what the questions may be, before focusing on the answers. You start with open listening, and only later do you search for themes and patterns in the stories that emerge. Even those of us not trained in the technique of grounded theory can benefit from the spirit of the technique by acknowledging as we begin the research that we do not know the answers. And while the target customer will not give you the answers outright, he'll give you clues so that you yourself can discern patterns.

To help you cultivate the beginner's mindset, internalize that in this interaction, *you* have lower power than the customer to whom you are speaking. Social psychology research demonstrates an inverse relationship between power and perspective-taking. In conversations where the participants have unequal power status, the person with the lower status tends to be more astute at taking the other's perspective. Researchers at Northwestern University showed that "power leads individuals to anchor too heavily on their own vantage point, insufficiently adjusting to others' perspective." So, recognizing the customer to whom you are speaking as the one with higher status helps you to attune and empathize.

A parting word on the listening mindset: let it become your default state. Rather than adopting it surgically, only to discard it when you finish the research exercise, train yourself to be an excellent customer listener all the time. Consider making informal customer research a regular practice. Interact with your customers routinely. Here are a few stellar examples:

- David Neeleman, who founded JetBlue Airways and served as CEO for its first seven years, worked the cabin regularly. "Each week I fly on JetBlue flights and talk to customers so I can find out how we can improve our airline," he has said.
- When developing a men's razor for the India market, Proctor & Gamble's Gillette razor team conducted ethnographies and learned about how shaving differs in India versus Gillette's other markets. The research resulted in Gillette Guard, which is designed for easy cleaning without running water.
- Howard Schultz, CEO of Starbucks, hangs out in Starbucks cafés almost every day. The lessons he's learned by observing his customers and staff and how they interact with Starbucks' offering have led to significant changes, including adding nonfat milk as an option for lattes.

A continual listening mindset will help your brand to be ever more relevant and meaningful to your target customer. It can be your brand's turbocharger.

DESIGN YOUR RESEARCH

To create an ironclad brand strategy, you need penetrating and subtle insights. You will use a qualitative research method to explore and uncover these insights.

In the social sciences and in marketing, qualitative research methods are for open-ended searching. The sample size is relatively small, and the goal is to detect insights on the problem and to develop hypotheses for the solution. In contrast, quantitative research is used for closed-ended studies, particularly to validate or confirm. For example, you might use a survey to quantify the size of a market opportunity, interest in a product concept, or receptivity to specific ad copy. The sample size is larger with quantitative research because the objective is empirical validation. While qualitative yields subtle insights, quantitative brings numerical conclusiveness.

Ideally, as a marketer and leader, you continually employ both qualitative and quantitative research methods. You do qualitative research to unearth hypotheses, cultivate empathy, and explore subtle insights. You do quantitative research to validate and size opportunities that come out of those hypotheses. Then you return to qualitative methods to learn how your shifts are performing for customers.

My favorite qualitative research method, and the one I'll be illustrating most in this chapter, is one-to-one phone interviews with customers. The privacy and psychological safety of one-to-one phone conversations encourage revealing, candid discussion. This tool also brings the advantage of being expedient and practical—no travel, no fancy technology, just a phone call. You may learn so much that you make these calls a regular part of your work as a leader, to keep you in a customer-centric mindset.

There is no rule about how long the interviews should be. It will depend on how familiar your target customer is with your category and how skilled you are at interviewing. I find thirty to forty minutes works well, as it's usually enough time to get beneath the surface but compact enough that you aren't demanding undue time from your interviewee. Regardless of length, it's customary and polite to give the interviewee some form of compensation (e.g., Amazon or Target gift cards) for the time they spent with you on the phone.

Similarly, the number of interviews you need to conduct to get a useful set of data is also malleable. If you are truly talking to your target customer, and you are asking carefully crafted and open-ended questions with a beginners' mind, you are likely to see patterns emerge after just a few calls. Until you get very experienced in phone interviews, I recommend that you aim to interview at least fifteen people. If after fifteen you are hearing the exact same responses, you may not need more. Conversely, if you have spoken with fifteen people and still don't see common themes emerging, keep interviewing until the themes are consistent.

While preparing for the interviews, I recommend that you get an audio recorder so that you can record and later transcribe your conversations. Actual customer verbatims are powerful for channeling the customer and sharing your interview findings with others. Audio recording the interviews will allow you to capture the vibrancy of customers' actual verbatims without having to scribble like a maniac while interviewing. At the beginning of the conversation, obtain the customer's explicit permission to record the interview.

COMPOSE YOUR DISCUSSION GUIDE

As you prepare for your interviews, put on your journalist hat. This approach is effective in many communication realms. When asked how he writes jokes, comedian Chris Rock replied, "Forget

FOCUS GROUPS AND ETHNOGRAPHIES

Beyond one-to-one interviews, the most common types of qualitative research for brand development are focus groups and ethnographies.

Focus groups involve a moderator and a group of participants (typically six to eight, but I've invited as few as two and as many as ten) sitting around a table or in group video conference sessions. This research method has the benefit of getting participants riffing and building upon one another's ideas. When the chemistry is right, the social energy can foster subtle insights. On the flip side, that same social dynamic can go awry. Sometimes participants will posture for others in the room, and sometimes dominant personalities shut down quieter ones, thwarting the more vulnerable (and therefore useful) insights. It also takes skill to facilitate these effectively, so if you do go this route, partner with an experienced moderator.

In ethnographies, researchers observe, rather than interview, the target customer and do so while the customer is using or buying your offering. This can yield direct knowledge of how a customer acts with your offering, rather than how he says he acts with it. Anthropologists have long known how revealing ethnography can be. They also know its pitfalls, such as the Hawthorne Effect: the phenomenon in which research findings are skewed as an inherent result of their being studied.

A derivative of ethnography popular among marketers is the "shop-along." I once did shop-alongs with Starbucks customers while concepting the brand positioning for Starbucks' breakfast offerings. We met our target customers outside their favorite Starbucks locations, stood with them in line, watched their eyes as they scanned the pastry case, and asked them questions, such as why they had skipped the scones in favor of the hard-boiled eggs. The shop-alongs unearthed insights about what the customer was trying to accomplish through his breakfast, which enabled us to focus the brand accordingly.

One can also combine research methods—for example, focus groups with follow-up ethnographies. I used this combination once for Clorox2, a color-safe bleach laundry additive. During the focus groups, most participants reported doing laundry every single day and using Clorox2 in every load. When we visited one of these participants in his home for an ethnography, I noticed that the box of Clorox2 displayed the graphic design we had changed two years earlier. With thirty loads per box, the customer was likely using Clorox2 not once a day but once a month or even less. Having observed this, we saw that the customer actually was not using or valuing our offering as much as he had claimed, allowing us to probe accordingly.

being a comedian, just act like a reporter. What's the question that hasn't been asked?" This is how we get to real truths, how we uncover original and useful insights. In both comedy and in business, this leads to your audience feeling deeply recognized, seen, and known—the basis of any human connection. In comedy, this connectedness sparks laughter. In business, it sparks trust.

When you start these conversations, put the person at ease by giving him some time to warm. To facilitate this, structure the conversation so that you are starting at a high altitude and then narrowing little by little. This orientation is more aligned with the target customer's actual way of experiencing the problem your offering solves. He thinks first about himself and his day and his life, and then about the context in which your offering is relevant, and then (maybe) about your brand or offering. So, orient yourself the way that *he* is oriented, which is starting general and only later converging on your brand.

To facilitate this orientation of high-to-low-altitude interviewing, prepare your questions in three parts. The first set of questions seeks to gain a sense of your customer's life and inner world. The second set of questions narrows to the context of your offering. Only toward the end do you pose questions about your offering and brand.

Here's an example of questions I might prepare if I were doing the brand strategy for the United Airlines First-Class Lounge, aimed at those who travel regularly for work and usually fly business class.

PART ONE: YOUR CUSTOMER'S LIFE (HIGH ALTITUDE)

1. Tell me about you. What do you do? What is your typical day like?
2. Tell me about the last time you had a particularly good day. What happened? What made it good?
3. Tell me about something that you really worry about.
4. What do you like about your job, your career? What do you wish you could change?
5. What are some of your favorite brands? What makes you love them?

PART TWO: HOW THE CUSTOMER RELATES TO THE CATEGORY (MIDDLE ALTITUDE)

1. How often do you travel for business?

2. How do you feel about business travel? Is it a necessary evil? Is it a secret guilty pleasure? Are you just resigned to it?

3. When you first realize you need to book travel for a work trip, what is your dominant feeling? What are the other feelings that emerge?

4. How do you approach travel planning for work? What services do you use? How do you relate to those services?

5. How do you feel about each of the airlines that you use? What makes you feel this way?

6. Do you use any private airport lounges? How often? To what extent does it depend on whether it is business or leisure travel? On whether someone else is paying or whether you are paying?

7. What do you like and dislike about these lounges?

PART THREE: YOUR OFFERING AND YOUR BRAND (LOW ALTITUDE)

1. When I say, "United Airlines," what comes to mind?

2. How is United Airlines different from other airlines? How is it similar?

3. If United Airlines were a movie star or a character in a book, who would it be? What is this character like?

4. What do you most like and dislike about United Airlines?

5. What are the images and words that come to mind when I say, "United Airlines First-Class Lounge?"

6. How is United Airlines First Class Lounge similar, different, better, or worse than the alternatives?

During and after your interviews, take notes. Use what psychologists call "metacognition" by asking yourself: What did I just learn? What surprised me? What confused me? When did the tone of the conversation change from dull to excited or excited to dull? Are there any areas I want to learn more about by asking different questions in my next interviews? How was this conversation similar and dissimilar from the others?

CONDUCT YOUR RESEARCH

Now you have prepared and are dialing your customer on the phone to conduct your interview. Here are some tips for fruitful customer research:

1. RESIST THE TEMPTATION TO JUMP TOO SOON TO THE LOW-ALTITUDE QUESTIONS ABOUT YOUR PRODUCT.

You might get so excited to hear what the customer thinks of your offering that you neglect to learn about him first. Beware of this temptation and resist it. Understanding the context leads to the animating insights that undergird a powerful brand strategy.

2. FOLLOW YOUR PREPARED QUESTIONS AS LOOSELY OR TIGHTLY AS YOU'D LIKE.

You may find that as you go, some questions are really resonating with your interviewees, while others are falling flat, so feel free to shift your questions accordingly.

3. TAKE NOTES.

Write or sketch as you interview. There is something about holding physical pen and paper that helps one listen with presence. As long as your interviewee verbally agrees to it, you may record the conversations so that you can go back and listen for emphasis later.

4. LET THERE BE SILENCE.

After you ask a question, be quiet while your interviewee responds. After your interviewee finishes responding to a question, like a good reporter, zip it. Make sure she really is finished responding. Give him space to elaborate. That silence is when some of the most revealing insights emerge. As Stoic philosopher Epictetus said, "Nature hath given men one tongue but two ears, that we may hear from others twice as much as we speak."

5. LISTEN BETWEEN THE LINES.

Inhabiting the beginner's mind is far from passive—it is a highly active state. Dan Pink wrote in *To Sell Is Human* that "the ability to move others hinges less on problem solving than on problem finding." You are not so much listening for overt problems you can solve as you are listening for the problem behind the overt problem.

Listen not only to what your customer is saying but to what he is not saying. Notice not simply the letter of what he is saying but also the spirit of what he is saying. The customer will not give you an eloquent, perfectly packaged insight that you can then plop into your brand strategy. When you listen empathetically, you can listen between the lines and crystalize the insights yourself.

6. DON'T CORRECT, INFORM, OR TEACH.

Do not chime in. Do not correct or offer suggestions or advice. Don't do it! Don't get your dander up if your interviewee says something you know to be untrue. If your interviewee were to say he lacks access to your first-class lounge when you know that, as a frequent flyer, he is indeed granted that access, don't correct him. He would respond by clamming up, because he would then view you as the teacher. You are the student here, so bury your reactions and listen.

7. ASK WHY.

Follow up with "why?" and then again, be quiet while she responds. Keep asking "why?" or "tell me more about that" until you've reached a void, until you feel you have grasped the root.

Entrepreneur Eric Ries wrote in his book *The Lean Startup* about the Five Whys, an investigative method of getting to the root of an idea or problem by asking "why?" (or a version of that) five times. Here is how this could play out with our United Airlines First Class Lounge example.

> Me: When you first learn you are scheduled for a work trip, what is your dominant feeling?
>
> Customer: Stress.
>
> Me: Why?
>
> Customer: My family gets really annoyed when I travel for work.

Me: Why is that?

Customer: I'm the person who drives everyone around and makes everyone feel taken care of, so when I'm gone, everyone is stressed and a mess. I feel guilty.

Me: Tell me more.

Customer: I guess I feel I'm shirking my duty if I am gone. And my family is the most important thing to me, so that feels bad.

Me: Why do you think that is?

Customer: It makes me feel like I'm failing, and not just that, but failing the most important part of my life.

Me: Say more about that.

Customer: I'm pulled in different directions constantly and I never feel like I am doing enough in any of the areas of my life.

This customer is thinking about what she is leaving behind while she travels, surfacing guilt, feelings of nurturing, and overwhelm. This tidbit may only come up once, or you may hear elements of this emerge repeatedly during your target customer conversations. If it is indeed a pattern, that forms a highly useful insight that can help you position your brand in a more accurate, human way.

8. DON'T BE SHALLOW.

It is not the customer's job to give you the insight. Don't expect to get answers you can apply carte blanche. The goal of the research is to give you clues to understand your customer. You are seeking to learn, connect dots, and integrate—not to simply record and then regurgitate. You will be the one to distill insights from these clues, and you'll use those insights to lead, not follow.

In that United Airlines example, if you had heard multiple interviewees use the word "stress" when describing their feeling about work travel, a shallow interpretation might be that your brand needs to mitigate stress immediately before flights. That would be shallow. When you follow up with "why," you might learn that the word "stress" was hiding the more useful clue that the stress was not about the flight. Work travel stress for these customers was less about work travel than it was about their time not spent at home. Knowing this can help you empathize with them and build your brand using that deeper insight. Rather than mitigating stress at the airport, you could ideate ways to mitigate stress at home during the customer's absence.

This chapter has been as much about your own mindset as it has been about that of your customer. The quality of your insights directly stems from the openness you bring to these conversations. Once you have cultivated the listening mindset and spoken with customers, you have the insights you need to lay out and examine the learnings. You can move from data collection to data examination.

CHAPTER 9

STEP 3: EXAMINE

Ironclad brand strategy is rooted in what you uniquely offer that your customer deeply wants. Now that you have gathered insights from target customers, it's time to examine that data and channel it into your brand building.

Articulating your brand is not about creating something out of thin air. It's about discovering something latent. It's identifying what customers want that you are uniquely able to satisfy, and then building your promise around that. In this step, we will inventory the insights we have about our customers, our competitors, and our company, so that we can spot the overlap that is already there and start to cultivate it in earnest.

We will examine what we know in three parts:

- Compile Your Insights
- Articulate Your Target Customer Profile

- Assemble Your Uncommon Denominator Framework

COMPILE YOUR INSIGHTS

Start by synthesizing your customer research. Your goal is to transform raw notes into a report that you and your team can easily reference and share. There are lots of ways to do this, and you should let your personal style inform your approach. Here are some suggestions for compiling insights.

SET ASIDE YOUR NOTES

- Ask yourself: "What did I hear that I want to be sure to remember? What was surprising? What came up every time in some form? Were there any words or images or phrases or metaphors that multiple people used? What were the dominant emotions I perceived?"
- Imagine what you would say to a colleague about what you learned. If you had three minutes to relate the major findings, what would you share?
- List the big insights that emerged, either in actual list form or in a non-linear way. You might write one insight per sticky note and cluster them by theme. Draw a mind map or spiderweb of connected ideas to help reveal patterns. Choose a mode that feels natural to you to visualize the learnings.

REVIEW YOUR ORIGINAL NOTES WITH A FINE-TOOTHED COMB

- After your brain dump, review your notes for other highlights you previously may have missed.

- Ask one to two teammates to identify what they consider to be highlights or what surprised them. Those fresh eyes can help you see what you missed or underappreciated.

SUMMARIZE AND IDENTIFY THE IMPLICATIONS

- Articulate the themes from the disparate observations you have just made. Keep these themes granular and distinctive from one another. Your goal at this point is to discern five to ten major insights that you can leverage while building your brand. You can do this with a list, a table, a picture, a few paragraphs—however it will be most accessible to you. (I provide an example in table form below.)
- Arrange these insights in order of high-to-low altitude, the gentle progression toward your offering that we introduced in the last chapter. Start with what you learned about the bigger picture of your target customer's life. Then articulate the insights about how she relates to your category. Finally, write what you learned about how she relates to your brand.
- Include customer quotes from your conversations to illustrate each insight.
- Note the implication of each insight for your brand development: what might you incorporate into your brand strategy?

This insights summary is for a fictional meal delivery service.

INSIGHTS	IMPLICATIONS
Moms. Target customer identifies first and foremost as a mother. "It's the best and hardest job."	Our brand should validate her as a good mom.
Health-conscious. Prides herself on making virtuous nutrition and fitness choices. "I would never let junk food into our house."	Our meals must be healthy and assuage her anxiety about non-nutritious food.
Frustrated and hurt by kids not eating food. "I spend all this time chopping and roasting vegetables, and then they wrinkle their noses."	Our brand should be the one that solves the tasty-but-nutritious predicament.
Resistant to meal delivery services. Considers them a form of cheating. "Cooking is my job."	Our product experience should be participatory so that she feels we are complementing her rather than replacing her.
Indifferent to our brand. Neither likes nor dislikes our brand. "Yeah, I've heard of it. They're all alike."	We have a big task ahead in distinguishing ourselves from this largely similar competitive set, in her mind. We may find our breakthrough position in this insight.

ARTICULATE YOUR TARGET CUSTOMER PROFILE

Once you have crystalized your major insights, capture your target customer (which you focused on in Chapter 7) in an easy-to-use and easy-to-share one-page customer profile. This serves as a useful touchstone, not only for brand building but also for fostering a customer-centric culture within your organization. A concentrated articulation of your target customer is a go-to tool for you and your team to reference.

Some do this by generating a customer persona with photos or illustrations. Others create a day-in-the-life for this person. Still others write a paragraph in the first person of the target customer describing herself. I like to create a profile of my target customer in table form, describing her in terms of demographic and psychographic traits, behaviors, and beliefs.

CHART YOUR INSIGHTS

Organize insights about your target customer into the following three categories:

1. **Demographics and Psychographics:** Start by describing the basics of your target customer. What are her demographic characteristics (age, income, gender, ethnicity, geography, life stage)? What is her personality? Likes and dislikes? Attitudes and aspirations? Worries and scarcities? How does she think about herself? Who and what influences her?

2. **Behaviors:** Understand your customer's baseline behavior so that you can consider how to shift that behavior. How, when, and where does the customer use your offering or your competitor's offering? What prompts her to use it? How, when, and where does your offering fit into the larger context of your customer's day? Is your offering an afterthought, or does your customer plan to use it? Does she embrace your offering, or does she wish she could avoid it?

3. **Beliefs:** Since behaviors tend to be rooted in beliefs, identifying your target customer's underlying beliefs helps you understand where your brand fits into her reality and, therefore, how to talk about and deliver your offering. Articulating your customer's belief system helps you influence behavior. What does your target customer believe about your category? Is she receptive to it? Resistant to it? What are the beliefs underneath that receptiveness or resistance?

Here is a chart of this for the same fictional meal delivery service we used as an example before.

DEMOGRAPHICS AND PSYCHOGRAPHICS	BEHAVIORS	BELIEFS
Female, ages 30–45	Juggles numerous activities; between her own commitments and her children's activities, she is always in motion	Being a mother includes feeding her family well
Works outside the home, identifies as a working mother		Family dinner is nourishing both physically and mentally
Upper-middle class	Serves dinner for the family every night, even after a busy day	Family dinners correlate with successful children
Skews urban and suburban		
Highly educated	Grocery shops 2–4x a week. Indexes high on grocery delivery but not on meal delivery	Despite her busyness and overwhelm, it is worthwhile to cook for her family
Slight skew toward married but a fair proportion divorced or separated		
Life stage: in the "crunch period" of life, when kids still require heavy work and career is escalating simultaneously; super busy; time feels scarce; worries that she is not giving enough to her children; worries that she herself is not "enough"	Works out regularly	The experience of cooking is integral to the experience of family dinners
	Intermittently reads and saves recipes but not loyal to single source	
	Regularly discusses time-saving hacks with her friends. Willing to trade money for convenience	Food is the foundation for a healthy life; family time is the foundation for a successful life

ASSEMBLE YOUR UNCOMMON DENOMINATOR FRAMEWORK

It is time now to use what you have distilled to parse out your competitive advantage. I devised a framework that helps you isolate that advantage. Called the Uncommon Denominator framework, this Venn diagram lays out an examination of what you know about your customer, your competitive set, and your own business. From this, you arrive at the core of your business strategy, which is the answer to the question Scott Galloway posed in *The Four*: "What can you do really well that is also really hard?" Your strategy is not just about what you can do well, but what others cannot do well. It's not just your strengths, it's your uncommon strengths.

The framework's three circles represent your customer's desires, your competitor's strengths, and your own strengths. As a Venn diagram, the Uncommon Denominator framework has several overlaps. There are two overlaps that are particularly salient. The Common Denominator zone is the overlap of all three circles. The Uncommon Denominator zone is the overlap of what your customer wants and your strengths—notably *not* including your competitor's strengths.

Figure 9.1. **Uncommon Denominator Overview**

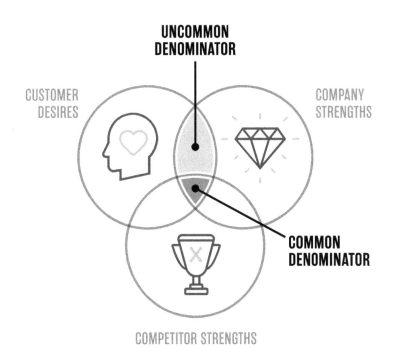

THE COMMON DENOMINATOR

The items within the Common Denominator zone are your category benefits: the things that your customer desires, that your competitor is good at, and that you are good at. So, if your brand is a pancake mix offering, your Common Denominator includes "delicious" pancakes. Your customer wants pancakes that are delicious, your competitor is good at making delicious pancakes, and you are good at making delicious pancakes.

The Common Denominator is important because it moves you into the customer's consideration set. Being delicious is the cost of entry into the "pancakes" category. But the Common Denominator is the beginning, not the end, of the story. Mistaking the Common Denominator for the central brand idea is the single biggest error that I see in brand strategy development. If it is common, then you do not own it. If you do not own it, it will not work hard to grow your business.

THE UNCOMMON DENOMINATOR

Now consider the other critical overlap, the Uncommon Denominator. This is the intersection of what your customer wants, what you're good at, and what your competitor is *not* good at, or has chosen not to focus on. This overlap forms the basis of your brand positioning. Drawing from this zone enables you to move from a brand that meets a need generically to a brand that meets a need uncommonly.

Generically, your pancake mix offers your customer "delicious." Great start, but you should not get too excited about this. Of course your pancakes are delicious—they are pancakes. They *should* be delicious. Move on to what only you bring to the pancake mix market. Perhaps your pancake is unbelievably thin and crispy and uses your Swedish grandmother's recipe. These are things your customer wants, that you provide, and that your competitor does not bring. They are Uncommon Denominator ideas.

EXERCISE: FIND YOUR OWN DENOMINATORS

Now identify your Common Denominator ideas (benefits that you must bring but do not own) and your Uncommon Denominator ideas (benefits that you *do* own). For this exercise, you're going to need a spacious piece of paper or whiteboard.

1. Draw a large Venn diagram: three circles, two on top, one on the bottom, and all three overlapping in the middle.
2. Label the top left circle "Customer Desires," the bottom circle "Competitor Strengths," and the top right circle "Company Strengths."
3. Next to your Customer Desires circle, list what your customer wants. Refer to the insights and target customer profile you created earlier in this chapter. As you know from your customer interviews, while some customer desires are ones your customers overtly expressed, others you have discerned by listening between the lines. Write all insights—explicit and implicit—near this circle.
4. Next to your Competitor Strengths circle, list how your competitors excel. Remember that your competitor could be a direct competitor, an indirect competitor, or a substitute. You could be competing against a behavior, the status quo, or an adjacent type of product. Use what you know about your

market and your customers to list the strengths and benefits your competitor brings.

5. Next to your Company Strengths circle, list what you are good at. What is special about your business? What are you especially proud of? From what do you draw passion or purpose? What are you better at than anyone else? What is your business model strength, your economic strength? If you have investors, what inspired their belief in your business? What inspires *your* belief in your business? Think about this from all dimensions—from functional to emotional, from pragmatic to philosophical, from grounded to inspirational. You might write details about your intellectual property, your technology, your heritage, your recipes, your culture, your origin story, and the features and benefits that emerged during your customer research.

6. Label the center overlap—the zone where all three circles intersect—"Common Denominator." Label the top overlap—the zone where your customer's desires overlaps with your strengths and *not* with your competitor's strengths—"Uncommon Denominator."

7. Copy details into these overlap zones. Write the ideas that show up in all three circles inside your Common Denominator zone. Write the ideas that show up in Customer Desires and Company Strengths, but not in Competitive Strengths, inside your Uncommon Denominator zone.

Figure 9.2. **Uncommon Denominator for Batter Pancakes**

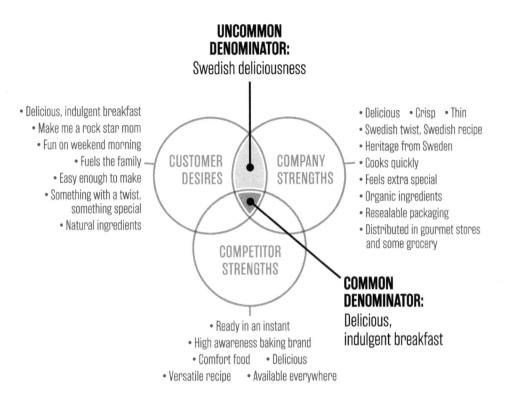

UNCOMMON DENOMINATOR:
Swedish deliciousness

• Delicious, indulgent breakfast
• Make me a rock star mom
• Fun on weekend morning
• Fuels the family
• Easy enough to make
• Something with a twist, something special
• Natural ingredients

CUSTOMER DESIRES

COMPANY STRENGTHS

• Delicious   • Crisp   • Thin
• Swedish twist, Swedish recipe
• Heritage from Sweden
• Cooks quickly
• Feels extra special
• Organic ingredients
• Resealable packaging
• Distributed in gourmet stores and some grocery

COMPETITOR STRENGTHS

COMMON DENOMINATOR:
Delicious, indulgent breakfast

• Ready in an instant
• High awareness baking brand
• Comfort food   • Delicious
• Versatile recipe   • Available everywhere

WHAT IF THERE ISN'T MUCH DIFFERENCE BETWEEN YOU AND YOUR COMPETITOR?

First, recognize that this is not sustainable if you are aiming to be a profitable, growing business. You *must* be different to create value for both your customer and your business. There is a word for not being different: commodity. A pure commodity confers zero margin, because when an offering is the same as its alternatives, it can only compete on price. Remember our nine criteria from Chapter 6 and how they together create differentiation. If you are not the only, you have not yet narrowed enough, are not yet asymmetrical enough, are not optimally distinct enough.

Second, consider that you may be more different than you are appreciating. You simply need to pinpoint more assiduously and expand upon your distinguishing strengths. Return to the Company Strengths circle and dream bigger. Where do you (or could you at some point) hugely shine? Which of those does your customer care about deeply? What might you be able to help her care about? Leverage every aspect of your offering.

CHOOSE AN UNCOMMON DENOMINATOR TO BUILD

At this point in brand strategy development, you choose the most compelling theme in your Uncommon Denominator zone. This is the one you will build up into a focus point of your brand.

Of the ideas in that intersection between customer desires and your strengths, which do you have the most heart for? Which feels the biggest, the most ownable? Which feels sharp-edged? Which has the potential to satisfy both rational and emotional customer needs?

The answer may be immediately clear to you. You may look at the Uncommon Denominator zone of your Venn diagram and intuit the strongest idea. Or perhaps everything in that overlap feels "right," and so you would need to reflect further to arrive at the Uncommon Denominator you want to develop.

EXERCISE: CHECK YOUR DENOMINATORS AGAINST THE NINE IRONCLAD CRITERIA

Evaluate the Uncommon Denominators against the nine criteria we discussed in Chapter 6. How would each of your Uncommon Denominators score in the following?

1. **Big:** Is this Uncommon Denominator big enough to matter? Does it meet a significant customer need? Will the customer feel moved to engage with this benefit, buy it, and be loyal to it? Does this idea allow you room to expand, evolve, and scale?

2. **Narrow:** Is it narrow enough to own? Can you dominate with this strength? Do you have a right to win? This "narrow" law checks you on the "big" criterion. You want the Uncommon Denominator you focus on being big, but also specific and ownable.

3. **Asymmetrical:** Is it truly differentiated? Can only you bring this to your customer? Does it capitalize on a dramatically asymmetrical strength? To what extent, with this idea, does your strength outsize your competitors' strength? To what extent is it un-copy-able? Could you build a moat around this?

4. **Empathetic:** Is this benefit rooted in an empathetic insight about your customers? Is this truly something your customers want? Does it genuinely have their interests at heart? Does it

honestly make your customer better, happier, more fulfilled? Will it bring your customer meaning? Does it serve a higher good? Is it generous?

5. **Optimally Distinct:** Has your benefit struck the balance between familiar and different? Can your target customers' minds easily grasp your offering so they feel its "warm glow of familiarity"? At the same time, could they be amazed by the distinctive newness you bring? Do you present an option comfortable enough for customers to comprehend what you're offering—and compelling enough to get them to stay?

6. **Functional *and* Emotional:** Does this benefit idea bring both a functional and an emotional boost? Can it appeal to both your customer's heart and her brain? Does it balance rational with aspirational? Does it have elements that satisfy your customer's thinking mind while also lighting up her feeling mind?

7. **Sharp-Edged:** Inside this idea, is there a concrete benefit? How granular is this idea? Is it single-minded? Is it simple but not simplistic? Is it truly a choice, rather than a safe non-choice? Does it allow you to be indubitably clear to customers what you are (and are not) bringing them?

8. **Has Teeth:** Is this not just true but demonstrably true? Can you prove it, show it? Is it a credible promise? Does your customer believe you can bring this? Is this anchored in fact?

9. **Delivers:** Can you honestly deliver on this, consistently and broadly? Can you nail not just the letter of the promise, but also the spirit of the promise? Can you deliver across the big things and the small things? Across the easy things and the hard things?

As you choose your strongest Uncommon Denominator, be

assured that nothing is carved in stone. Hold your answer lightly. If you get farther into this brand strategy development exercise and aren't liking what you chose now, you can come back to this step.

BEING ONLY OR BEING BEST

Sometimes it's hard to tell whether your strength is yours alone. Perhaps your competitor is arguably strong in this area, but you are *exceptionally* strong at it. Is that enough? Could that strength be your Uncommon Denominator?

In most cases, no. In most cases, you need to be the *only* one with that strength. That exclusive hold makes your position asymmetrical and sharp-edged, two of the criteria for ironclad brand strategy. There is one exception. If your offering confers a 10X (or better) improvement on your competitor's offering, *and* your customer cares about that 10X improvement, this Uncommon Denominator may be the one you build.

If you are going with a best, rather than an only, promise, tread carefully. Attaining and sustaining such a 10X threshold is demanding. In most cases, you are better off focusing on what only you can do and leaving the rest of the market to fight we're-better-than-you battles. You are better off changing the game altogether.

THE UNCOMMON DENOMINATOR AND GETTING TO OPTIMALLY DISTINCT

In Chapter 6, we discussed the notion of being optimally distinct— that ideal balance of familiar and different, of being recognizable but surprising as well. The Uncommon Denominator framework can be a useful tool for attaining that balance, helping you integrate familiar and recognizable (Common Denominator) with different and surprising (Uncommon Denominator). You are similar to your competitors by virtue of your Common Denominator, which is good—it breeds familiarity and puts you in your target customer's mind. You are different from your competitor by virtue of your Uncommon Denominator, breaking away from the sea of sameness, igniting customers' own desire to be different. Using these in conjunction helps your customer to both let you in and see you as different. This helps you offer a warm glow of familiarity while also stirring curiosity with your distinctiveness.

In this chapter we examined the insights that customer research unlocked and synthesized the learnings to shine a light on your Uncommon Denominator, your brand theme. Focusing on the Common Denominator at the expense of the Uncommon Denominator does your business a disservice. It will get you in the door, but it won't set you apart. Ultimately, you win by delivering more value to your customer than others do. The Uncommon Denominator is the essence of your value. It is that thing that you want to express and magnify and expand throughout your business. In the next chapter, we will articulate your Uncommon Denominator into a specific and logical argument.

CHAPTER 10

STEP 4: LADDER

In the previous chapter, we zeroed in on the positioning territory to explore—the Uncommon Denominator zone. In this chapter, we specify the promise within that zone that we can support with fact, and that we can leverage to provide a large emotional reward. We do this through the benefit ladder framework.

This is perhaps the most critical step in the Ironclad Method. When you develop your brand's "ladder," you distill your business's value proposition into an argument that is at once aspirational and grounded. The ladder depicts the levels at which your business benefits your customer, from the functional and grounded to the emotional and transcendent.

In this chapter, we will introduce the benefit ladder concept and guide you into building one. Your brand's benefit ladder will serve as the crux of your brand strategy, so pay close attention. Here is what we will cover:

- What Is a Benefit Ladder?
- Why Should a Brand Ladder Up?
- Build Your Benefit Ladder
- Select Your Emphasis
- Sum Up Your Positioning Statement

Figure 10.1. **Benefit Ladder with Bounce as an Example**

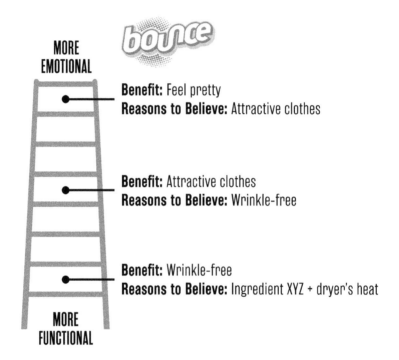

MORE EMOTIONAL

Benefit: Feel pretty
Reasons to Believe: Attractive clothes

Benefit: Attractive clothes
Reasons to Believe: Wrinkle-free

Benefit: Wrinkle-free
Reasons to Believe: Ingredient XYZ + dryer's heat

MORE FUNCTIONAL

WHAT IS A BENEFIT LADDER?

Let's time travel for a moment. It's 1975, and Procter & Gamble has just created Bounce dryer sheets. But no one knows what dryer sheets are. It is a completely new type of product, and it's a strange one at that. Bounce wants customers to add squares of fabric—or are they paper?—to their laundry dryers with their wet clothes.

So, what does Bounce do? Bounce identifies the specific functional problem it solves and then makes that the brand's doorway into the customer's life. The problem Bounce solves is wrinkly clothes. Wrinkles, you may recognize, are a buzzkill for the laundry-doer of the household. After you've done laundry, you want your clothes to look clean and neat, not wrinkled and sloppy. And Bounce dryer sheets solves that problem in a snap. If Bounce were to have drawn an Uncommon Denominator diagram at that time, "wrinkle-free" would have been in the Uncommon Denominator zone.

Bounce satisfies a functional problem (wrinkly clothes) with a functional benefit (when you use Bounce in your dryer load, your clothes will be wrinkle-free). This is a big promise. No other product has easily solved the wrinkly clothes problem. To make that big promise credible, Bounce articulates its concrete "reasons to believe": the heat of your dryer combining with Bounce's wrinkle-relaxing ingredient results in wrinkle-free clothes.

Jump ahead a few years. Wrinkle-free clothes is still Bounce's emphasis, its brand promise. Bounce messages "wrinkle-free clothes" broadly, and soon their target customers readily grasp and accept that Bounce delivers the benefit of clothes that are wrinkle-free. Target customers believe the promise because it makes intuitive sense that a dryer's heat with Bounce's ingredient can relax wrinkles. And when they use Bounce, it does result in wrinkle-free clothes.

This is satisfying an unmet need and doing so uniquely—it is a hard-working brand position for Bounce. But in time, Bounce seeks to expand the wrinkle-free promise to become more emotionally resonant. Bounce wants to "ladder up"—to continue to put the offering higher in their customers' minds through an increasingly large benefit.

Bounce ladders up the functional benefit of wrinkle-free clothes to the higher-order benefit of "attractive clothes." Bounce promises attractive clothes, and the reason to believe this audacious promise is Bounce's previous promise: wrinkle-free clothes. Wrinkle-free is now so widely believed that it can serve as support for the larger promise of "attractive clothes." Bounce no longer needs to explain the ingredient and heat reasons to believe, because wrinkle-free is now accepted implicitly.

The customer now hears that Bounce makes their clothes attractive. A big promise—but credible, because customers already know Bounce makes their clothes wrinkle-free. In time, Bounce owns in customers' minds this larger benefit of attractive clothes.

Let's move forward a few years again. Bounce ladders up from an emphasis of attractive clothes to the even higher-order benefit of "feeling pretty." That is another big promise. But customers are ready to believe it, because they have accepted implicitly that Bounce brings attractive clothes, just as previously, they came to accept that Bounce makes clothes wrinkle-free. Bounce first earned wrinkle-free in the customer's mind, thereby earning the way up to attractive clothes. They then earned attractive clothes in the customer's mind, thereby earning the way up to feeling pretty. The brand's emphasized promise becomes: with Bounce dryer sheets, you can feel pretty. Why? Because your clothes look attractive. Why? Because they're wrinkle-free.

This string of benefits with supporting reasons to believe forms what is called a benefit ladder. A benefit ladder spells out the layers of your benefits from product features and specifications at the bottom, to functional benefits in the middle, to emotional benefits at the top. Each rung is a benefit, which is supported below it by a reason to believe in that benefit. The ladder illustrates the levels of value a brand is delivering to customers, from the rational to the aspirational and the points between. It shows the brand's means, ends, and the relationship between those means and ends.

Here's something to notice: benefits on the ladder serve as both promises and as support for larger promises. Sometimes a benefit is the promise a brand will emphasize, while other times that same benefit can serve as a reason to believe for a larger benefit on a higher ladder rung. Initially, "wrinkle-free" was Bounce's promise, but once it was able to ladder to "attractive clothes," the role of wrinkle-free changed to a supporting role for the larger promise of attractive clothes. Later, the role of attractive clothes changed to a supporting role for the larger promise of "feel pretty."

The benefit ladder can help you, as the leader, to internalize a fundamental truth that enables all excellent brand building: customers do not buy products. Customers buy the reward they enjoy *as a result* of the product. Your products' features at the ground level of the ladder only bring value insofar as they enable a benefit the customer cares about. No matter how cool your product, no matter how proud of it you are, no matter how much work you spent developing it, for the customer it is merely a means to an end. The bottom rung of the ladder is only useful insofar as it propels him to the next rung.

So, as you identify your features, know the "why" they enable. As you ladder your features to functional benefits, know the emotional reward of those functional benefits. Aaron Woodman, general manager of Microsoft Windows Marketing, explained his thought process about this: "You're looking for space that emotionally gives permission for people to opt in, but it has to come through within rational reasons to believe, and ideally, those two things are in concert. [The customers] can feel they've made a rational choice and even talk about it like that, even if the reason was actually more emotional." Customers sometimes use functional benefits to rationalize their emotion-driven choice.

Here are some examples of the product-reward relationship:

CATEGORY	PRODUCT	REWARD
Cars	Four-wheel suspension, so that the drive is smooth, so that the customer enjoys a luxurious driving experience.	The customer is not buying your four-wheel suspension. He is buying the smooth, luxurious driving experience that your four-wheel suspension enables.
Running shoes	Lightweight shoes, so that his run is comfortable, so that he can complete a marathon.	He is not buying your lightweight shoes. He is buying the comfortable run that will propel him to complete his marathon.
Water filtration system	Active carbon filter from charcoal, to purify your water, so that the customer can enjoy healthy hydration.	He is not buying your technology that removes impurities. He is buying clean water and its resulting healthfulness.
Ski wax	Microcrystalline wax, so that you can ski fast, so that the customer can feel like a bird.	He is not buying your wax technology that slicks his skis. He is buying fast skiing and the resulting sensation of flying.
Corporate accounting software	SAAS model, so that rules are always up-to-date, so that taxes are reliably compliant.	He is not buying your SAAS model. He is buying the way he looks smart and promote-able to his executives.

WHY SHOULD A BRAND LADDER UP?

After all of Bounce's work and media spend to own "wrinkle-free clothes," why did they move up from that prized position? Before we dig into the explanation, see if you already know the overall answer intuitively. Here's a hint: how much do you imagine someone would pay to feel pretty?

Compare that to how much someone would pay for a piece of cloth drenched in a wrinkle-relaxing ingredient.

So, this is it. This is why we care about moving up the ladder, and ultimately, why we care about brand. It helps us to expand the value of our business. The higher you are on the ladder, the larger your benefit, and the greater and more meaningful the value you are bringing your customer. This heightens the customer's purchase intent, willingness to pay, and propensity to become loyal—which in turn strengthens your sales. Moving up the ladder is how we deliver ever more value to our customer, thereby continually increasing the valuation of our business.

Let's revisit the value equation we discussed in Chapters 2 and 6.

Customer Value = Benefit − Price

As this equation states, you have two levers for increasing customer value—increasing benefit or decreasing price. You can deliver customer value (and therefore purchase intent, willingness to pay, and loyalty) by enlarging your benefit or by shrinking your price. Shrinking your price erodes your margins and limits your value, since most of us can't decrease our price below zero. We focus instead on the first lever of this equation: increasing benefit. Expanding your benefit increases your offering's appeal, which increases customer value *without* decreasing price and eroding margin. The larger the benefit a brand offers, the more people will buy, the more those people will pay, and the more delighted and loyal they will become. So, this is the first reason it's a good idea to move up the ladder: topline sales with bottom line profits.

The second reason to climb the ladder is competitive insulation. By increasing the vertical distance on the ladder between your brand and that of your competitor, you can reinforce your differentiation, because it is hard to copy emotional benefits and easy to copy features. The higher your brand is on this ladder, the harder it will be for your competitor to match your benefit. Eventually, most features and attributes become table stakes in any category, as they're easily copied. Even legal patents eventually expire.

So, laddering up prevents you from needing to engage in costly feature proliferation and one-upmanship for its own sake. While others are catfighting over who relaxes wrinkles best, you've moved on to enabling your customer to feel pretty. Once you've earned that upward motion on the ladder by truly relaxing wrinkles and making clothes attractive, it tends to be difficult for a competitor to copy "feel pretty" with credibility. This is how your emotional benefit becomes your competitive moat.

And the third reason to ladder up is that doing so enables headroom for you to grow. Brands that own higher-order benefits can extend to other categories. This is a ladder to the sky, so the higher on the ladder a brand resides, the more categories it can play in and grow laterally. If you are about enabling customers to feel pretty, you could enter categories beyond laundry additives. Consider Nike, who owns the high-order benefit of "victory" and plays not just in athletic shoes but also in apparel, gear, and equipment. High on the ladder, your room for growth is more spacious. As Robert Neer, Director of Best Buy's Technology Development Center, said, "The ladder helps you keep answering the question 'why?' Why should we care about such and such feature? Why is the customer better off because of that attribute? It connects the features to the world, and it also connects the emotional reward to the real world, rather than something amorphous."

Since that upward motion on the ladder is a good thing, how far up do you claim? Too low, and you are leaving money on the table, opening yourself to copycats and limiting your lateral growth. But before you race to the top of your benefit ladder, know this: you can only go as high on the ladder as your current target customer gives you permission to go. He will give you permission to climb higher when he is aware of and believes in your brand's functional benefit.

If Bounce had launched in 1975 to a customer who'd never heard of dryer sheets with a benefit of "feel pretty," that customer would have been puzzled or simply would have ignored this inexplicable promise from this unknown laundry brand. Worse, he may even have deemed the promise disingenuous, losing Bounce his trust forever. Because of this, for your business, your promise should be enough of a stretch to be a big value to your customer, but not so much that you lose credibility and your doorway in.

The benefit ladder enables brands a reality check: what benefit is meaningful and believable to your target customer? Be honest with yourself about how high your brand has a right to climb. Strike the balance of low enough to satisfy his rational mind, while high enough to engage his aspirational heart.

BUILD YOUR BENEFIT LADDER

Now it's time to build your brand's benefit ladder. I suggest doing this in two steps: first sketch it and then refine it. Deconstructing it like this prevents overwhelm and analysis paralysis.

To get started, review the Uncommon Denominator you chose in the previous step in the Ironclad Method, detailed in Chapter 9. You're going to use that Uncommon Denominator to inspire the elements of your benefit ladder.

Brainstorm all the components of this Uncommon Denominator, from features to functional benefits to emotional rewards. From elements equivalent to Bounce's wrinkle-relaxing ingredient, to those equivalent to attractive clothes, all the way up to feeling pretty. Write all of these down. You may already have written many in your "Company Strengths" circle during the previous step, so feel free to use those. Later you will edit to refine, so right now, be unfettered and ideate.

After you have ideated free form, on a large sheet of paper or white board, draw a simple ladder on the left side of it, leaving lots of room to write. Arrange your brainstormed elements hierarchically, with features toward the bottom, functional benefits toward the middle, and emotional rewards toward the top. In my Uncommon Denominator exercise in Chapter 9, I introduced a fictional pancake mix brand, so now, here is what my pancakes brand benefit ladder sketch might look like:

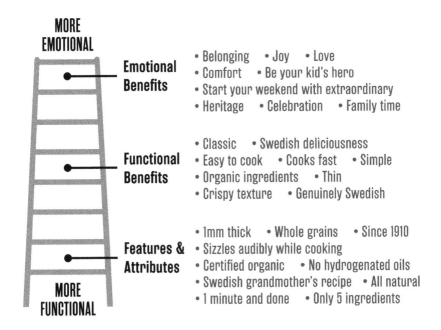

Figure 10.2. **Sketch of Benefit Ladder for Batter Pancakes**

MORE EMOTIONAL

Emotional Benefits
- Belonging   • Joy   • Love
- Comfort   • Be your kid's hero
- Start your weekend with extraordinary
- Heritage   • Celebration   • Family time

Functional Benefits
- Classic   • Swedish deliciousness
- Easy to cook   • Cooks fast   • Simple
- Organic ingredients   • Thin
- Crispy texture   • Genuinely Swedish

Features & Attributes
- 1mm thick   • Whole grains   • Since 1910
- Sizzles audibly while cooking
- Certified organic   • No hydrogenated oils
- Swedish grandmother's recipe   • All natural
- 1 minute and done   • Only 5 ingredients

MORE FUNCTIONAL

Once you have a sketch, play with the benefits you could potentially promise and test them against your gut and against the ironclad criteria in Chapter 6. Identify the benefit that you have the most heart for. This will be your brand promise. Then connect your brand promise to its reasons to believe on the lower rungs, and the end reward on the higher rungs of the ladder.

On my Batter Pancakes sketch, the benefit of Swedish deliciousness resonates with me, so I'm going to make that my brand promise rung. I identify the functional benefits that enable the promise of Swedish deliciousness: thin, crispy, and genuinely Swedish. I am able to deliver Swedish deliciousness because of these three reasons to believe, which support the larger benefit of Swedish deliciousness.

Each of these reasons to believe have their own supporting

features, too. Supporting the "thin" reason to believe is the feature that it cooks in less than one minute. Supporting the "crispy" reason to believe is the feature of the sizzling sound the pancake makes while cooking. Supporting the "genuinely Swedish" reason to believe is the recipe my Swedish grandmother brought with her when she immigrated to the United States. Batter Pancakes bring Swedish deliciousness because they're super thin and crispy and genuinely Swedish. Why? Because they take less than a minute to cook, make a sizzling sound on the stovetop, and are made from my Swedish grandmother's recipe.

Now we have refined the middle to bottom of the ladder, so we turn to refining the top rung of the ladder, the emotional end reward. Let's say I heard during my customer interviews that special pancakes like ours engender a feeling of anticipation and excitement and joy about the weekend. One of my customers put it in a way that I like, which is that when she serves Batter Pancakes, "we start our weekend with extraordinary." So, I am going to pick that as the end reward on my ladder. With Batter Pancakes, you get Swedish deliciousness so that your family can start the weekend with extraordinary.

Your benefit ladder works only as a whole. A ladder with only a bottom, middle, or top rung is not useful. So, do not indulge the false binary that your brand is *only* functional or *only* emotional. Your functional benefit could be extremely compelling, but you should still know the customer's emotional reward for it. Even when Bounce messaged wrinkle-free, the business recognized that it was ultimately delivering attractiveness and used imagery of beautiful people and clothes to cultivate that perception.

Conversely, if you have high customer awareness and acceptance of your functional benefit, such that you can focus on the emotional end reward at the top of your ladder—super. Just don't forget the functional benefits that uphold that end reward. When Bounce climbed the ladder to "feel pretty," the business continued to invest in wrinkle-free technology, bolstering the delivery on that promise. Treat the customer as the whole person she is—rational and emotional. Nurture all parts of the ladder so that your brand can serve your whole customer, regardless of where he is on his journey with your brand. This will guide your brand's growth with both firm footing and aspirational meaning.

Here is how my Batter Pancakes' refined ladder looks. On the middle rung is Swedish Deliciousness, supported by pillars of Thin, Crispy, and Genuinely Swedish, and reaching up to the end reward of Starting the Weekend with Extraordinary.

Figure 10.3. **Benefit Ladder for Batter Pancakes**

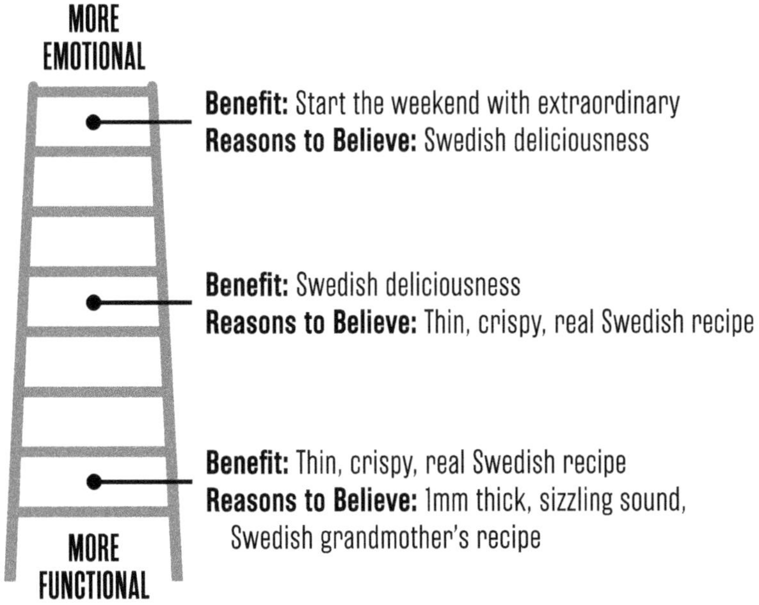

MORE EMOTIONAL

Benefit: Start the weekend with extraordinary
Reasons to Believe: Swedish deliciousness

Benefit: Swedish deliciousness
Reasons to Believe: Thin, crispy, real Swedish recipe

Benefit: Thin, crispy, real Swedish recipe
Reasons to Believe: 1mm thick, sizzling sound, Swedish grandmother's recipe

MORE FUNCTIONAL

Now, take your sketched benefit ladder and write your refined benefit ladder only with the vital elements you chose from your sketch. Once you have done this, check with your gut. Do you *like* this? Do you want it to be your guide as you grow your brand? If not, go back to your sketch and refine again, trying on different benefits as your promise. If you do indeed like it, then pressure-test your ladder against the nine criteria for an ironclad brand strategy, much like you did when you narrowed to your Uncommon Denominator in the previous step. Here are some questions about the nine criteria to help you do this:

1. **Big**—Is this benefit idea big enough to matter? Will the customer find it significant?
2. **Narrow**—Is this idea contained and distinct? Are the elements on this ladder precise?
3. **Asymmetrical**—Do you dramatically outperform your competitor with this strength?
4. **Empathetic**—Would your customer really want this? Is this generous?
5. **Optimally Distinct**—Does it both understandably meet a need and provide an enhanced solution?
6. **Functional *and* Emotional**—Are there solid rungs on each level of the ladder? Could it satisfy both his rational and emotional desires?
7. **Sharp-Edged**—Is this a single idea, rather than an amorphous conflation of ideas?
8. **Has Teeth**—Could you prove this? Is this credible?
9. **Delivers**—Will you be able to deliver on this set of benefits every time?

If after doing this you are not satisfied, go back to the sketch and try different benefits until it rings with truth. Once you have that, move on to the next step of choosing your emphasis.

SELECT YOUR EMPHASIS

Now you have your benefit ladder with top, middle, and bottom rungs. This ladder will likely serve and guide you for the foreseeable future. By design, though, it is flexible. Although the ladder rungs will remain in place, where you shine the spotlight will evolve with the brand. Bounce has the same basic ladder now as it had in 1975, but while in 1975 it emphasized the rung of wrinkle-free clothes, it now emphasizes the rung of feeling pretty. Same ladder—still supported by attractive and wrinkle-free clothes—just a different selected emphasis.

Whether something is a benefit or a reason to believe is relative. Today's selected emphasis (e.g. wrinkle-free clothes) becomes tomorrow's reason to believe in tomorrow's promise (e.g. attractive clothes). You shine the spotlight on the rung that makes the most sense given what your customer and business need today.

Now you will choose the emphasis on the ladder you built, where you will shine the spotlight for your brand at this point. This decision of where to emphasize hinges on where your customer is on his journey with your brand. Choose to shine the spotlight on the rung of your ladder that is as high as your customer currently permits you to go, but no higher. The higher the better, until it is too high.

The common errors here are choosing emphasis on the ladder that is either too low (the features and product attributes) or too high (the intangible, ethereal benefits). The wrong focus will frustrate your brand-building efforts, so let us look at each of these two errors so that you can avoid them. We will then discuss that middle ground that most brands will emphasize. Meet customers where they are.

COMMON ERROR #1: TOO LOW

If you are too low on the ladder, as we have discussed, features will not create high enough value for your customer that she will be moved to buy and pay meaningfully for your offering. The customer will be unlikely to feel significant goodwill for it, to bond with it, or to become loyal to it. Since features are easily copied, even if right now you do differentiate because of that feature, you likely will not own it for long. And, features anchor you in a small idea and category, not enabling lateral growth. If you love your feature, that's great. Keep making it awesome! That will support your upward motion.

But remember that your customer does not care about your feature for its own sake. He cares about the benefit she enjoys because of that feature. He does not care about a state-of-the-art wrinkle-relaxing ingredient, but he does care about wrinkle-free clothes. Identify the functional benefit your feature delivers, and make sure it's one your customer wants and that you alone can bring.

COMMON ERROR #2: TOO HIGH

When your focus is too high on the ladder, you are not providing accessible scaffolding for the customer to believe your promise.

Starting with a functional doorway in enables the customer to grasp what he would be buying. Bounce did not start with "feel pretty." If it had, customers would be confused, because back then, they didn't even know what a dryer sheet was, let alone believe its aspirational end reward. If you focus on the top of the ladder prematurely, you confuse your customers and they will not let you in. Worse, they may find you disingenuous and will not ever trust you with a second chance. You have to earn your way to the top.

GOLDILOCKS AND THE LADDER'S MIDDLE

The linchpin of a ladder is its middle. The middle is low enough to be accessible to the customer—sharp-edged, believable, rationally easy-to-grasp. Focusing on the ladder's middle enables you to deliver substantial value, gain a sizable and defensible position, and appeal to emotions. The middle reconciles what the customer needs now with where the customer would like to go.

So, for most brands, the spotlight tends to be near the middle. That is the Goldilocks balance of rational and emotional, satisfying the mind while also lighting up the heart.

But, focusing on the middle can become an issue if it prevents you from perceiving the exceptions to the rule. For example, a brand can be high on the ladder when they enjoy high customer awareness and strong belief in the functional benefits. Bounce is in this place now, as is Trader Joe's, Apple, BMW, and Patagonia. If you consider your favorite brand as a consumer, I bet that it is high on this ladder. And I bet for you it had to earn its way to that place before it earned your favor. So, if your brand enjoys high awareness and belief among your target customer, you will emphasize the top of the ladder.

Also, a brand can be low on the ladder when the proposition is difficult to grasp and believe, necessitating a concrete doorway in. For example, Netflix started with a functional promise of "no late fees." Today, Netflix is a massive-promise entertainment brand, but the doorway in was the "no late fees" promise. Zappos started with "free shipping both ways." Today, Zappos is perhaps the most-lauded customer service brand in the world, but it began simply with free shipping. The humble functional promises of no late fees and free shipping were the doorways into these now-world-class disruptive brands.

Select from an empathetic understanding of your target customer. Where can you give him value that is both big and believable to him? Remember to do this while also striving for upward motion on the ladder, as this is what creates the most value for your customer, and correspondingly, the most value for your business. The higher and lower rungs support this upward motion. Regardless of your emphasis, the rungs below and above give you a line of sight—why you ultimately matter, and how you get there. The aggregate ladder also helps you serve your customer holistically, both the rational and emotional parts of him, delivering on both his functional and aspirational needs, seeing who he is now along with who he wishes to become.

Nurture the entire ladder. Customers need a functional doorway in, and then they will love you for the big emotional benefit you bring them. By solving the wrinkle-free clothes problem, they will let you promise attractive clothes and eventually even feeling pretty. Seek to deliver on this whole set of benefits with everything you do as a business.

SUM UP YOUR POSITIONING STATEMENT

Once you have built your benefit ladder and selected an emphasis, you have completed the hard work of identifying the components of your positioning. Now weave these components from the past few chapters into a positioning statement to reference as you grow. Gather up your target customer profile and frame of reference designation from Chapter 7, and your brand promise, reasons to believe, and reward from this chapter.

Here is the template for your positioning statement:

To [the target customer], [our brand] is the one [frame of reference] that [brand promise]. That's because only [our brand] brings [reasons to believe] so that you can [end reward].

Your positioning statement illuminates the basic facts about your brand:

- Who? (your target customer)
- Where? (your frame of reference or category)
- What? (brand promise)
- How? (reasons to believe)
- Why? (end reward)

For my Swedish pancake business, here is the positioning statement that results from the choices I've made in the previous steps:

To moms with kids at home, Batter Pancakes is the one pancake mix that brings Swedish deliciousness. That's because only Batter Pancakes brings super thin pancakes, with a crispy crunch, and with genuine Swedish heritage, so that your family can start the weekend with extraordinary.

As a leader, when you have an idea, or someone presents an idea that would require an investment in time, money, or cognitive energy, your positioning statement is your decision-making litmus test. Would such-and-such activity help me to make my positioning statement even more true? If no, do not pursue. If yes, consider pursuing. For example, if my product developer had an idea to change my ingredient sourcing for Batter Pancakes that would allow me to make a claim about organic ingredients but would increase my costs and would not be consumer-noticeable, I go to my positioning statement. Would this organic investment increase my ability to deliver on Swedish Deliciousness? No, it would not, so I would not pursue.

Now do this for your business, using this positioning statement format:

To [the target customer], [our brand] is the one [frame of reference] that [brand promise]. That's because only [our brand] brings [reasons to believe] so that you can [end reward].

Once you have this positioning statement, congratulate yourself. You've defined the crux of your brand's position. This is the central nervous system of your brand. It will inform and infuse everything your business does.

A final note: benefits do not need to be lofty to connect with the customer. How lofty the benefit depends on the target customer and what this person needs in this context. Sometimes, your brand promise might be mundane, like lightweight shoes.

Other times, a promise will be transcendent, like the feeling of victory.

What makes a promise right is its truth for your customer. Use empathy to reach that truth. That which appears functional and rational (lightweight shoes) is actually the most empathetic gift we could give and would make someone feel heard, understood, and cared for.

Remembering that your brand in relationship with your customer helps you find meaning for your customer. So, next, we're going to articulate your brand's character, which further enables customers to bond with your brand.

CHAPTER 11

STEP 5: CHARACTERIZE

Human beings connect better with other human beings than they do with abstract entities, as we are a highly social species. When you allow your business to show up with the characteristics of a person, you are working with, rather than against, the way that people naturally bond.

In this chapter, we will define the character of your brand, imbuing it with personality and tonality. We articulate the qualities of your business as though your business were a person.

Brand strategy is an articulation of what you stand for, of what your business means to your customer. In the last chapter, we defined your benefit ladder and emphasized your brand promise—the value that a customer will enjoy as a result of being in a relationship with your business. In this chapter, we will define something more right-brained—the character of your business. As Jonathan Zabusky, CEO of Seamless, put it to me, "Brand is what you want to be. What is the character you embody that will not change, even when everything else does change? It's what you want to be and what you want to be thought of by all of your stakeholders."

When you define the character you will embody, you accomplish at least three good things for your business.

First, when your brand has character, your target customers more easily see it, bond with it, and want it. People are more likely to buy from—and remain loyal to—a brand they understand and relate to readily.

Second, brand character is another source of differentiation for your business. Most businesses do not do this well. They either have no personality, or they adopt a trite category personality, which feels shallow and stale to customers. Thoughtful articulation of character helps ensure your brand is original and true, not clichéd or contrived.

Third, explicitly defining your brand's character helps you scale by empowering your employees to live your brand. The character articulation enables you to push to others decision making about the brand expression. Your people can embody the brand even when you as the leader are not there to guide them. The act of defining your character inclines you toward it.

To achieve these three goals, we'll do the following in this chapter:

- Understand Your Character
- Detail with Personality and Tonality
- Provide Nuance with Edge
- Use Brand Character as Style Guide and Checklist
- Connect on the Levels of What, Why, and How

- Zig against Your Competitors' Zag
- Embody Your Character Consistently

UNDERSTAND YOUR CHARACTER

So where do you start? This goal of defining your business's character can feel squishy and overwhelming. It can be tempting to gloss through this step, resting on the cliché character of the category.

To ease the overwhelm and the temptation to adopt superficial category characteristics, I offer you a framework that enables you to consider your business through the lens of storytelling. This framework helps you organize and crystalize your brand's substance so that you can represent it with all that you say and do.

DON'T REINVENT THE CHARACTER WHEEL—THE TWELVE BRAND ARCHETYPES

As humans, we are hardwired to connect with stories. We relate to one another via shared elements of experience. Even two people from vastly different backgrounds can bond when they swap stories about their lives. The details may reflect differences, but the reactions, tensions, emotions, goals, and decisions—the plot points and character descriptions that make a story a story—help us see each other human to human.

We can learn about stories from the work of Swiss psychologist Carl Jung. Jung studied storytelling across cultures, time, and distance. He found that no matter where you go in human history, and no matter where you go on earth, there are only a handful of stories that have ever been told. And in these, there are only twelve basic classes of characters who have appeared. We are not only programmed to like stories, but we are hardwired to relate to specific characters in those stories.

In *The Hero and the Outlaw*, authors Margaret Mark and Carol S. Pearson introduced character archetypes to the realm of brand building. They examined the most loved brands of our time and discerned that these brands each embody one of the twelve Jung archetypes. Arguably, these brands are powerful partly *because* they embody one of these twelve primordial characters. Since brands, like stories, work with human cognition, it fits that brands, like stories, connect best when taking on familiar human characteristics.

These three Jung character archetypes strive to achieve mastery and harness risk:

- **The Hero,** whose goal is to save the day. FedEx is a Hero brand—especially for businesspeople on deadlines and anxious parents at Christmastime.
- **The Outlaw,** whose goal is to destroy what is not working. Outlaw Harley-Davidson gives customers not just access to the open road, but freedom from society's constraints.
- **The Magician,** whose goal is to transform the ordinary into the extraordinary. Throughout Disney experiences, this Magician brand promises and delivers the magic of a fairy godmother.

These archetypes are driven to establish stability and control:

- **The Caregiver,** whose goal is to nurture and support. The Caregiver brand Volvo strives to care for humanity, from the child-friendly playrooms in Volvo dealerships, to pioneering safety features—that it even permits its competitors to use—to protect the humans in their competitors' cars.

- **The Ruler**, whose goal is to call the shots. Ruler American Express is self-possessed and authoritative. Their commanding tagline for decades was "Don't leave home without it."
- **The Creator**, whose goal is to unleash creativity. The Creator brand LEGO fosters play, building, and imagination, enabling the creation of skyscrapers, models of plant cells, a modular skate house, a giant piano, a treehouse, a space shuttle launch pad, even a full-size, functional, high-end racing car.

Belonging and enjoyment motivate these three character archetypes:

- **The Jester**, whose goal is to spread laughter and fun. Jester Taco Bell brings levity and humor to the otherwise earnest, edgeless fast food category.
- **The Lover**, whose goal is to indulge the senses. Lover Godiva chocolates fill the consumer with sensory delight and escape.
- **The Everyman**, whose goal is to keep it real. With an Everyman Toyota in your life, you can rely on your car to serve you without drama for years.

The final three archetypes seek independence and fulfillment:

- **The Innocent**, who represents purity, simplicity, nostalgia. Innocent brand Ivory has expressed pure-white cleanliness in a gentle, unadorned, unadulterated soap ever since it was introduced in 1892.

- **The Explorer,** whose goal is to chart new territory. Explorer Patagonia frees you to explore your own love of wild and beautiful places through the outdoor sports of climbing, surfing, skiing. snowboarding, fly fishing, and trail running.
- **The Sage,** whose goal is to share wisdom. Sage Mayo Clinic imparts wisdom through patient care, research, and education, and is respected the world over for its gravitas and excellence.

EXERCISE: PINPOINT YOUR CHARACTER ARCHETYPE

Now that you've given some thought to the twelve Jung character archetypes, you are going to determine your business's archetype, using both instinct and analysis. Since you cannot convincingly manufacture your character, you will articulate and then express the kernel of character you already are. This can be aspirational, as long as it's rooted in a fundamental truth about what you value. Your brand character is the way that your brand acts and talks, the way that it delivers your brand promise and end reward with its own distinctive ethos.

1. **Do you just know your character archetype instinctively?** Many leaders I work with immediately identify one or two of the archetypes from their gut. This is useful data—note it.
2. **Review what you know about your customers and your category.** Refer to the Ironclad Method step on listening (Chapter 8) during which you heard your customers discuss your business. How do customers relate to your business? What role in the customer's story does your business play? How do they relate to your category?

3. **Map the brand characters for your competitors.** What characters do each of them embody? Do this for direct competitors, yes, but also for indirect competitors (whatever your customers are doing instead of purchasing from you). You may find reviewing the Competitive Strengths circle of your Uncommon Denominator framework (Chapter 9) helpful at this point.

4. **Review insights about *your* brand.** Talk to your team. Be reflective about your business and your origin story. What feels true about your personality and values and goals and reason for existing? Are you fun-loving? Audacious? Caring? Playful? Charismatic? Affectionate? Sincere? Kind? Rebellious? Cerebral? Forthright? Determined? Again, employ your listening skills to really hear your team's opinions, humbly, with an open mind, and without judgment.

5. **Try on archetypes that resonate.** Pretend your business is a given archetype. Does it feel like you? Try others on until you find one that does.

6. **Play with the Jung archetype quizzes on the web.** Pretend your business is a person and then answer the quiz questions as though you were that person.

7. **Try to whittle it to one archetype.** A lot of times we can narrow it to two, and the last narrowing is hard. Feel which one is primary and which is secondary. Instead of blending two archetypes, see if you can choose one but will embody the characteristics of another, too. Starbucks is an Explorer Archetype with undertones of Sage. T-Mobile is an Outlaw Archetype with undertones of Jester.

8. **Hold the archetype exercise lightly.** If the archetype exercise feels forced, let it go and perhaps revisit it another time.

For some, the archetypes just do not click, and that is okay. It is merely a tool, so it if is not helping, don't force it. For those who do find the archetypes clarifying, still hold this lightly. This is the beginning, not the end. In the next section, you will be adding meat to the bones to make it yours.

SMALL BUSINESSES AND STARTUPS: KNOW YOUR BUSINESS CHARACTER NOW, SO YOU'RE READY TO GROW

When your business is yours alone, the character of the business is likely *your* character. For startups, the business character reflects the founders' collective character.

When your business is tiny, you implicitly know your character and expressing it is effortless. If you are planning on remaining tiny, implicit may be all that you need. But what about if you want to grow? Articulate your character now while it is clear and concentrated. When a business scales to an expanding team whose members may never have met the founders, those employees should know the brand character.

This is where the brand strategy step of delineating character becomes essential. By defining your business's character now, even if it seems obvious to you, your business can embody that character as it grows, thereby building a genuine and enduring relationship with customers at scale.

DETAIL WITH PERSONALITY AND TONALITY

Identifying your brand's archetype is a significant start because you have framed your brand around a recognizable character. Now you will define your brand's personality and tonality to give your character granularity and substance, and to make it distinctive to you. Each business has its own way of showing up as its archetype. For example, Disney and Tesla are both Magician archetypes, but these two brands feel completely different from one another in personality and tonality. While Disney's Magician is whimsical and light, Tesla's is sophisticated and debonair.

CHOOSE THREE WORDS THAT TOGETHER CONVEY THE PERSONALITY OF THE BRAND

Your brand personality is how your brand comes across to your customers. Think of it as describing the personality of a friend, or family member, or person you admire. What would your brand, if it were a person, be like?

If I were describing my college roommate Katie, I would describe her as *buoyant*, *wickedly organized*, and *outgoing*. If I were to describe my first boss, Jon, I would describe him as *patient*, *sweet*, and *brainy*.

NEXT, CHOOSE THREE WORDS TO CONVEY YOUR BRAND'S TONE OF VOICE

Your brand tonality is the manner in which you speak, both literally how you sound and what kinds of words and vocal emphasis you use. If your brand were a person, how would this person talk? What would this person sound like? My college roommate Katie's tonality is *bubbly*, *cheery*, and *sassy*, while my first boss Jon's tonality is *warm*, *friendly*, and *approachable*.

If you feel stuck, here's a way to spur your thinking as you identify your three personality and three tonality descriptors:

First, write a few phrases or sentences about what kind of person your business would be, and how they would speak. For example:

- Personality
  - The kind of person who always takes the high road even when, or especially when, no one is looking
  - Sits at the bar, not at a table in the corner
- Tonality
  - Speaks with a booming voice
  - Talks to you as a peer, not as a teacher or mentor

Next, crystalize each of those phrases into a single word.

- Personality
  - The kind of person who always takes the high road even when, or especially when, no one is looking might distill to a personality descriptor of noble.
  - Sits at the bar, not at a table in the corner suggests your brand personality is open, curious, or friendly.
- Tonality
  - Speaks with a booming voice becomes a tonality descriptor of impassioned or energetic.
  - Talks to you as a peer, not as a teacher or mentor becomes a tone that is informal or easygoing.

PROVIDE NUANCE WITH EDGE

Now you have your character archetype, and you have portrayed it with a handful of personality and tonality descriptors for your brand. Next, we give those descriptors edge. Establishing edges to your personality and tonality gives dimension to your brand's character. It shows where your brand falls on the spectrum of a given trait.

People are nuanced. Some people who are friendly are downright chummy, friendly in an overt and perhaps even loud way. Other friendly people are more quietly so. By defining your character edges, you are applying a fine-grain sandpaper to refine your brand from caricature to real person. Characterizing with this level of acuity also improves your ability to push brand decision making outward. The vivid portrayal empowers your team to express your brand in a single, bold voice.

EXERCISE: ESTABLISH YOUR CHARACTER EDGES

Write your three personality descriptors and your three tonality descriptors with some blank space on either side of each word.

Write another word to the left of each word, this one conveying the same idea but not quite as strong as your descriptor. Then, write a word to the right that is an exaggerated version of your original descriptor.

For example, if I had chosen *noble* for my personality descriptor, I might write to its left *moral* or *honest*. My brand's personality is more than just moral and honest; it's noble. To the right of *noble*, I might write *altruistic* or *self-righteous*. Those take the concept too far. My brand is *noble* but not *altruistic* or *self-righteous*.

For my tonality descriptor *friendly*, I might choose as my

not-strong-enough word, *approachable*, and my too-strong word, *chummy*. My brand personality is more than approachable but less than chummy. Friendly is just right.

Figure 11.1. **Character Edges for Batter Pancakes**

	NOT FAR ENOUGH	JUST RIGHT	TOO FAR
		"The Creator"	
PERSONALITY	Intelligent	Bright	Smart alec
	Caring	Action-oriented	Activist
	Friendly	Open	Gregarious
TONALITY	Novel	Fresh	Flashy
	Upbeat	Light	Playful
	Concise	Direct	Blunt

USE YOUR BRAND CHARACTER AS STYLE GUIDE AND CHECKLIST

When you ask people on various teams, both internal and external to your business, to bring your brand to life, they cannot read your mind. They can only embody your brand independently if you define your brand character overtly, boldly, and granularly, and then empower them to breathe life into it. This definition you created becomes their guide in your stead, so that they may give a single voice to your brand character throughout all touchpoints—ad copy, social media, direct mail, how the phone is answered, how emails are signed—ensuring that your brand is expressing your true character every time.

Consider the brand edges as a checklist for brand expression. If you are evaluating the messaging someone on your team has created, and you are not liking what they wrote, rather than saying, "I don't like it—it feels off-brand," reference the checklist. What, specifically, makes it off-brand?

A client of mine once had a vague sense the copy his team was developing for email newsletters was off-brand but could not put his finger on why until he referenced the brand edges. He noticed that the brand edges said "energetic but not frenetic." The copy was rife with hyperbole and exclamation points, which he could identify with this checklist as "frenetic" and therefore too caricatural for this brand. Knowing this edge, the copywriters felt empowered to work without constantly getting the head of marketing involved with copywriting decisions. They also improved their own brand expression skills. This resulted in a happier team, a happier leader, a more consistent expression of the brand, and thus a more scalable business.

CONNECT ON THE LEVELS OF WHAT, WHY, AND HOW

Brand positioning is about making your business easier to see, buy from, and have a relationship with. So, good positioning, like good human relationships, is layered and multifaceted and holistic. It includes the logic argument (your brand promise and reward). It also includes a personality and tonality (your character). A differentiated promise, end reward, and distinctive brand character form the basis of a meaningful customer relationship, and it can make everything that you do in your business come alive with heart and soul.

Until now, we have been talking about character as a separate layer—the "how" on top of the brand's "what" and "why." Brand strategist Catherine Carr, who introduced me to the idea of the brand archetype years ago while we were collaborating on a project, taught me a deeper dimension to the character archetype framework. A business that feels great resonance with its chosen archetype might find that it not only shows how a brand acts and talks, but it also infuses the brand's very promise. An archetype can be the way that a business comes across (the how), but it also can be part of the benefit a business brings (the what and why). It can be a layer—a personality—but it can also be the very fabric of the offering.

I know both these approaches to work, and you should embrace the one that feels the most genuine to you. Character could be a layer that gives outward style, or it could infuse the promise itself. As Carr advised me, "Each archetype contains a wide emotional range. You can go as deep as you want, as long it feels authentic for your business."

Geico is an example of the layered approach. Geico's brand promise (its what) is low-cost insurance. The Jester character, expressed through the brand's gecko mascot, is the *how* that is layered on top of Geico's very rational promise. Geico is a distinctive and treasured brand. This layering of the Jester personality is effective for Geico. Insurance is not funny, but the company's style is, and its customers are drawn to that humor.

In contrast, consider Disney. Disney's promise is to create magical moments, and its character is the Magician archetype. Its what, why, and how *all* stem from the Magician. Instead of Magician being a layer, Disney epitomizes Magician through and through. This is effective, too. Disney is one of the world's most meaningful and most valuable brands.

I noticed this deep and broad character expression with my client Cypress Grove, which we discussed in Step 1 (Chapter 7). Cypress Grove is a brand that, like Disney, embodies the Magician archetype. Magician also imbues Cypress Grove's promise and end reward of *elevating moments to extraordinary*. The Cypress Grove team felt this archetype so deeply that they even brought the idea of magic into their tagline: "Fine Cheese Alchemy." Pamela Dressler, CEO of Cypress Grove, told me "As soon as we learned about the twelve archetypes, we all quickly gravitated toward the Magician. It felt like us, like what we strive to do and be. Cheese is conjured from milk through an alchemy-like process. How can three simple ingredients—milk, culture, rennet—produce such an amazing variety of cheese? It's magic, right?"

ZIG AGAINST YOUR COMPETITORS' ZAG

Here's the exciting part from a bottom-line perspective. Brand character can be another source of differentiation and, therefore, a competitive advantage. You can be different not only through your value proposition—the promise that you bring your customer—but also through your personality. Being the same personality as your peers is blah, undifferentiated, edgeless, and therefore hard for your customer to see—engendering little love. Embodying a character that is distinct from the other options your customer is considering makes you stand out and, therefore, is itself a competitive advantage.

When choosing your character archetype, consider what is true to your character and consider it in the context of your category. Channel your customer and view the characters of your business and category through your customers' eyes. Select an archetype that both expresses your truth and zigs from the category.

You can take advantage of the fact that your category is cliché by pushing away from that archetype to be more distinctive, more different—more human. You can recognize this in some of the best-loved brands:

- **An Explorer in a Caregiver World**
  - When Starbucks began selling coffee in 1971, most coffee brands were either the Caregiver or the Lover archetype. A woman created a morning for her husband in which the best part of waking up was Folgers in his cup (Caregiver). Dear girlfriends reminisced the cute stranger from their visit to Paris as they sip International House of Coffee (Lover). The Caregiver and Lover were so pronounced in the coffee category that they were category clichés.
  - Starbucks bucked this cliché by embodying the Explorer archetype, beginning with naming the business after the first mate in *Moby Dick*. By drinking Starbucks coffee, customers discover new things and explore new flavors, regions, and sensations. Starbucks zigged while the others zagged, allowing its brand to be both meaningful and distinctive at the same time.
- **A Caregiver, Lover, Jester, Sage, Hero, Magician, and Ruler in an Explorer World**
  - In contrast to the Caregiver- and Lover-dominated coffee category, the car category cliché archetype is the Explorer, presumably because cars literally move around as explorers themselves. Notice that the most compelling car brands are *not* the Explorer archetype. In a category

of Explorer blah-ness, a brand might show up as a Caregiver (Volvo), a Lover (Volkswagon), a Jester (Mini), a Sage (Audi), a Hero (BMW), a Magician (Tesla), or a Ruler (Mercedes). Among a tedious flock of Explorers, being adventurous means being something other than adventurous.

- **A Jester in a Ruler and Everyman World**
  - The staid insurance category is filled with Rulers and Everymen, into which Geico breaks through as a Jester.

Here's a fun test: Google your category and look only at the images. Notice the colors, fonts, and shapes of your frame of reference. When I searched for *insurance companies*, my screen filled with shades of dark blue, capital letters, and italicized fonts. In other words, Ruler. "You're in good hands," says Ruler All State. "Let Prudential be your rock," says Ruler Prudential. Beyond the dark blue are spatters of red and blue Everymen: "Like a good neighbor, State Farm is there." And then amid this sea of blah is a funny little gecko with his hands on the approachable "Geico" font. It makes me smile to see this gecko among these stern and earnest brands. Geico zigs as a Jester while the rest of the category zags as Rulers and Everymen.

EMBODY YOUR CHARACTER CONSISTENTLY

At every level of your business, consistently embody your character to earn trust. Just like with a person, how you act matters more than what you say. Embodying your defined character with everything you do will win trust when consistent, and distrust when inconsistent.

Over the last twenty years, neuroscience has shed light on the way our brains detect patterns that result in trust and distrust. Our limbic systems have evolved to detect inconsistent patterns as signals for threat—a signal to beware, to not trust. Lack of consistency signals to my brain that I am not safe.

Recently, while leaving a friend's home after dinner, I walked down the stairs from the front porch and jerked to a stop. It was dark, and even though my eyes couldn't see anything, my body froze. A split second later, a dog on a walk with its owner lunged angrily at me, missing my face by inches.

In hindsight, I see that my brain stem perceived threat and reacted quickly and intelligently with a "freeze" response. It perceived an aggressive pace and an unknown shape, likely an animal, jumping toward me. That surprise and inconsistency alerted my threat response and I froze, saving myself a trip to the ER.

This happens with interpersonal interactions and business communication as well. You might feel vaguely uncomfortable—consciously or not—when there is an incongruence between what a person or business is saying and what they are doing.

When a person or business acts inconsistently, your metaphorical forearm hairs stand on end. If a business acts fun and Jester in its advertising, but it then sends you stern emails with heavy fine print, the inconsistency erodes trust. You will think twice about entering into or deepening the relationship.

Much of this "characterize" step is less about creating than it is about making the implicit explicit. You may have already thought a great deal about the character of your business but have not taken the time to codify it into plain words. When you select the character archetype most true to your business and then define it overtly, everyone who represents your business has a beacon to express what you do consistently. When distinctive and true, your character will attract customers. When your behavior aligns consistently with that character, your business earns customer trust. It is not contrived, but it does take effort and courage to put a stake in the ground. Doing so will incline your business toward your North Star.

CHAPTER 12

STEP 6: STAGE

You now have in place the principal elements of your ironclad brand strategy. In this chapter, we apply these brand strategy elements according to where your customers are in their journeys with your brand.

First, we'll discuss the framework of the customer journey. Then we'll dive into the customer mindset and messaging goal at each journey stage, so that you can influence the customer sequentially. Lastly, we'll tailor the messaging ideas from your benefit ladder so that all the brand's creative can match messaging to the appropriate journey stage. All of this will connect the dots between your brand strategy and the deep customer engagement of an ironclad brand. We will take these one by one:

- Sequence the Customer Journey
- Grasp Each Distinctive Mindset
- Tailor the Message by Stage and Mindset

SEQUENCE THE CUSTOMER JOURNEY

Customers move through stages as they enter into and then deepen their relationship with your business. You may be familiar with the notion of the sales funnel, commonly attributed to Elias St. Elmo Lewis, who codified the framework in 1898. The sales funnel is often referred to as the first formal marketing theory. While this funnel has been called many different things, and has seen many permutations and evolutions, the principle the sales funnel illustrates remains even today: your relationship with your customer is a journey.

The funnel illustrates that as customers come to your business, they travel through stages of a funnel with increasing levels of commitment to your offering. A customer begins as a prospect who is *Unaware* of your brand. That person then becomes *Aware* of your brand, then begins to *Consider* it, then *Purchases* it, then becomes *Loyal*. In much the way a friendship develops first with an introduction, then with an initial conversation, then with continued experiences, your relationship with your customer moves through progressive stages. Each customer and prospective customer is at his own distinctive stage in his relationship with your business. Recognizing this enables you to meet the person with the most effective message at each stage.

To make full use of this customer journey framework, we are going to modify the sales funnel construct in two ways:

1. Replace the phrase *sales funnel* with *customer journey* to foster a human, customer-centric orientation. A customer does not consider himself to be an object in your funnel, so nor should you. A journey reflects the two-way nature of your relationship. As with all mutually beneficial relationships, you

are giving to each other. Your customer does not represent a wallet you are trying to access at the end of a funnel, but a human being with whom your business is making a reciprocal commitment.

2. Rather than the shape of a funnel that ends at a tapered bottom, the customer journey shape resembles an hourglass. While a funnel ends once a customer makes a purchase, the hourglass continues well past purchase, expanding as we enrich our relationship with that customer. In the lower half of the hourglass, new and existing customers themselves fuel the engine, bringing in more sales and more customers as the love deepens. Commonly, businesses disproportionately nurture the customer at the beginning of the journey when building awareness, consideration, and conversion. Ironclad brands lavish love on existing customers just as much, recognizing that the purchase is a beginning, not an end.

GRASP EACH DISTINCTIVE MINDSET

There are five basic stages of a customer's journey with your brand. Step into the shoes of your target customer and imagine his mindset toward your business at each stage. This insight will enable you to expand the relationship progressively, moving him from one stage to the next. I view the chain of five stages— Unaware to Aware to Considering to Purchasing to Loyal—as linked by the corresponding customer mindsets of *See, Like, Believe, Commit,* and *Love.* To get from Unaware to Aware your communication goal is that they *see* you. From Aware to Considering, the goal is that they come to *like* you. From Considering to Purchase, your goal is to help them *believe* in you, which will inspire them to *commit*. From Purchase to Loyal, you are igniting their *love*.

See, Like, Believe, Commit, Love. Let's examine the journey in detail, step by step:

Figure 12.1. **Customer Journey Stages Overview**

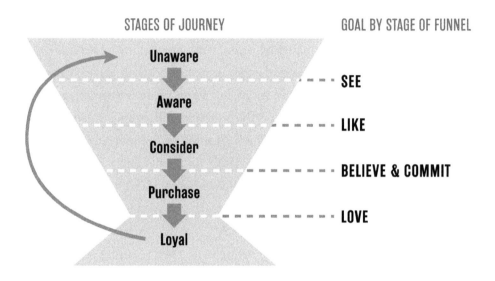

1. UNAWARE → AWARE

See, Like, Believe, Commit, Love

At this stage, your target customer is not aware your brand exists. Their mindset toward your brand is blank, and you are simply giving them an easy way in to begin a receptive mindset. Your only goal when communicating with Unaware customers is to make them Aware of your brand. It is to make them *See* it. Later, you can make them *Like* it, *Believe* it, *Commit* to it, and *Love* it. Right now, you are merely gaining their attention.

To do this, make it easy for them to see your brand by leveraging what about your brand is already familiar to them. Give them a handle, a doorway in, perhaps employing their existing mental file folders with a familiar category descriptor or a familiar functional benefit. What *are* you to this person? You may simply be describing fundamentally what your brand is so that they can easily file it into their head. Once they see you, you can later "fill" that frame—that file you have started—with meaning.

Remember that your target customers' attention is scarce. The other stimuli you compete with to gain customers' initial awareness are vast, loud, and ubiquitous. The only way to succeed at breaking through the clutter so that they will attend to you is by making it extremely easy for them. Do the cognitive heavy lifting for your customers by making your doorway in simple and accessible.

Paul Tiffany, professor of strategy at UC Berkeley Haas School of Business, explained that brand helps us do that: "Brand is your chief way to fight for space in the mind. Brands tap into the way our brain learns. And a brand, like a relationship, evokes a reaction in your mind that, once there, is really hard to change. That's also why it's true that first impressions count so much. They form a neural pathway that is hard to shift."

Andrew Sherrard, as CMO of T-Mobile, described something similar. "In the modern world, what do you think is the single most scarce resource? It's attention, by far and away. It's not information, it's not capital, it's attention. And it's getting more precious, because the cost of it is going up, because supply of things you could be attending to is increasing exponentially. Brand gives customers and employees shorthand to make it easier to attend to you."

2. AWARE → CONSIDERING

See, *Like*, Believe, Commit, Love

Customers at the Aware stage know your brand exists, but they are not yet Considering. At the previous stage, you helped the Unaware customer become Aware by enabling them to *See* your brand. At this step, you help the Aware customer to Consider your brand by exposing them to what will make them *Like* it. Doing so will move them from Aware to Considering.

This is where your ironclad brand promise that you articulated in the Ladder step starts to bear fruit. You worked hard to develop a brand promise that was meaningful and likable to your customer and unique to you, and now you will put that promise to work. If it is indeed your target customer with whom you are communicating, this will pull him from Aware to Considering, from *Seeing* it to *Liking* it.

"Having a strong brand just makes everything *easier*," related Leigh McMillan, General Manager for White Pages' Consumer Business. "When customers come to us already having a baseline value of what we do for them, our efforts to build affinity with those people are so much more likely to be fruitful."

3. CONSIDERING → PURCHASE

See, Like, *Believe*, Commit, Love

At the Considering stage, the target customers are intrigued. They like you, so they are considering your offering. The goal at this stage is to reinforce that liking by enabling customers to *Believe* your promise. They see you, they like you, now you want them to believe you.

To inspire this belief in you, you typically communicate to the Considering customers your brand's reasons to believe that you established in your Benefit Ladder (Chapter 8). The specific context and type of marketing tactic will determine the way you convey your reasons to believe, but regardless of the tactic or words, your goal is to make your promise credible in the mind of your customer.

The Considering stage differs from previous stages in that you tend to have more communication real estate and more time, because there is now goodwill. With Unaware and Aware audiences, you need to communicate what you are and what you promise in a nanosecond, as the attention stimuli you are competing with are formidable. But with a Considering audience, you likely have a handful of seconds—sometimes even minutes, depending on your communication tactic—because you have already broken through the clutter to hold their attention and interest.

This luxury of real estate and time is something you earned by communicating only one stage at a time. If you had conflated the stages and crammed multiple communication goals into one tactic, your customer would not as easily progress through the stages, so you would not be given as much of their time and attention.

4. PURCHASE

See, Like, Believe, *Commit*, Love

At this stage, customers are on the precipice of purchasing your offering. Your goal is to make it easy and satisfying to pull the trigger. They have come to *See, Like,* and *Believe* your brand. You now want them to convert that interest into a purchase. Here, your job is to reduce friction by giving them exactly what they need to make that purchase. This could be a quick "buy now" button; a money-back guarantee; an express lane; plenty of available sales-people to help; fast check-out; thirty-day free pricing; not needing to walk far or scroll far to pay. And then once they have purchased, right away make them glad that they did. Make the opening of the package fun. Send them welcome notes. Minimize the time between his parting with his money and him enjoying the product.

5. LOYAL

See, Like, Believe, Commit, **Love**

Once customers have purchased, your goal is to make them *Love* your brand, to inspire loyalty such that they become frequent customers who evangelize your brand to others. Use your compelling product experience and post-purchase communication to deepen your customer relationships. Make it worth their while to stay. Remind them why they chose you. Allow them to feel smart for doing so.

When you give a lot to your customers, they become loyal to you. They *Love* you. They embrace you. They tell their peers about you. Those peers are often your target customer, too. When they tell their peers about you, the loyal customers themselves become marketing engines for your business. Your loyal customers inspire new prospects to *see, like,* and *believe,* so now you have new customers entering the journey already aware of and considering your brand.

At the point where customers purchase, the tapered part of the hourglass gives way to a flared out opening where your current customers deepen their relationship with your business by buying more from you and evangelizing you to their peers. This flow then becomes a virtuous cycle. Loyalty breeds more and more goodness for your customer and your business. You treated them like family, so they will treat you like family.

The math of loyalty is compelling: the cost of keeping a current customer is lower than the cost of acquiring a new one, especially with frequent repeat purchases. Even better, your marketing ROI improves sharply when current customers themselves evangelize your brand to new customers.

But really, beyond the math, this is a moral imperative. It is your duty and privilege to delight your customers. They have given you money or time in exchange for enjoying your promise, so live up to your end of the bargain by delivering and overdelivering on that promise. This is your chance to serve these people you set out to serve. It is your chance to shine.

TAILOR THE MESSAGE BY STAGE AND MINDSET

Now that you understand the customer journey as five distinct stages, prepare a messaging hierarchy to support it. A messaging hierarchy is an outline that lists the ideas that will fuel specific messaging copy for each individual stage of the customer journey. Later, when creative is being developed, this hierarchy will empower your copywriters to write language that meets your customers where they are.

Let's look at some examples of *See, Like, Believe, Commit, Love*.

A NEIGHBORHOOD BIKE STORE

Your target customers became Aware, having walked by your storefront and seen your sign posted outside reading *Jake's Bikes*. They now *see* you and file you in their head as a bike store. They then read the tagline written below your name sharing your brand promise "Bikes That Fit Like a Glove." Because their own bikes at home are uncomfortable, they do not ride as much as they wish. Your brand promise resonates with them and they *like* you. They are Considering you.

The next time they are in your neighborhood, they walk into your shop to look around, and a salesperson strikes up a conversation. The customers learn from the salesperson your reasons to believe, which are that all bikes are custom-fit on the premises, and that you provide unlimited tune-ups for five years for a continued fit. Now the customers *Believe* the promise, and you have paved the way for them to *Commit* to purchasing a bike with a quick check-out process without long forms to sign or long lines to wait in.

With their new bikes, the customers relish the most comfortable bike-riding experiences they have ever had, enjoy no-hassle tune-ups regularly, participate in your monthly group rides, meet new cyclist friends, and feel younger than their years. Now these customers *Love* you.

A B2B MACHINE-LEARNING SOFTWARE PRODUCT

Your target customers became Aware of your brand having seen your company's name featured as a sponsor to the annual industry trade show. They now *See* your brand. They then begin to Consider it after your CEO gave the keynote at that trade show and the theme (your brand promise of human-powered machine learning) resonated with them. They now *Like* your brand. Then they invite you to pitch to them in your offices a month later, and you share your sales presentation with all of the reasons to believe—your data modeling technique, your team of PhD data scientists, your flexible pilot program. Now they *Believe* your promise, helping pave the way to their signing your simple proposal for a pilot partnership. Then they experience your pilot and can transform their business because of the human-powered machine learning you delivered. Now, these customers *Love* you.

SILK PAJAMAS SOLD VIA YOUR ECOMMERCE SITE

Your audience became Aware after a Google search for luxury pajamas. They now see your brand. They then begin to Consider it after reading your tagline "The Original Stretch Silk Pajamas." They now *Like* your brand, so you communicate to these Considering customers greater detail to seal their belief in your promise: your exclusive silkworm-rearing process, your patented stretch sewing technique, an image of a person luxuriating in a well-appointed king-size bed while wearing the pajamas, a testimonial from a rabidly happy customer.

Now they *Believe* your promise, and you pave the purchase path with visible "buy now" buttons on your website. They receive their pajamas in the mail the next day, and the box itself presents like a gift. Wearing them that night, the pajamas make them feel like royalty. After multiple wears, they seem to get better with age, increasingly supple and cozy. These loyal customers now post on Instagram photos of themselves lounging in your pajamas, garnering you yet more customers.

As you build each customer relationship, your job is to give your customers exactly what they need—and only what they need—to progress in their journeys. To advance this progression, identify for each stage of the relationship the specific messaging idea that will help them move to the next stage. Articulate for yourself your customers' mindset at each stage, as well as the message that will inch that mindset along to engage the person more deeply with your brand.

For each stage of the journey, recognize what you are trying to move the customer to do. Consider the appropriate message by asking these specific questions:

- How do we make someone who is unaware of our brand aware of it?
- How do we encourage an aware person to consider us?
- How do we motivate someone who is considering our brand to purchase our offering?
- How do we instigate the actual purchase conversion?
- How do we inspire and deepen delight for a current customer?

Here are two tips to building a messaging hierarchy that tailors message to mindset:

- **Do not write actual customer-facing language.** Instead, identify the single messaging idea that your copywriting team can later translate into copy. Focus only on the idea, not on crafting beautiful language. In fact, at this stage, keep your messaging idea so bare that the language borders on bland. As Roman stateman Cato the Elder advised orators, "Grasp the subject, the words will follow." Later, your creative team can dress it up.

· **Keep each messaging idea singular and precise.** Stick to one messaging idea for each stage. You may be tempted to develop a sentence or paragraph so great that it will serve all your purposes, all the stages of the customer journey. Resist this temptation. There is no one magic message that will advance all customers at all journey stages.

TAILORING MESSAGE EXAMPLE

As you prepare to leverage your benefit ladder and positioning statement to assign a single message to convey at each stage of the journey, let's walk through this entire journey with our Batter Pancakes brand as an example.

Figure 12.2. **Customer Journey Messaging Hierarchy for Batter Pancakes**

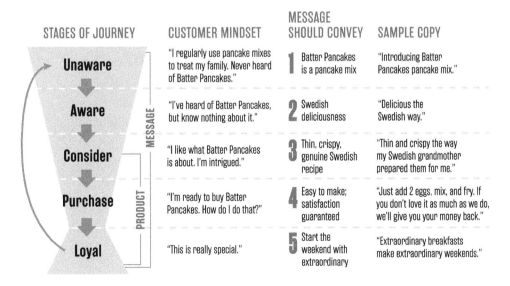

STAGES OF JOURNEY	CUSTOMER MINDSET	MESSAGE SHOULD CONVEY	SAMPLE COPY
Unaware	"I regularly use pancake mixes to treat my family. Never heard of Batter Pancakes."	1 Batter Pancakes is a pancake mix	"Introducing Batter Pancakes pancake mix."
Aware	"I've heard of Batter Pancakes, but know nothing about it."	2 Swedish deliciousness	"Delicious the Swedish way."
Consider	"I like what Batter Pancakes is about. I'm intrigued."	3 Thin, crispy, genuine Swedish recipe	"Thin and crispy the way my Swedish grandmother prepared them for me."
Purchase	"I'm ready to buy Batter Pancakes. How do I do that?"	4 Easy to make; satisfaction guaranteed	"Just add 2 eggs, mix, and fry. If you don't love it as much as we do, we'll give you your money back."
Loyal	"This is really special."	5 Start the weekend with extraordinary	"Extraordinary breakfasts make extraordinary weekends."

RIGHTING A MESSAGING WRONG

Getting granular in this way as you define your customer journey enables you to meet your customers exactly where they are. Instead of trying to come up with a message that attempts to do everything and winds up being confusing, you move to each touchpoint one at a time and give the one message to move your customers one stage farther into their journeys. I'll give you an example of when I failed to do this—and, therefore, failed to connect with my target customers.

When I ran Clorox Bleach Pen, I got to know a lot about stain removal, laundry, and the way that customers related to their laundry. Everyone has had the experience of having to toss an article of clothing either because it had a stain on it or because bleach splashed onto it, creating a stain. The Clorox Bleach Pen solved these problems. Instead of tossing that striped shirt with the wine stain on it, you could bleach it with the Bleach Pen. Instead of risking the harsh and uncontrolled liquid bleach getting on the colored portion of your clothes and rendering them unwearable, the Bleach Pen controlled that ingredient in a gel form dispensed through a squeezable pen.

We knew that we were solving a significant, unmet need in laundry, and the strong sales bore this out. Clorox Bleach Pen became the darling of the laundry aisle and of our company. The pens flew off the shelves in the first two months of launch, prompting in-house excitement (we're beating our numbers!) and fear (what if we run out of supply?) and satisfaction (we are really filling a need here!). But more astounding for me, the general manager of this business: we were delighting the hell out of our customers. They were giddy.

To paint the picture of how unusual "giddy" was in my world, let me remind you of my other Clorox brands, like Glad, Hidden Valley Ranch, and Formula 409 surface cleaner. While garbage bags, salad dressing, and grease cleaners are necessary and our solutions were excellent, sexy they were not. There were no communities of people camping outside stores awaiting our latest version. No, with our brands, we often got a thumbs-up but seldom passion.

During focus groups of early adopters of the Bleach Pen, I remember my astonishment as the moderator had to ask participants to stop interrupting each other. "I used it to save my son's baby clothes that I'd thought were long gone!" "My kids use it to decorate colored T-shirts for DIY projects!" "Did you know you can use it on grout?"

With this insight, we proceeded to develop a TV ad campaign around how much adoration there was for the Bleach Pen. The tagline was "the bleach you love to use" and featured consumers discovering clever and creative applications for the offering.

We aired the commercials, and our current customers loved it. They saw themselves in it.

But the audience we should have been reaching was our Unaware audience, as we were a new product with relatively low household penetration. These people had never heard of the Bleach Pen and were not moved by the TV spots at all.

What happened? We conflated our journey stages. We did not recognize that our audience was in a different place than we were. We had confused a post-purchase delighter (bleach that is fun and gratifying to use) with a purchase driver (salvage stained clothing with a controlled form of a strong stain remover). Even our rabidly happy customers did not come into the category because they wanted a bleach that was fun to use. They had purchased a Bleach Pen because they had an article of clothing that seemed unsalvageable, and they had wanted to try a very strong but highly controllable stain remover to fix it. Consumers had come in for a functional reason. We served up an emotional post-purchase delighter to an audience not ready for it, and it did not land with them.

Recognizing our mistake, we created a new campaign around "bleach you can control," and sales soared again. That correctly tapped into the purchase driver that resonated with our target customer. People came in because of seemingly unsalvageable stained clothes and stayed because it was so satisfying and fun to use.

I begin by seeking to make my Unaware target customers Aware target customers. To these customers, I will give just our name and category descriptor: Battered Pancakes pancake mix. An activity where I will focus on this message is the development of my business's logo and visual identity. I will resist the urge to get fancy or promote-y at this point. My name and descriptor should be in clear, easy-to-read font and color treatment, as the goal is merely to give target customers a way to *See* our brand.

Exposed to that single message, my customers are now Aware, but not yet Considering Batter Pancakes. I inch them along the journey by communicating the brand promise: Batter Pancakes brings Swedish deliciousness. A tactic to express this message might be a digital ad, or a print ad in the Sunday paper. Again, I do not overreach by messaging the aspects that make this promise believable. My goal is merely to make these customers *Like* our brand.

Now that they have been exposed to our promise, the customers have *Seen* and are *Liking* Batter Pancakes—they are Aware of and are Considering our brand. We now share our reasons to believe: our pancakes are thin, crispy, and use my Swedish grandmother's recipe. The medium for this message might be a cooking podcast or long-form piece of content on an online community for moms who love to cook. This helps customers to go from *Liking* to *Believing*, from Aware to Considering.

At the shelf or online, they are now looking through our packaging to learn how easy it would be to buy and make these pancakes. We display a simple price and a money-back guarantee, paving the path for them to *Commit* with a Purchase.

The product itself then plays the star role in our deepening relationship by delivering on the promise and bringing them other post-purchase delighters. Of course, the pancakes must deliver on Swedish deliciousness: they are delicious in a distinctively Swedish way that is both familiar and different at the same time. In addition, where can we surprise and delight customers? Can we feature an easy-to-open-and-close box with an innovative zip mechanism? Can we feature stories and images on the back of the box for them to enjoy during breakfast preparation? Does the pancake sizzle audibly while cooking, wowing the cook and others in the kitchen? Are there interesting but accessible recipes to include? Perhaps a way to join a community of cooks who love to make brunch?

These customers have parted with their hard-earned money for our promise, so I am going to work to delight them. If successful, this unleashes a cascade in the lower hourglass where they become frequent customers, telling their friends about Batter Pancakes, posting photos of pancake creations on Pinterest, sharing their own Batter Pancakes-inspired recipes. Our goal at this phase is *Love*—that they love the whole brand experience so much that they further deepen their relationships with Batter Pancakes.

WATCH OUT FOR PITFALLS

The necessary ingredient for tailoring messaging is genuine empathy for your customer, combined with respect for his journey stage. Just as it would be tone-deaf to propose marriage on the first date, it is tone-deaf to try to move an Unaware customer to a Purchasing one in a single move. Potential customers are unlikely to Consider your offering if your first interaction with them is a push to buy.

The major pitfalls at the messaging phase are of two flavors:

1. **One-size-fits-all messaging.** There is no single message, no matter how good, that can get a person through every stage of the journey in one message. Sometimes I see people squeeze many ideas into one sentence, thinking since it is still a single sentence that that qualifies as a single message. It does not. Select one idea only for each stage.

2. **Proposing marriage on the first date.** Conflating stages of the journey, either coming on too strong too soon (conflating the Aware or Considering stage with the Purchase stage) or bragging about your product features to someone not yet liking the promise (conflating Considering or Purchase stage with the Loyal stage). Take your fences one at a time.

These mistakes are easy to make, particularly when you yourself are proud of your product, and when you yourself are farther along in the journey than your customer. After all, you have been seeing this offering, liking it, believing it, committing to it, and loving it for quite some time—maybe years. So, you have to use your imagination to see that your customer needs to be brought along at their pace, not at your pace.

In this chapter, you thought about messaging as the one thing that will transition a customer from Unaware to Aware, and then from Aware to Considering, and so on until your whole product experience delights them into a Loyal customer. Respect the journey as the progression of stages through which all relationships blossom.

Now we will move to activating on-brand creative using the work you just completed.

CHAPTER 13

STEP 7: ACTIVATE CREATIVE

When you activate creative, you put to use your ironclad brand strategy. The creative and messaging you develop—company name, logo, About Us page, packaging, photos for your web site, Facebook ads, billboards, sales demos, and all of the other things you do to communicate your brand for your audience—happen now.

Denny Post, CEO of Red Robin, reflected, "Brand is strategy. A wise colleague who was a creative director told me 'give me the freedom of a tight strategy.' The tightest brand strategy creates from the beginning a focusing function so you know what's in and what's not. It is very freeing for a leader."

The role of your creative tactics is to progress customers farther into their journeys with your business. Before developing any piece of creative, allow your ironclad brand strategy to help you set the strategic directive and goal. This will establish the conditions for creative communication that works.

In this chapter, we will:

- Harness the Alchemy of Creative Development
- Set Direction with a Creative Brief
- Evaluate Creative with Confidence

HARNESS THE ALCHEMY OF CREATIVE DEVELOPMENT

A brand strategy is both a creative and a logical exercise. You have used both your gut and your brain to develop your brand strategy. We will continue this multidimensional approach with the development of creative.

Before creative development, articulate a deliberate directive for the tactic at hand. This sets you up to operate intuitively but within logical constraints, allowing there to be alchemy in the creative development process.

Here are two examples of resonant creative that resulted from exacting logical directives.

SHAKESPEARE, BEEP BEEP!

Shakespeare, most would agree, was wildly creative. His literary works have stirred readers and theatergoers for centuries. But consider this: Shakespeare used strict constraints to create his plays. He wrote verse in iambic pentameter, requiring a line of verse with five metrical feet, each with one short or unstressed syllable followed by one long or stressed syllable. Within the demands of the iambic pentameter, Shakespeare produced volume upon volume of cherished and enduring literature.

And consider the Road Runner cartoons. Creator Chuck

Jones was said to have defined strict rules to guide development of every episode. These rules are at times downright wacky. From "Rule #4: No dialogue ever except Beep Beep" to "Rule 6: All action must be confined to the desert," Jones's rules were his constraints, the edges of his canvas. Within this framework, Road Runner writers invented stories, tricks, and solutions in these adored mini-dramas.

1. The Road Runner cannot harm the Coyote except by going "beep beep"

2. No outside force can harm the Coyote — only his own ineptitude or the failure of Acme products.

3. The Coyote could stop anytime — if he were not a fanatic. (Repeat: "A fanatic is one who redoubles his effort when he has forgotten his aim." — George Santayana)."

4. No dialogue ever, except "beep-beep!"

5. The Road Runner must stay on the road — otherwise, logically, he would not be called Road Runner.

6. All action must be confined to the natural environment of the two characters — the southwest American desert.

7. All materials tools, weapons, or mechanical conveniences must be obtained from the Acme Corporation.

8. Whenever possible, make gravity the Coyote's greatest enemy.

9. The Coyote is always more humiliated than harmed by his failures.

These fruitful blends of structure and imagination illustrate exactly what resonant creative requires, too. Embrace the blend, and your creative will move your audience.

THE PERFECT RELATIONSHIP

Remember that brand is the relationship between a person and a business. If you ask yourself, "What's a brand I really love? What do I love about it?" I bet your answer is multidimensional, just like any relationship. It has a grounded, functional appeal to appease your intellect. It has an inspirational appeal that stirs your emotions. Left brain, right brain; mind, heart.

I'll explain with an example of a brand I love: Trader Joe's. The stores sell Icelandic yogurt, grass-fed ground beef, chili-lime Thai cashews, local beer, and also mini orchids. While I shop, I can enjoy free samples of coffee while my kids enjoy the in-store scavenger hunt. The Trader Joe's staff are friendly and eager to help. The low prices make me feel like I'm a smart shopper.

Many of those things are emotional: I feel positive emotions when I shop there. Many are logical: the stores have the groceries that I want and need and that delight my family and respect our bank account. If you take away either the emotional or the logical, it's not a full brand.

Like Shakespeare and the Road Runner cartoons, Trader Joe's abides by its own stringent rules to deliver its promise in a way only Trader Joe's can. And like Shakespeare and the adored Road Runner, Trader Joe's is an unequivocal success: at around $8 billion in annual sales, Trader Joe's sells twice as much per square foot as does Whole Foods.

Whether Shakespeare, Road Runner, or Trader Joe's, stories and brands span the mundane to the sublime, the rational to the emotional, the sensory to the verbal. If you think of your brand as encompassing all these things, just like any rich relationship, customers are more likely to bond meaningfully with you. And structure helps you span these elements.

If your comfort zone is in thinking of brand as a creative exercise, great. But don't forego the logical structure to help guide and unlock that creativity.

If you prefer to live unbound by rules, don't be afraid of

structure, because it's the foundation for creativity that ignites your audience.

Your best brand building doesn't come from rigid rules or serendipity alone. A brand is most moving when you have used both your left brain and your right brain to create and express it. By developing your ironclad brand strategy *before* developing creative output, you are taking a page from Shakespeare and Chuck Jones. You are using constraints, boundaries, and edges to make your creative effective.

Even if you yourself are going to be the person to develop the creative communication, I still encourage you to break the work into two pieces: the directive first, and the execution second. Strategy first, then tactics. Now while your head is clear, designate the idea you want to convey with your needed constraints, and only then begin creating.

SET DIRECTION WITH A CREATIVE BRIEF

A mentor once told me that "you always get the creative you deserve." The way that you "deserve" effective creative is by developing an ironclad brand strategy and using it in a crisp directive for your team to use to develop the creative you need.

Twenty years since receiving my mentor's advice on deserving creative, I am still amazed at its stark and consistent truth. Single-minded strategic direction will result in creative that sings. Vague creative direction will result in flat creative. Every. Single. Time. No shortcuts, no being indecisive. You did the hard work of developing your ironclad brand strategy, so remain disciplined by bringing that same laser focus and decisiveness to your creative development.

Your tool for setting this strategic direction is a creative brief, addressing these questions:

What is the creative for? Is it a tagline? A name? A billboard? A package? A home page? A video? A business card? An Amazon product description?

For example, perhaps for my Batter Pancakes brand, I have decided to drive awareness through an outdoor billboard, and I need creative design to put on that billboard.

Who is your target audience for this piece of creative? This might be your brand's target audience, or a smaller subset of your target that will interact with this creative in question. Where in the customer journey is this person right now?

For my Batter Pancakes billboard, my target audience may be "moms with kids at home who have heard of Batter Pancakes but know nothing else about it, and who drive on I-95 in Northern California." They are Aware of my pancakes mix but are not yet Considering it.

What is your desired customer action after having interacted with this copy? Be specific about what you want your customer to do differently as a result of interacting with this creative.

For Batter Pancakes, the desired customer action may be that the target customers look for Batter Pancakes next time they're at the grocery store. The goal is to move them from Aware to Considering.

What is the net takeaway? If they remember nothing else from this creative, what will be that one thing they remember? Refer to the customer journey of tailored messages you delineated in the Stage step.

For Batter Pancakes, the net takeaway should be the brand

promise of Swedish deliciousness. This billboard must convey, if nothing else, that Batter Pancakes brings Swedish deliciousness to customers.

What is your brand personality and tonality? You identified your brand personality and tonality in the Characterize step of building your ironclad brand strategy. Now, you simply include that thinking in the brief so that your creative team when developing the work can embody that personality and tonality.

For Batter Pancakes, the brand personality is *youthful*, *fun*, and *energetic*, and the tonality is *lighthearted*, *direct*, and *engaging*.

What are your executional mandatories? What must be present for the creative to be viable? What are the nonstarters? These can be the picky things you know must be used. Without being overly prescriptive, note here the things that for whatever reason you know must be part of the creative in order for it to work. "Must feature a photo of a mother and a child." "Must be X size." "Must use our brand color orange."

For Batter Pancakes, I may require as an executional mandatory that copy includes the word *Swedish* but not the word *Scandinavian*, and that the font presents large enough to be legible from 150 meters away.

A word to leaders who have hired creative partners to develop the creative output: do not micromanage your creators. The executional mandatories section is not an excuse for you to prescribe the creative to the creative developers. Overly prescriptive creative briefs will result in non-inspiring creative because your creative team could not stretch their wings. You have hired creatives because they are better at it than you are, so let them do their jobs.

EVALUATE CREATIVE WITH CONFIDENCE

Now you have written your creative brief and you've shared it with your creative team. When they come back to you to share the creative output they have developed, evaluate that work according to the brief. Do *not* evaluate creative in a vacuum. Never. Do not hamper your own hard work! Always evaluate according to your creative brief, which you developed according to your ironclad brand strategy. This sets up your springboard for effective creative.

To evaluate creative, I suggest a three-angle technique called HOPE—Heart, On-Point, and Execution. Here are the three steps to the HOPE technique:

Heart. Pay attention to your immediate gut reaction to the creative you are reviewing. Don't think about it; just notice your response. Did it make you smile? Did it surprise you? Did it give you goose bumps? Did it make you feel known, seen, recognized? Do you just *like* it? This is purely a subjective, nonanalytical response, so you only need to note your gut reaction and then set it aside for the moment.

On-Point. Is this piece of creative on-point? This is the chance for your analytical brain to weigh in. In my observation, this angle requires practice and is where many get lost, so take your time here.

Go back to your brief and review the goals you set forth in this directive. Get yourself in the mindset of the target audience that you identified, and the context of their taking in this piece of creative. Review carefully the net takeaway that you identified as critical that the creative delivers. Read again the brand personality and tonality that all your brand's expressions should embody.

Now look at the creative. Does it express the net takeaway you need it to express? Does it embody the brand's personality and tone? Be analytical at this point. Your prefrontal cortex now gets its chance to weigh in on the creative in question. It is an exercise in comparing what you asked for with what has come back. You are looking for an alignment between your brief's directive and the creative in front of you.

Execution. Imagine that this piece of creative has been executed and is in the wild. What will it look like? How will it be perceived? What details could go wrong or right?

If you are evaluating your brand's name, is it something that is legally available? Is there a domain name available for this brand name? Is the name idea memorable? Will it be flexible enough you can grow with it? Rich Barton, founder of Expedia and co-founder of Zillow, once blogged that when he names companies, he draws inspiration from the game Scrabble. High-value Scrabble letters like *Z*, *X*, and *K* are the most memorable because they're harder to place. This translates in business too. There aren't a lot of business names starting with *Z* out there, and brands like Zillow, Zulily, and Zappos can then enjoy the white space on the web and in consumers' minds.

If you are evaluating a logo, consider how it will appear in all its surroundings. Will the colors reproduce well on screen and on paper? If your budget is tight, having a logo with seven colors is more expensive to print than a logo with two colors. Is your color combination visible to the colorblind (8 percent of men)? Does the logo work well in black or gray, when color printing isn't possible? If your company is international, are your colors appropriate across cultures?

If you are evaluating a package design, will it visually pop off the shelf when compared to competing products? How does the package fit into standard retail shelving—will it take up enough space to make an impression? Is it different enough from surrounding packages that shoppers will notice it?

Most people have a natural inclination to lean toward one of these three angles—Heart, On-Point, and Execution. Many who are new to evaluating creative rely on Heart. Many seasoned marketers favor the On-Point step. For still others in both groups who in general tend to be detail-oriented, they may immediately zero in on the Execution aspects. It's natural and even desirable to have a primary orientation—the trick is not to stop there. Know your tendency, and then use this framework to ensure you are looking at this creative from all angles, not merely the angle of your comfort zone.

Let me share with you an experience in which I was glad for all three checkpoints of HOPE. I had created the brand strategy for a startup that had developed a new-to-the-world health and wellness service, and we wanted the business to have a big, magical, evocative name that could not only hold the bigness of this new idea but would be an umbrella for us as we created new offerings. One of the names we were considering and that many of us (including me) really loved was Madrigal, a type of song. It felt evocative of harmony and spaciousness, like our business's brand promise.

At the *E* stage of the HOPE framework, we evaluated how this name could come to life for our business. Although it was an available brand name for our space, by digging around on the internet, we learned of an association to this name that was problematic, to say the least. If you have watched the TV show *Breaking Bad*, you might recall Madrigal Electromotive, the parent company of the show's illegal drug ring. It would not have been good to name our health and wellness company a name many associate with an illicit drug.

Take the time at this critical step to avoid a logo that doesn't print well in black and white, a tagline that translates poorly to half of your international market, or naming your company after a meth lab.

Once you've completed all three steps, go back through them again. The second time you look at the creative, your subtly different lens may yield a nuance you did not originally perceive. Review:

- Do you like the creative?
- Does it express the point that you need it to express?
- Does it have executional challenges or advantages?

Figure 13.2. **HOPE Framework for Evaluating Creative**

Heart

- Identify your immediate, gut reaction.

- Don't think about it; just notice your response.

- Ask yourself: Do I like how it makes me feel when I first see it?

On Point

- Before looking at the creative, review the brand positioning and the brief.

- Focus on the tone and personality. Think about the net takeaway this piece of creative should express.

- Ask yourself: Is this creative on point? Does it express the net takeaway? Does it embody the brand's personality and tone? Does it solve the directive outlined in the brief?

Execution

- Imagine this creative already in play in the marketplace.

- If a logo, consider how it will look on paper, on a screen, in black and white?

- For packaging, consider how well it will fit and stand out on the shelf alongside similar products.

- Ask yourself: Are there tactical, pragmatic advantages to this approach?

Bring it all togther
After completing the 3 steps, go back through them again.

Ask yourself: Do you like it? Does it express the point that you need it to express? Does it have executional challenges or advantages?

NAMING YOUR BUSINESS

There are whole books on naming brands—my favorite is *Hello, My Name is Awesome* by Alexandra Watkins. Here is a high-level way of thinking about brand names.

Your name and descriptor together are your business's first impression, and your most valuable real estate as a brand. It will be your primary tool to take a customer from Unaware to Aware, and yet it will also be the name you live with for years and decades after your customer has begun a relationship with you. Naming can feel hard and high-stakes because it is costly to change your name once it has a foothold in the market.

You might think of names as living on a continuum from, on the left, highly descriptive, like Salesforce or Onlineshoes.com, and on the other extreme right, highly evocative and fanciful, such as Oracle or Slack or a made-up "empty vessel" names such as Zappos. The appeal of a descriptive name is that in the beginning when you are trying to get Unaware people Aware, your name can work hard to tell people what you are. On the other hand, the appeal of an evocative name is that as you grow, you've built in flexibility to move from the category you begin with. In the short term, descriptive names are helpful in gaining quick awareness. In the long term, less literal, more evocative names provide flexibility for growth.

To balance short- and long-term needs, use all your brand's real estate: your brand name, descriptor, and tagline, with your name being the hardest to change. If you pick a more fanciful name like Zappos, you may need, especially in the beginning, to lock it up with a category descriptor that tells what you sell, for example, "Zappos Online Shoes." This helps you with the short-term need of educating Unaware customers what you basically are. On the other end of the spectrum, if you pick a descriptive name, ensure that your descriptor and tagline infuse that with more life and inspiration. For example, Salesforce's tagline has been "Crush your sales goals with ease"—bringing more pizzazz and long-term relationship fodder to their descriptive name.

PRACTICE EVALUATING CREATIVE

When you as a consumer see a piece of creative, do this exercise: reverse-engineer the creative brief that was behind this creative execution. You may even want to use the HOPE technique. For example, if you saw the Miele vacuum billboard in Figure 13.3 while driving, you might react like this:

- **Heart:** I like that! It's fun and kind of shocking!
- **On-Point:** My net takeaway is that that brand of vacuum cleaner has a highly powerful engine. If that is their brand promise, they have conveyed it well.
- **Execution:** That image hanging off the billboard was probably expensive since it's not a standard billboard shape. They must have decided that it was worth it, despite the expense.

Do this whenever you see a piece of creative, whether you

like the creative or not. Your evaluation really will get better with practice, and when you get skilled at spotting the brand strategies of others, you will be sharper about your own.

The creative review process is one of the most elusive parts of brand activation. Creative evaluation is a subtle blend of art and science, heart and mind. Great creative taps into the way that human beings think and find meaning.

The power of all the work you have done to articulate your brand strategy is that you now can evaluate what comes out of your business according to that strategy. So, USE IT! Don't revert to subjective responses. Make it a practice never to evaluate creative unless it is using your brand strategy as a directive.

I am often asked to weigh in on a piece of creative, such as a tagline, or a video, or a name, or an About Us page. People say something general such as "What do you think of this copy?" My response tends to annoy them. I say, "I don't know, because I don't know what your strategic directive was. Show me your brief, your strategic directive, and then I could weigh in on the extent to which this creative expresses that intent."

By the way, so could you! When you set the strategic directive, you can react to creative based on adherence to the creative brief, rather than merely a subjective response. You have built a robust brand strategy so that you, too, can make decisions with integrity to your brand.

CHAPTER 14

STEP 8: ZOOM OUT

With your brand strategy in place and ironclad, we now zoom out and view the business as a forest of trees in which your brand lives. In this chapter, we will identify how you will deliver on your brand throughout everything the customer experiences.

David Aaker, widely considered the "father of modern branding," told me that brand's power to connect dots is what originally sparked his interest in brand. As a business strategy scholar, he saw that the prism of brand could translate business strategy into a graspable leadership tool. "Leaders can get stuck. Brand strategy is a way to implement the business strategy. It helps you tell employees and customers what you're going to stand for, because without that, the business strategy will fail." Brand strategy brings business strategy to a level that is useful every day.

This works in reverse, too. "What's more," Aaker related, "a brand strategy can be a vehicle for getting clarity on the business strategy itself. You might find while developing your brand strategy that you don't have a well-articulated business strategy. So they help one another become more clear."

The frameworks we explore in this chapter zoom out in two dimensions. The 4 Ps framework shows the breadth of decisions that enliven and reinforce brand, while the 3 Ds shows the sequential moments of a customer's engagement.

- Position with Breadth
- Position with Depth
- Surround the Ball

POSITION WITH BREADTH

Your brand position is the uniting idea that your business expresses broadly, across every decision it makes that touches customers, from the product to the price to the place of sale to the promotion. These elements, called the 4 Ps of marketing—form a classic framework that catalogs the levers that combine to bring to life a business's brand. Often called the "marketing mix", the 4 Ps is a framework for marketing decision making first proposed by Harvard Business School's Jerome McCarthy in 1960, and later popularized by Phillip Kotler of the Kellogg School.

The 4 Ps framework allows you to use every angle to let your business be a conduit for its promise. These elements work in concert to strengthen your brand. Let's look at each.

PRODUCT

Your product is the thing your customer purchases to experience your brand promise. Product can be a physical thing: a car, a massage chair, a TV. Product can also be a service: a taxi ride in that car, a pedicure on that massage chair, a Netflix subscription on that TV.

What your customer is buying includes all your brand's benefits, from functional to emotional, from tangible to intangible. This includes your product design, packaging and labeling, warranties, return policy, customer support, assortment of sizes and flavors.

Remember from Chapter 10 that your product is the vehicle for your promise. Customers do not buy the product for the product's own sake. They buy what they will enjoy as a result of your product. Think about the product from the customer's standpoint, not from yours. Think of it as what the customer is buying, rather than strictly as what you are selling.

Product tends to be the most arduous and least forgiving brand lever. No amount of strength of the other three Ps can compensate for a product that does not deliver the promise. At the same time though, many businesses spend so much time and energy on the product that the other levers are afterthoughts. This is as much of a mistake as developing a weak product.

PRICE

Your price is the money your customer pays to experience your brand promise. The price P includes all elements of pricing, from the absolute numerical amount you charge, to the optics of how you convey pricing, to the flexibility and customizability of pricing options, to discounts, rebates, credit terms, and payment methods. As with all the four Ps, the price lever has the power either to reinforce or to erode your brand position.

Again, consider the equation:

Customer Value = Benefit - Price

Your customer's value from your brand is all the good things your brand brings (benefit) minus what he parts with in exchange (price). The more Uncommon Denominator benefit you deliver, the more value your customer enjoys, and/or the more you can charge that customer. This is why we spend as much time as we do defining your benefit—your brand promise. It is the hero of your value proposition.

There are two reasons it is better to focus on increasing benefit than on decreasing price, as you try to create customer value. First, the obvious reason: decreasing price erodes your margin. Second, there is a floor to price decreases. Most cannot charge less than zero for your offering (at least not for very long), so reducing price can only increase customer value by a finite amount. In contrast, there is no ceiling to benefit. One could continue to increase benefit ad infinitum while still preserving and even improving margin. Focus your energy on making and delivering a promise so big, meaningful, and uncommon that price plays the lesser role in the customer's value. Then use the price *P* as a signal for your big promise.

PRICE SIGNALS QUALITY

Let price be another way you build your brand using the entire value equation. Here is an example. Smirnoff Vodka successfully fought a price competitor, Wolfschmidt, which sold for one dollar per bottle less than Smirnoff, by *raising* its price by one dollar per bottle. Using the extra revenue from the price increase to expand advertising, Smirnoff bolstered the brand's image and, therefore, the brand's perceived benefit: the increased price served as a signal of the product's superior quality and prestige. Smirnoff actually *increased* value with the price increase, because they made an even larger increase to the brand's perceived benefit. In this sense, price works together with product to reflect a benefit's resonance.

Base your pricing decisions on the customer value equation. Rather than lowering price to increase value and demand, how can you amplify your benefit? Can you expand value without lowering price? Rather than increasing price in a vacuum to pad your margins, make sure you have earned that price increase by amplifying your benefits at least as much as your price increase. When determining your price, do not begin at the bottom with your internal cost structure anchoring your price. Rather, begin with the top, creating huge value for your customer because of the huge promise you make and deliver, and then use that as the starting point to land on the appropriate price point.

PLACE

Place is the channel through which your customer purchases your offering. It includes geographic distribution and coverage, location, retail partnerships, inventory, shipping, transportation, and logistics. The place lever is your opportunity to make it easy for your customer to access, from the physical store location to the virtual one, from the fully owned to a shared marketplace, from direct to indirect modes. Make your product available where it makes sense for your customer to purchase it.

A recent homerun on this principle is the sale of vitamins and supplements in many physicians' offices. Patients who have just heard from their doctor that they need more calcium can purchase calcium supplements as they leave the physicians' office. Not only are these customers avoiding an extra errand, they also know they are choosing a brand and formulation their physician endorses, particularly meaningful in the confusing realm of non-regulated supplements. In this case, by virtue of convenient place, the customer value further increases.

PROMOTION

Now for that scene stealer, the promotion *P*—the sexiest of the four *P* levers. In order for your customer to enter into a relationship with your brand, your customer needs to know about and want your offering. Promotion is your communication to generate that knowledge and desire. Promotion decisions include the message you are communicating, the balance of tactics you are using to communicate that message, and the frequency of each message. Infuse your brand throughout your communication touchpoints, from advertising to PR to social medial to content marketing to email outreach to search engine marketing and beyond.

Etymologically, *promote* derives from the Latin *pro* ("forward") and *movere* ("move"). The promotion lever is everything you do to move your brand out there in front of people, so they know about it and desire it. Promotion is what you say, how you say it, what you look like and sound like, and how you feel to target customers as they interact with your communication and your offering.

Promotion should both express and reinforce your brand strategy, regardless of the size of your organization or budget. The more your promotion communicates the elements of your ironclad brand strategy—promise, reasons to believe, character, frame of reference—the more you can make of your marketing resources.

THE 4 PS IN CONCERT

Brand relationships upheld by only one thing, one *P*, will not hold up. Use all of them. In fact, if you can think of other *P*s (whether they start with *P* or not), all the better—use them. In consumer packaged goods, sometimes we add *packaging* as a fifth *P*. Some service industries have added three more—*physical evidence*, *people*, and *process*. I recommend that you not get too fancy at first. Begin with the original four Ps. The goal is to harness the major levers so that you can surround customers with your brand in every way they experience it, on all levels, on all sides, in manners both big and small.

The reason you need to employ all 4 Ps, if not more, is that your customer experiences all of them, not only one or two. Here is how one Starbucks customer might describe his Starbucks experience:

My favorite Starbucks is on my way to work, and I go most days as part of my morning routine. When I walk into Starbucks, I immediately feel lighter. There's music playing. There are warm colors on the walls. I smell coffee being ground and hear the espresso machine humming. The barista smiles at me. She knows I like the Veranda blend. The coffee tastes wonderful, and I can grab a box lunch to eat later (my favorite is the Protein Box). I love the holiday-themed paper cup and look forward to that every year. When I leave, I'm holding the Starbucks cup and feel invincible for a few moments of the day. I feel like I've treated myself, and in some ways, four dollars is indeed a lot to spend on coffee. In other ways, it's the best I feel all day, which is worth a lot more to me than four dollars.

He mentioned product (coffee, Veranda blend, protein-packed lunch). He mentioned price (four dollars). He mentioned place (the location near his work, the ambiance, the aromas, the sights and sounds, and the barista's smile). He mentioned promotion (the holiday cup). If Starbucks were to charge that much merely for coffee (product) without surrounding the customer with these other brand elements, would this customer be so happy? Would he even be a customer?

POSITION WITH DEPTH

While CEO of Clorox, Don Knauss often encouraged us to consider everything we did according to our "three moments of truth" with our target customer. He echoed that to me in a recent conversation. He said, "When you focus and allocate resources, make sure that you are covering all three moments of truth: desire, decide, and delight." These three moments are when we:

1. Create *desire* for what we offer
2. Motivate customers to *decide* to purchase it
3. Cultivate *delight* from experiencing our offering

The first moment, desire, is our set of activities to bring target customers from Unaware to Aware to Considering. We create desire by making it effortless for them to *See* us, *Like* us, and *Believe* us.

We support the second moment, decide, through our marketing activities near the point of purchase that convert an interested customer into a purchasing customer. We make it easy for them to find and purchase our offering, whether in a physical retail store, on the Internet, or through a person-to-person interaction. The packaging is accessible. The price is compelling.

The third moment, delight, is the set of activities that makes the customers glad that they purchased. We do this through the compelling product experience as a whole, including the product proper as well as all of the services and communication that we wrap around that product, from customer service to community building to post-purchase messaging to continual product improvement. Delight is how you ignite loyalty that can endure even during tough economic times. "During the recession, on the Glad brand, even with our about 30 percent price premium, we held share," Knauss told me. "And a lot of it was due to understanding the 3 Ds, but particularly the third *D* about delighting people."

An ironclad brand strategy brings your brand to life across all the three moments of truth equally, making the journey rewarding for the customer and rewarding for your business. "With all 3 Ds," Don Knauss advises, "you should be answering for customers the fundamental question, why should I buy this brand instead of another?"

SURROUND THE BALL

As you might expect, these breadth and depth frameworks go hand in hand. Use them together to apply your brand strategy both broadly and deeply so that it can shine through all your customer experiences of your brand. Come at your brand from four breadth angles and three depth angles and you've effectively surrounded the ball. Here is what this might look like for two different car brands.

Figure 14.1. **Positioning Wide and Deep—Volvo Example**

Brand Position: Safety

3 MOMENTS OF TRUTH	PRODUCT	PRICE	PLACE	PROMOTION
1 Desire (Awareness & consideration)	Car itself looks safe to a casual observer. Boxy, stable-looking.	Priced at high end of mid-priced cars. Not high-end because not luxury. Not low because safety's a big promise.	Volvo dealerships are visible and appealing from the road. Easy and safe to drive in and out.	Tagline: "For Life." Images of families safely driving and enjoying nurturing experience.
2 Decide (Conversion)	Learn during test drive that Volvo pioneered the 3-point seatbelt, and now is pioneering pedestrian airbags.	Price is transparent and clear. It feels psychologically safe. No bait and switch.	Safe place for your kids to play in a toy room with a babysitter while you talk to the dealer.	Statistics and stories of passengers in Volvos surviving collisions only because they were in a Volvo.
3 Delight (Loyaly & retention)	Turning radius is phenomenal. Defroster and heater work faster than any car you've ever driven.	Volvo covers cost of maintenance if maintenance issue could threaten safety.	Feel like the dealer is your friend you can trust. You want to refer others to this dealer.	Volvo ads continue to reinforce safety and wisdom of Volvo, making you feel happy about your purchase.

Volvo's brand position is safety. Let's see how Volvo infuses safety across all 4 Ps and through each of the 3 Ds.

PRODUCT

A person who falls into the definition of Volvo's target customer notices Volvos on the road, and the car itself looks safe: boxy, stable-looking. Before the customer is even in the mode of car shopping, Volvo is on his mind as a safe-looking, and therefore *desirable*, car.

Moving through the journey to the *decide* phase, during the test-drive, the customer learns that Volvo pioneered the three-point seatbelt, and now, Volvo is pioneering pedestrian airbags.

And after purchase, the Volvo product *delights* the customer with a phenomenal turning radius, a superfast defroster and heater—all features that make the Volvo safer and more enjoyable to drive.

PRICE

Before car shopping in earnest, this customer knows that his *desire* is for a premium car but not for a luxury car. Volvo is accordingly priced at the high end of mid-priced cars. This puts Volvo in this customer's consideration set.

Moving through the journey to when the customer is shopping at the dealership and *deciding*, he notices that the price is simple, transparent, and explicit. It feels psychologically "safe." No bait-and-switch tactics here.

Even after purchase at the *delight* moment of truth, Volvo still uses the price lever to reinforce the safety promise: the dealership covers the cost of his repair issues when the issue is safety-threatening.

PLACE

Before car shopping, during the *desire* moment, the customer sees the Volvo dealership along his usual driving route. Volvo dealerships are visible and appealing from the road and are easy and safe to drive into and out of.

While he is at the dealership *deciding*, there is a safe toy room for his kids to play in while he speaks with the dealer.

After purchasing his Volvo, he feels as though the dealer is a friend he can trust and, *delighted*, will heartily refer others to this dealership.

PROMOTION

The target customer notices a Volvo print ad while flipping through a *Time* magazine. The ad features *desirable* images of a family driving safely, boasting the tagline "Volvo. For Life."

Moving through the journey, while at the dealership considering a Volvo purchase, he learns of the features that show how Volvo can be so safe: the forward-collision warning with automatic braking, blind-spot warning system, lane-keeping aid, and distance alerts. The dealer demos some of those features so that, while *deciding* on a purchase, the customer can actually sense the safety of the car.

After he has purchased his Volvo, when he receives monthly newsletters from his Volvo dealership with safe driving tips and information, he feels assured, proud, and *delighted* that he has made a wise choice for his family.

Figure 14.2. **Positioning Wide and Deep—BMW Example**

 Brand Position: Driving Performance

3 MOMENTS OF TRUTH	PRODUCT	PRICE	PLACE	PROMOTION
1 **Desire** (Awareness & consideration)	Sleek, beautiful design. It looks fast.	Luxury price point for a luxury car.	BMW dealership itself looks elegant and prestigious on the outside when you drive by.	Tagline: the ultimate driving machine. Images of driver enjoying driving.
2 **Decide** (Conversion)	Test-driving, learn no coffee cup holders for drivers in this model, so the driver can instead feel the car.	No gimmicky sales at BMW dealerships.	Dealers who work at BMW are car enthusiasts, some are even professional race car drivers.	The messaging when you are nearing pulling the trigger on buying the car is classy, not aggressive.
3 **Delight** (Loyalty & retention)	While driving, you feel the hum of the engine and the wheels on the road. Sensory delight.	Price includes dealership cleaning your car gratis any time.	Dealer follows up with you to see how you are enjoying the hum of your car.	Sense of club membership and camaraderie with other BMW drivers.

PRODUCT

While casually considering buying a new car, the target customer notices BMWs on the road. The cars are sleek and elegant in design. They look fast.

Further into his journey, he is at the BMW dealership, and while test-driving, he learns that there are no coffee cup holders in this model. The dealer explains that this is so that he can feel the experience of driving, not relax as a passenger would.

After the customer has purchased a BMW, he can *feel* the hum of the engine and the wheels on the road. Driving the BMW is sheer sensory delight. Every time he drives the BMW, he loves it more.

PRICE

The customer is at a point in his life in which he wants and can afford a luxury car. He is only considering cars in the luxury tier. BMW is priced near the other luxury car brands, and so is in his consideration set.

At the dealership, price is whispered rather than shouted. There are no sales, discounts, or cheesy rebates. The price cards are displayed quietly but cleanly.

After the customer has purchased a BMW, the customer can keep coming back to the dealership for complimentary detailing forever.

PLACE

The customer notices the BMW dealership while driving to work, and from the outside, it looks elegant and prestigious.

Further into his journey, when he visits the dealership to browse, he learns that BMW salespeople are themselves bona fide car enthusiasts. Some are even professional race car drivers.

After the customer has purchased a BMW, the dealer follows up to ensure she is enjoying the hum of the car and to let him know about some little-known features she can turn on to amplify the driving experience. The customer feels a bond with the dealer, with whom she now likes to geek out about car engineering.

PROMOTION

In an airline magazine, the customer notices a print ad of BMW with the familiar tagline: "the ultimate driving machine." The ad depicts a driver enjoying driving. No kids with Cheetos in the backseat, just the driver, the car, and the road. This customer is enchanted.

While shopping for his BMW, all of the signage and messaging at the dealership are restrained and classy in tone, emphasizing the fine engineering of the BMW.

As a BMW owner after purchase, his BMW dealership provides a sense of "club" and camaraderie with other BMW drivers. BMW drivers regularly stop in casually for a cup of coffee and to talk cars with fellow BMW owners.

EXERCISE: IDENTIFY YOUR PS AND DS

Now it is your turn. Identify how your brand positioning can come through in each of the 4 P levers at each of the 3 D moments of truth.

Think about how your positioning comes through in your product, price, place, and promotion at the early stages of your relationship with your target (when you are trying to create desire), at the mid-stages (when you are trying to help them decide to purchase), and at the later stages (when you are trying to ignite delight).

Pull out a large piece of paper. Draw a grid on the page, with four columns across (one for each *P*) and three rows down (one for each *D*).

Product Column: For Product, consider how your offering itself creates Desire. What hooks can you build into your product that can generate interest, make your product something that people want to become aware of, that people want to consider buying?

Then moving through the journey to the Decide phase, how

can your product itself help you to convert interest into a sale? What about your product helps a person go from thinking about buying it to actually buying it? This could be a demonstration of your product. This could be a very visual side-by-side of using your product, or not using your product. This could be an illustration on your web site or packaging or at point of purchase in retail.

Finally, how might your product deliver and over-deliver on your promise? How can it Delight beyond your customer's expectation?

Price Column: Then, move on to Price. How can your price and your price structure lure your target customer? You can think of this as the absolute price, but also as the way that you convey price.

If your brand is luxury, your price point is high. Optically, you would not cheapen it by ending it with a ".99" rather than a whole digit. If your brand is mass, your price point is also mass, and perhaps optically you sweeten it by showing the savings between your offering and an alternative.

Moving farther along in the journey to Decide, how can your price and your communication of price itself spur purchase? This could be the idea of a scarcity tactic such as "We're only offering this price for the next thirty-six hours."

Lastly, how can you allow price to be your asset in creating loyalty and retention? Can you use price to show your customers that you appreciate them? Can you give freebies or discounts or upgrades to loyal customers?

Place Column: Now consider the third *P* of the framework, Place. How can the place where people buy your offering itself instigate Desire for your offering? Maybe it's your beautiful and easily discoverable website, or your convenient retail location with easy parking, or your warm business-to-business referral partners.

Moving down the journey to Decide: how can you make use of the way that your product is distributed to turn purchase interest into an actual purchase? For example, if you have an online offering, perhaps you provide a highly-visible "buy now" button on your web site, making the customer purchase nearly effortless. Or, like the supplement brands described earlier in the chapter, how can you think innovatively with respect to your channel? How can place itself make your offering easier, more natural, to buy?

Lastly for place, how can the place where your customer buys your product, improve their experience of the product itself? The Apple Store is a magnificent example of allowing place itself to Delight. Customers come to learn, troubleshoot, and play on the in-store devices, increasing the engagement and loyalty for Apple customers. During the busy holiday shopping season, a mall near my home provides free valet parking to shoppers and serves complimentary hot spiced apple cider. The place itself becomes an enhancement of the brand experience.

Promotion Column: Now we are at the final *P*, promotion. Promotion is the one that most of us have already thought about while articulating our brand, so I expect this will feel natural. To ignite Desire among target customers, what can you say and show about the offering?

Moving to Decide, what can you say, show, and demonstrate to help the customer reach for his wallet? This could be a limited time offer, a money-back guarantee, or a gift with purchase.

Finally, what messaging, imagery, or storytelling after the purchase can make that purchase ever more Delightful to the customer? How can you keep talking to the customer after they have purchased? How can your communication make them ever more pleased they made the decision to buy? How can you use communication to further deepen your relationship with that customer?

The point of using these tried-and-true frameworks is to surround the ball, to use every angle you can to allow your business to be a conduit for your promise. Zooming out is a tool for inviting brand to drive your decisions from big to small, from early in the journey to late, from the obvious aspects of your offering to the hidden. When you zoom out, you enable yourself to view the breadth and depth of how your brand can come to life. The more you let brand radiate to all of these elements, the more true your promise will be, and the more it can grow the relationship between you and your customer.

PART 3

AMPLIFY YOUR BRAND

EXTEND YOUR STRENGTHS

DEEPEN LOVE

TELL STORIES

You have created your brand strategy methodically, thoroughly, and honestly, informed by your target customer's point of view. Now, let that hard work be worthwhile. Let your brand be as big as it deserves to be. Let it guide you at your highest level. Let it not be merely for marketing tactics, pricing, or your next messaging campaign, but rather, let it infuse everything. Let it not be just for customers or just for employees; rather, let it inspire everyone. Let brand fortify everything you do to grow with purpose.

To begin, let's re-ground ourselves in what a brand is, and why we even care about brand. Brand is your business's relationship with its audience—the promise you own inside the heads of customers. Your brand is your business's backbone, as well as a personification of its character. It is your only enduring competitive advantage. Everything else can be copied or can erode. Brand is the very crux of commerce—and the very crux of why your business deserves to exist. It articulates the reason customers ought to come to you and stay with you. Nurture your brand so it can serve as your ownable beacon for growth.

Consider the following three chapters to be a guide as you bring to life the brand you just defined. How can you expand your business's ability to deliver on your brand promise? How can you further deepen customer love? What stories will you tell?

Figure 9.1. **Uncommon Denominator Overview**

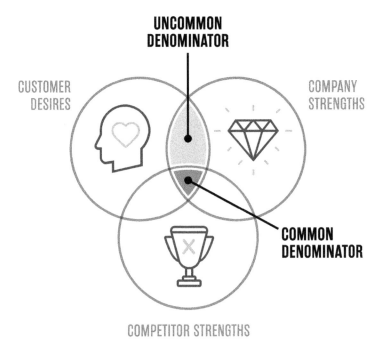

Recall your Uncommon Denominator—the thing that makes your business both uncommon and customer-relevant. Now, you will amplify that Uncommon Denominator. You do so through three forces: extending your strengths (Company Strengths circle); deepening customer love (Customer Desires circle), and storytelling (moving Company Strengths and Customer Desires circles closer together). In this final part of the book, we explore each of these forces for amplifying your brand.

Extending your strengths gives you a bigger delivery of your promise. Chapter 15 explores how you can systematically double down on your strengths, as a business and as a leader. When you extend your business's strengths, you increase the size of the Company Strengths circle, thereby increasing the surface of area of your Uncommon Denominator.

Figure 15.1. **Extend Your Strengths to Increase the Uncommon Denominator**

By making your promise more and more relevant and meaningful to customers, you deepen customer love. In Chapter 16, we discuss how you can offer more of what people need and that you have a differentiated ability to bring. By deepening customer love, you broaden the size of the Customer Desires circle, which in turn expands the surface area of your Uncommon Denominator.

Figure 15.2. **Deepen Customer Love to Increase the Uncommon Denominator**

Finally, in Chapter 17, we tell stories. This increases the Uncommon Denominator surface area by moving the Company Strengths and Customer Desire circles closer to one another. Storytelling binds our customer with our business, just as telling and listening to stories binds human beings together. By telling stories, we heighten the overlap of our customer with our business.

Figure 15.3. **Tell Stories to Increase the Uncommon Denominator**

Some of you might be wondering about that third circle, the Competitor Strengths circle, and what's happening to it as we increase the Uncommon Denominator. The answer is: the more you amplify your Uncommon Denominator, the more your brand becomes the only relevant option for customers. Competitors become decreasingly relevant to you and to customers.

So, our focus is not on your competitors' circle, but on the two circles that we have the power to increase, the two circles that represent the relationship between our customer and our business. Your brand becomes your increasing competitive advantage when you focus on the Uncommon Denominator—the thing that you are good at, that your customers want, and that your competitors cannot bring. When you extend your strengths, deepen customer love, and tell stories, you are operating on all cylinders, increasing the surface area of your Uncommon Denominator.

In these final three chapters, consider the internal ways you can amplify brand, continually expanding your business's ownable and relevant meaning.

Figure 15.4. **Use All Three Ways to Increase the Uncommon Denominator**

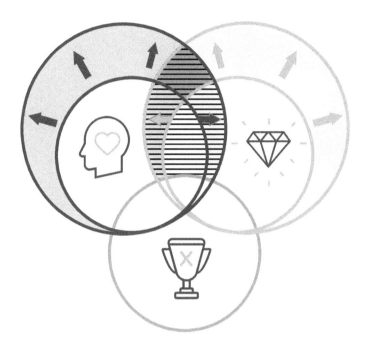

CHAPTER 15

EXTEND YOUR STRENGTHS

Now that you have created and are activating your ironclad brand strategy, lead with it—build upon it dynamically, to extend your strengths.

Clayton Christensen, Harvard Business School professor and authority in disruptive innovation, wrote in *How Will You Measure Your Life*: "Real strategy—in companies and in our lives—is created through hundreds of everyday decisions about where we spend our resources. As you're living your life from day to day, how do you make sure you're heading in the right direction? Watch where your resources flow. If they're not supporting the strategy you've decided upon, then you're not implementing that strategy at all."

Strive to live your brand. Make full use of it. Extend your ability to deliver on your brand in these ways:

- Enshrine Brand
- Operationalize Brand
- Innovate via Brand
- Prioritize According to Brand
- Decide with Brand as Litmus
- Resist Short-Termism

Before we explore these methods, I'd like to share a reminder about responsibility—everybody in the company is responsible for brand. As Denny Post, CEO of Red Robin, told me, "Brand is not somebody's job. It's everybody's job." For a brand to empower growth, marketing does not own brand, nor does PR, nor does product development. That would suggest that others do *not* own it. The business that sequesters brand in marketing, not thinking of brand in its full scope, will not derive the full power of its brand strategy. Anyone whose work touches customers should know and feel your brand so that it permeates everything the customer experiences. Everyone whose work touches customers owns brand.

This is a bottom-up, side-to-side, top-down, all-encompassing notion. Bottom-up in that people from junior to senior use brand as a guide. Side-to side in that all your company's functions support the delivery of the brand promise. Top-down in that the leader ultimately bears the responsibility to build brand, and with words and actions gives employees permission and encouragement to make brand-building the priority. Ultimately, the leader must drive brand. At the same time, brand will be most powerful when *everyone* is driving it. The more everyone is using your brand as the North Star, the more faithfully your brand will grow your business with ease, purpose, and scale.

Kristen Hamilton, CEO and co-founder of Koru, told me, "I used to think, oh, I'm not a marketing person so I need someone else to do my brand for me. But leadership needs to build the brand. You can engage an expert or marketing to help you and facilitate, but you the leader need to own it and make it yours and infuse everything you do with it."

ENSHRINE BRAND

Since you have now codified your brand into a singular definition, make it known to all who will be using it: employees, partners, agencies, and maybe even investors. Publicize your articulated brand strategy prominently, enshrining it. Share why you made the choices you made. Let it be known, loved, and embraced. These are a few ways to enshrine.

PUBLIC DISPLAY

To create this visibility to your North Star, post an encapsulation of your brand strategy in places where decisions are made. This can be a visible guide, reinforcement, and reminder for what your team is here to do, galvanizing people to express the brand. Over time, it can become enculturated to the point where folks barely need to look at it to reference its direction. They will effortlessly channel the promise, character, and reasons to believe as they make decisions. Figure 15.5 shows what a brand snapshot might look like for Batter Pancakes.

Figure 15.5. **Brand Snapshot for Batter Pancakes**

Brand promise	Swedish deliciousness
Brand personality	Bright, action-oriented, open
Brand tonality	Fresh, light, direct
Brand positioning statement	To <u>moms with kids at home</u>, <u>Batter Pancakes</u> is the one <u>pancake mix</u> that brings <u>Swedish deliciousness</u>. That's because only <u>Batter Pancakes</u> gives <u>super thin</u> pancakes, with a <u>crispy crunch</u>, with <u>genuine Swedish heritage</u>, so that your family can <u>start the weekend with extraordinary</u>.
Brand reasons to believe	Super thin. Audibly crispy. Swedish recipe.

BRAND STYLE GUIDE

Particularly for the designers and copywriters expressing your brand, a brand style guide is a useful enshrinement tool. How deep your style guide goes depends on how complex and large your organization. I've seen five-page style guides specifying only colors, fonts, and logo rules and offering light copywriting guidance. I've also experienced, with Clorox, a style guide that took over twelve months to complete, used a $500,000 budget, and wrapped with a launch party at a catered five-star space. You know your business and so can make the call about the detail level of your style guide. Even the smallest of businesses benefit from the explicit dos and don'ts of your brand.

This style guide is a utility, rather than a banner to be shown for posterity. A good style guide is, figuratively or literally, dog-eared and highlighted. People reference it regularly. It is not, however, a prison. Let your style guide grow as a living, breathing document that your people enhance as new direction becomes apparent. We discussed earlier my client who noticed that the brand's email copy was making heavy use of exclamation points, which felt overly bubbly for this Sage brand. The team added to the style guide a designation that exclamation points should be used no more than once per communication occasion. This addition keeps their tone on-brand consistently, efficiently.

RITUALS

Starbucks begins meetings with coffee tastings. Walmart begins and ends weekly store staff meetings with a Walmart cheer. Facebook conducts epic, all-night coding sessions dubbed Hackathons. Zappos offers my favorite ritual for systematically inculcating their brand promise: the Offer. After four weeks of paid training, each new hire is given this offer: "If you quit today, we will give you a $1,000 bonus." Only those committed to the spirit of Zappos customer service choose to stay, thereby enhancing Zappos's famous customer service promise.

Bold moves like this enshrine the brand for employees and for customers. They encourage employees to think big and to extend similarly big gestures to deliver on a promise. Stories abound of Zappos's ridiculously excellent customer service, such as representatives buying plane tickets to personally deliver items to customers during harried time crunches or in far-flung geographic restrictions.

Matt Crum, CMO of Meyerberg Goat Milk, explained to me,

"Once your rules of the road are in place, your business can consistently, faithfully deliver on your promise. If you don't have those positioning elements codified and visible, then brand manager X leaves, brand manager Y comes in, and suddenly things are different, things are changing, and the brand has gone off course from what's made it successful." Enshrining weaves the brand into the fabric of your company, so that no one person, team, or document represents the brand singlehandedly. By weaving brand into the fabric of your business, it lives and breathes as people move in and out. Enshrining your brand makes it integral and lasting.

Enshrining your brand is not a one-and-done thing. As a long-term rallying cry, brand is repeated and reinforced visibly. As Tarang Amin, CEO of e.l.f. Cosmetics who we met in Chapter 1, told me, "Your brand strategy only means as much as it's actually expressed every day." Make brand habitual.

By enshrining your brand publicly, you are saying, "Here is where you should focus. Here is us at our best."

OPERATIONALIZE BRAND

A brand is what it does, not just what it says. Operationalize your brand by elevating the activities in your business's value chain that have an opportunity to heighten your brand promise. Carter Cast, venture capitalist and former CEO of Walmart.com, gave me these suggestions for building brand into the nuts and bolts of your business:

1. Outline your business's activities and sub-activities, from sourcing through creation and customer use.
2. Consider your brand promise.

3. Identify your business's activities that could up-level your customer's experience of your promise.
4. Make your business best-in-class at those activities. Measure your success against your excellence on those activities. Align your goals to them and set key performance indicators for employees accordingly.

Cast and I discussed an example of a business he once managed: Frito Lay. Frito-Lay's brand promise is "fresh": crunchy and flavorful, not stale, soft, or faded. The company's activities might be broken down roughly as: (1) sourcing, (2) manufacturing, (3) packaging, (4) inventory management, (5) demand planning, (6) marketing communications, (7) shipping, (8) in-store messaging, and (9) post-purchase customer service. Each of these involves sub-activities as well. All are important, but a few are critical to a brand promise of "fresh."

"There are a handful of capabilities that really matter to the promise," Cast said, "where we have to get it right every time or we are violating our promise." For example, sourcing, packaging and storing, and marketing contribute disproportionately to freshness. Frito Lay must properly resource these activities and incentivize for fresh. Not for "cheap." Not for "novelty flavors." But for "fresh."

Another example of a business operationalizing brand by activity is Molly Moon's Ice Cream parlors. Molly Moon's brand promise is "simple happiness from homemade ice cream." The brand character is wholesome, lighthearted, and upbeat. What does one need to deliver happiness through premium ice cream? The ingredients must be of superb quality. The freezers must run at a consistent temperature to prevent ice crystals. And the ice cream servers need to have smiles on their faces.

To my delight, I recently noticed Molly Moon's infuse their hiring with brand language. A job posting in the shop window announced, in Molly Moon's color and font (not in black-and-white or in generic font): "Now Hiring Optimists." Not "Now Hiring Ice Cream Aficionados." Not "Now Hiring, Great Benefits." By recruiting optimists, Molly Moon's heightens their ability to deliver on the promise of ice cream happiness. They became excellent at recruiting in order to operationalize brand.

Here's another example of operationalizing brand, but this one more flawed. Waka Waka Power is a portable device for powering cell phones with solar energy. I bought one recently, and I perceived the Waka Waka promise to be "sustainable recharging." The headline on the website is "safe, sustainable solar for all," and the tagline is "Share the Sun." Waka Waka appears to be targeting people who care deeply about the earth and use mobile devices extensively.

And they do a lot right. The product works. It holds a long charge. The messaging and imagery are single-mindedly about sustainability. However, one element that failed the brand promise was the packaging: the device arrived in heavy and non-recyclable (let alone biodegradable) plastic. With a brand promise around sustainability, everything, including the packaging, must deliver on that. Waka Waka had not yet fully operationalized the brand throughout the value chain. With sustainable packaging, they could more fully deliver on their promise of sustainability.

Operationalizing is not easy, and it is a journey. Matt Oppenheimer, CEO of Remitly, told me that after articulating the Remitly brand strategy, he and his team had a new perspective on what more they needed to do: "We have doubled down on features that align well with our promise, that we otherwise wouldn't have known would be meaningful." Identify the big points where you must truly shine and then begin systematically building in excellence.

INNOVATE VIA BRAND

Innovate to increase your brand's relevance and draw. As you consider innovation, you likely are considering weighty questions such as: *What are we going to make? What do we choose to build? How fast? Of the infinite directions, which do we choose? What do we optimize for?* Before you innovate, look to your brand strategy, your North Star. Then ask yourself a single question: *out of the millions of ways we could do this, what is the way that will create the most value for our customer?* Your brand strategy can serve as a reference as you grapple with these high-stakes decisions.

I used brand as a guide for innovation decisions while developing new product concepts for Clorox. In the early 2000s, we had evolved the Clorox Bleach brand promise from "whiter whites" to "higher level of clean." With the "whiter whites" brand promise, we considered innovations that would heighten our ability to further whiten whites—for example, fabric brighteners and a dry powder bleach with white-boosting ingredients. Our advertising featured bright whites, contrasts, and aesthetic beauty because that was the functional benefit we represented. Whiter whites was the lens through which we considered our innovation decisions.

We evolved our brand promise of "whiter whites" to "higher level of clean" for several reasons. The most basic was the decreasing need for a product that delivered whiter whites, as people decreasingly wear predominantly white clothing. Another reason was the misfit with the portfolio of Clorox sub-brands. Our home care products such as Clorox Disinfecting Wipes and Clorox Toilet Bowl Cleaner promised and delivered "clean," not "whiter whites." "Higher level of clean" was our new brand promise to guide all our decisions, including innovation decisions.

Near this time, we were considering a new product concept for what became our Clorox Bleach Pen, which would distribute a controlled application of bleach to a partially white item of clothing. If we had been evaluating the Clorox Bleach Pen concept through the lens of "whiter whites," this innovation idea would have been off-brand and we would have discarded it. But we had a new brand promise: higher level of clean. The Clorox Bleach Pen did indeed improve our ability to deliver on a higher level of clean and, therefore, was an on-brand concept. It turned out to be a consumer hit as well.

PRIORITIZE ACCORDING TO BRAND

You haven't got time for mediocrity. Focus your energy and avoid wasted effort by prioritizing ruthlessly. This ruthless prioritizing requires courage. While some ideas are overtly poor ones, most are good ones. The hard thing is deprioritizing the merely good ideas to make room for the excellent ones. Your ironclad brand strategy helps you find this conviction. "What you decide *not* to do is probably more important than what you decide to do," Tom Peters wrote in *In Search of Excellence.*

Strive for a short To Do list and a long To Don't list. Instead of tackling a thousand good ideas, identify and prioritize a few that disproportionately add to your ability to deliver on your brand promise. Instead of getting an inch better at one thousand things, get a mile better at ten things. Make your priority list short and potent, granting employees the permission to forego "inch" activities and instead triple their focus on "mile" activities.

Now that you have done the hard work of crafting your ironclad brand strategy, you can feel emboldened to put nine hundred good ideas on the To Don't list. You didn't pick a brand promise lightly. You picked it based on your particular right to win (Company Strengths) and your deep customer relevance and meaning (Customer Desires). It would be a shame to have done all that and then to go back to a thousand "inch" activities that bring you tiny gains.

Observe all the things you are doing, your initiatives big and small. Go through them and answer honestly for each: will this *disproportionately* increase my ability to deliver on my brand promise? Put the nos, maybes, and even the less enthusiastic yeses on a To Don't list. Only the resounding yeses go on the To Do list.

DECIDE WITH BRAND AS LITMUS

If your ironclad brand strategy is your North Star, then you can use it as a go-to litmus test for decisions big and small. When facing a decision in the moment, ask yourself: Would doing X help or hurt my brand? Would it enable me to reach more of my target customers? Would it enable me to deliver on my promise in a more accessible, potent way? Would it enable me to bring my target customer farther along in her journey? Would it enable me to expand my promise to be even bigger, even more emotive? Would it further differentiate me from competitors who want to serve my customer in this space? When you use your brand as a decision-making litmus, over time difficult choices become reflexive instead of arduous.

Trader Joe's in recent years has had to decide whether to follow the approach of other grocery retailers and develop an online presence. That's a hard decision, as expanding to online commerce would increase sales considerably. But with the Trader Joe's brand as the filter, leadership has decided to say "no" to selling online. Trader Joe's president, Jon Basalone, shared on the Trader Joe's podcast, "For us, the store is our brand, and our products work best when they're sold as part of this overall customer experience within the store. And so we're not ready to give that up. For us, the brand is too important, and the store is our brand."

Next time you face a decision, use your brand as a litmus, as an arbitrator. Difficult decisions then can become a springboard for expressing your brand. Perhaps your business is at a significant crossroads, and you are considering whether to enter into a new market, or engage a new partner, or create a new form of distribution. Perhaps it is a smaller decision, such as whether to attend a conference or how to craft your script for a speech. Consider where the alignment is with your brand promise.

When you effectively communicate brand throughout the entire organization, you empower everyone to make these brand-aligned decisions. This will build a cohesive, high-integrity relationship with customers. It will also cultivate purpose and meaning for employees.

RESIST SHORT-TERMISM

David Aaker has dedicated his career to researching, teaching, and consulting on brand. One of the reasons he chose this focus was, he told me, because "I came to believe that business was too short-term oriented. Brand was a way to fight short-term-ism, so the business would be around for a long time, to get folks away from focusing solely on cost reduction."

Show me an enduring business, and I'll show you one that uses the principals of brand as the North Star for prioritizing. Leading a business means constantly negotiating competing needs. The overarching tension my clients relate is navigating the tensions between short-term and long-term needs, between surviving today and at the same time setting the conditions to thrive for years to come. Your brand strategy can be a tool for navigating this tension. It can serve as counterweight against short-term-ism as it focuses your attention on activities that will reinforce your brand, helping you not just survive but also thrive.

My favorite tool for balancing surviving with thriving is Stephen Covey's time management quadrants from his masterful book *The 7 Habits of Highly Effective People*. In this framework, which consists of a square divided into four quadrants, Quadrant I activities are both important and urgent. These are survival activities: firefighting, managing crises, hitting this month's number. If this were your body, this would be going to the emergency room when you are having trouble breathing. In contrast, Quadrant II activities are important but not urgent. These are thrive activities: relationship building, coaching your team, planning. If this were your body, this would be going to an annual physical, exercising regularly, and eating nutritious foods.

If you want your business to survive, Covey tells us, focus on Quadrant I activities, and it will indeed survive, at least for a while. If you want to thrive, focus on Quadrant II activities. Leaders will always have short-term pressure. Brand can counterbalance this by elevating the lens toward not only surviving the week but thriving for years.

As Covey said, focusing more on Quadrant II activities over time paradoxically reduces Quadrant I fire drills. Going to annual doctor appointments reduces your emergency room visits. This focus creates for your business an upward spiral of success rather than a downward spiral of fighting fires.

Brand strategy and the use of it are the ultimate Quadrant II activities. They help you thrive. Your brand strategy focuses your attention on activities that will drive long-term growth but might not get the attention for short-term quick hits. The high-value brands we have discussed in this book—from Volvo to Salesforce to Etsy to Slack to Zappos to Nike—spend so much of their time in Quadrant II that they rarely have Quadrant I crises. Each can do that because the brand is so clear and because leaders have decided to use it to be enduring. Be like these brands. Get extremely intentional about what you want to stand for in the mind of your customer and then focus on building that meaning with everything you do.

Most of us are mired in Quadrant I and would benefit from this counterbalance. Quadrant II is what makes your business thrive, and it will break you away from your peer businesses.

e.l.f. Cosmetics CEO Tarang Amin previously led Schiff Nutrition. As CEO of Schiff, Amin moved $15 million out of trade spending (short-term promotion) into brand building. He explained to me, "I told the whole world that we're going to do that, and yet I was amazed by how much the industry continued to rely on just trade dollars [Quadrant I, push-sales-today promotion tactics] to promote their brand. All the analysis was there, the data was there that trade spending eroded brand and therefore sales in the long term. Yet we were the only ones who made use of that knowledge." Schiff went on to be acquired by Reckitt Benckiser for $1.4 billion, at the time the highest multiple ever paid for a nutritional supplements company.

Amin went on to advise, "You can't neglect your brand and expect it to continue to be valuable. A lot of times there is neglect because of short-term measurement pressures. People think they can drive revenue right away by doing something off-brand. But you have to invest in the brand and nurture it to see its value."

Once you have established the strengths that enable you to own your optimal brand position, extend those strengths. Become increasingly capable of nailing your brand promise. This begins with recognizing that nailing the brand promise is everyone's job, and enshrining and operationalizing your brand so that all are equipped to bring your brand to life collectively. Everyone then can build the company with the brand as backbone, so that operations and innovations continually up-level the delivery of the brand promise. As you lead, ruthlessly prioritize resource allocation according to brand, allowing a company-wide focus on expanding the Uncommon Denominator. Then everyone can make decisions, big and small, according to your brand, your North Star.

CHAPTER 16

DEEPEN LOVE

Increase your Uncommon Denominator, and therefore your business value, by deepening customer love.

At the beginning of a brand strategy project with my clients, I ask them two questions: Which is a brand that you love, and why do you love it? I hear responses like:

- "I love Patagonia because they seem to be really concerned about the earth, as am I."
- "I love Slack because it keeps me up to speed and also makes me smile."
- "I love Gibson Guitars because they make me feel like a real musician."
- "I love Trader Joe's because what is usually a drudgery task is filled with whimsy."

- "I love Salesforce because they make me so much more effective in my career."
- "I love Crystal Mountain Ski Resort because it is for true skiers like me."

Want to know what I never hear? "I love X brand because their advertising is so awesome." Customers like brands because of the way those brands make them feel, not because of the way they message. Brands we love are the ones that make us feel understood, that reinforce our identity, that include in them a solution to a deep problem, and that help us transcend. These are the brands that become part of us and the brands that create enduring business value.

Successful brands foster customer love by embracing the following:

- Let Everything Matter
- Model Your Brand
- Reinforce the Ladder Rungs and Stretch Upward
- Plus It

Flourishing businesses earn customer love by caring about every big and little thing they do and say. They give more target customers more to love by expanding on what they do best. They steadily increase their benefits to customers while continuing to deliver on previously promised benefits. The leaders model their brand for their employees, creating a chain of people committed to deepening customer love.

Tully's is a coffeehouse chain in the Seattle area. At first blush, Tully's cafés look similar to Starbucks cafés: plush interior, premium-priced lattes and pastries, quality chocolate, and shiny espresso machines.

Recently, I met a colleague at his neighborhood Tully's Coffee, where we enjoyed a nice conversation and latte. While in the restroom though, I was struck by a tiny detail hanging on the back of the door. There was a clipboard, complete with chewed-up pencil attached by a filthy, tattered yard of string. On the clipboard, for every customer to read, were employee initials and time stamps to signify the time of the last cleaning.

It was a jarring sight. Blink, and instead of being in an upscale coffeehouse, this could have been a McDonalds. But at McDonalds, I would not have felt lied to. McDonalds lattes are half the price of Tully's lattes, congruent with their brand promise of value. At Tully's, the cues were mismatched, and spotting that incongruity made me feel gross. If I saw a house painted beautifully, and then when knocking on the door felt that the wood was soft from termites, I'd feel the same misalignment and loss of faith. The Tully's brand was sullied for me.

My read on this experience is that Tully's considers brand merely a marketing activity, and since the marketing team does not "own" store operations and cleaning processes, brand was not operationalized beyond marketing. But as a customer, I really don't care who owns the restroom's cleaning. If I am paying $4.50 for a latte, the restrooms should be nice, or I'll feel duped.

In the previous chapter, we explored steps to operationalize brand from the inside out, from beginning to end, from source to customer experience. This extends our strengths internally. Now, consider this in reverse, from the outside in, from the customer experience back to the source of that experience. Check yourself: from the customer's vantage point, have I *earned* the right to make this promise? Because as with all relationships worth having, there must be reciprocity. You have to earn a deep relationship with customers, not just because it's good for your P&L, but because it is genuinely good for the customer.

Earning stems from making and delivering on a big promise, not just with the letter of the law (a high-quality latte) but also with the spirit of it (the customer's entire visit—including the restroom experience—makes you feel like a queen). To deliver on the spirit and not just the letter, your brand permeates the entire customer experience. Align all elements of your customer experience to your brand promise. Continuously operationalize, enhancing your capabilities by infusing brand throughout the customer experience. Sweat even the seemingly small stuff to make the whole customer experience sounder, more compelling, and more aligned with your business's particular essence. Messaging and promotion are vital expressions of your brand, but so are the less sexy, less visible elements of the customer experience.

Customers experience brands holistically. While your company may necessarily be divided into functions and components of the customer experience, customers do not know or care about that. Don't relegate brand to marketing only, because the customer will smell a rat. This would be akin to the CEO relegating company culture to the HR department. Employees will smell lack of commitment if ethos and values do not shape every level and aspect of the business.

As Sangita Woerner, VP of Marketing for Alaska Airlines, related to me, "Brand cannot come just from marketing. The customer needs to feel it at every single touch point." And as Howard Schultz of Starbucks often says, "Everything matters."

Brand encompasses your customer's total experience of your business. Let it mold their experience. If it is an airline, customers do not experience just the advertising message, just the baggage cart, just the check-in, boarding, or in-flight experiences, or just the food, the seats, or the banter with the flight attendant. Customers experience all of that, and the result of those experiences is your brand. Consider all of these customer touchpoints individually and in their entirety.

Brand is also experienced across time and space. It is your customer's experience of your whole offering, from just learning about it to their using it for years. As Pamela Dressler, president of Cypress Grove Cheese, told me, "It can't just be a surface thing. Brand has to live in the employees so that, for example, when a customer service person picks up the phone, they live the brand's values. That is how you build trust, when you do this consistently and with excellence and authenticity, in good times and in bad."

Brand is all of it. Brand is your employees' sense of purpose in the company. Brand is your partnerships, your email signature and how you answer the phone, your online reviews, and the product updates you're doing for the new release. Brand is your pricing for new customers as well as for loyal ones. Brand is your culture and your Glassdoor ratings. Brand is how you treat an upset customer, a happy customer, and your vendors. Brand is a customer telling a friend about you. Brand is your culture, your values, the way you operate in your market. Brand is your paying suppliers fairly and punctually. Brand is the fabric of who you are.

Every touchpoint between your business and your customer is a way to increase their goodwill toward your business. Those little things (a) matter on their own and (b) combine to something big, showing the customer that you care. The more you imbue everything with your brand, the more it can deepen customer love.

MODEL YOUR BRAND

It will be easier for you to demonstrate your brand in everything your business says and does, thereby deepening customer love, if you have a committed team helping you. Demonstrate with your words and with your actions, formally and informally, with colleagues of all levels, that brand is the priority. Let your brand strategy guide you and let your people *see* that it is guiding you. This gives them permission and encouragement to use brand as their North Star, too.

Starbucks CEO Howard Schultz modeled brand in a big way in 2008. On February 26, this note was attached to the locked front doors of all 7,100 US Starbucks cafés: "We're taking time to perfect our espresso. Great espresso requires practice. That's why we're dedicating ourselves to honing our craft."

Schultz, who had led Starbucks since the late 1980s, took an eight-year hiatus in the early 2000s. When he returned as CEO, he perceived a disturbing growing gap between what Starbucks promised and what Starbucks delivered, as the quality of Starbucks coffee beverages had declined in his absence. He learned that it was becoming common for baristas to reheat milk, for example, watering down the primary ingredient of the café latte. This quality decline weakened delivery on the Starbucks promise, and customers were losing trust. Schultz sought to close that gap in a sweeping, expensive way: he closed all US Starbucks stores for an afternoon to retrain baristas in the art of espresso.

Closing the stores for training was a public demonstration of the brand's sacredness. Though expensive in the short-term—an estimated cost of $6 million that day—the move was invaluable in the long-term. Within the year, the brand was flourishing once again, despite the Great Recession.

Schultz's bold move did improve the quality of Starbucks' espresso beverages, and this modeling of brand deepened customer love. It signaled to customers, employees, and investors that Schultz and his team meant to nourish the Starbucks brand, prioritizing the brand promise fulfillment above a day's sales.

Marc Benioff, CEO of Salesforce, a cloud-based customer relationship management platform, models brand in a B2B environment. Enterprise software was long known for being complex and clunky. Benioff made Salesforce the CRM that is as easy and intuitive to use as Amazon had become in ecommerce. For example, Salesforce application Chatter is an in-house messaging tool that works with Salesforce's applications, an unusual social media offering in enterprise software. In similar style, Benioff makes the annual Salesforce conference, "Dreamforce," an event worthy of flying in for. Dreamforce is known for its lavishness and celebrity. In 2017, award-winning actor Taraji P. Henson spoke, and Alicia Keys and Lenny Kravitz performed. Benioff is displaying that people purchasing B2B software are still people and appreciate being treated as such.

REINFORCE THE LADDER RUNGS AND STRETCH UPWARD

In Chapter 10, "Ladder," we discussed reinforcing the rungs at the bottom of the ladder while steadily bringing the customer higher on the ladder. Bounce did this well when it reinforced its functional benefit rung by rung to ladder up from "wrinkle-free" to "attractive clothes" to "feel pretty."

Throughout that gradual upward progression to "feel pretty," the brand continued to invest in lower rungs such as "wrinkle-free." When Bounce promised wrinkle-free clothing, the company strived to be able to promise "attractive clothes." When Bounce was able to promise "attractive clothes," it still fulfilled its "wrinkle-free" promise, investing continually in wrinkle-free technology development. Halle Hutchison, VP of Marketing for pet care service Rover, told me, "Your product can be absolutely great, but you need to connect the dots for [the customer] so they understand how it represents what you stand for. They're not going to make these connections themselves, so help them." Help them to see and to feel how wrinkle-free clothes is enabling attractive clothes and feeling pretty.

The higher on the ladder you can deliver, the more value you provide to your customers. The more value you deliver, the more delighted your customers will be, the more loyal they will be, the more willing they'll be to pay handsomely for your benefit, and the more likely they will be to tell others.

Nike differentiates at the emotional level, by helping their customers be and feel victorious. A less inspired shoe brand might brag about their excellent sole or their revolutionary lace-up system. What would you value more: an excellent sole with patented rubber technology—or the feeling of victory?

Contrast Nike and Brooks, two beloved athletic brands with different brand promises. Nike promises a winning performance, while Brooks promises the joy of running.

Nike's innovations aim to enhance performance and speed. By adding a waffle pattern to the sole or by streamlining to an aerodynamic shape, Nike reinforces the bottom rungs of the ladder. When those functional benefits lead to faster running, the Nike customer can feel victorious, delivering on the higher-order promise of winning. Remember, though, that Nike brought customers along with them, connecting the dots as they went. First, they convinced track coaches and runners that the lighter sole, invented by legendary track coach and Nike co-founder Bill Bowerman, would give them speed. Then they actually ran faster. Then they won. With Nike all along showing them that lighter soles led to faster performances. Nike's tagline is daringly, winningly, "Just Do It."

PHIL KNIGHT DESCRIBING A SCENE OF VICTORY IN HIS MEMOIR, *SHOE DOG*

"As they crossed the tape we all looked up at the clock and saw that both men had broken the American record. Pre had broken it by a shade more. But he wasn't done. He spotted someone waving a STOP PRE t-shirt and he went over and snatched it and whipped it in circles above his head, like a scalp. What followed was one of the greatest ovations I've ever heard, and I've spent my life in stadiums.... This, I decided, this is what sports are, what they can do. Like books, sports give people a sense of having lived other lives, of taking part in other people's victories."

Now consider Brooks, whose brand promises pleasure in running. Brooks innovates by reinforcing the elements that lead to running pleasure, and particularly the sensory comfort of the shoe's fit. They invest in fitting broadly-varying foot shapes with a visceral springiness of the sole. At Brooks' corporate headquarters, called "Brooks Trailhead," runners can visit the biomechanics lab for a gait analysis that will reveal their "Run Signature" and the resulting "Sole Mate" shoe recommendation. Brooks actually does make running more pleasurable. Brooks' tagline is the lighthearted "Run Happy." Brooks earned this claim through excellent fit, allowing the dots to connect for customers, delivering to customers a happy running experience.

If today you deliver on the equivalent of "wrinkle-free," commit yourself to (1) delivering on that in spades; (2) delivering on a promise that is a rung higher—the more emotional benefit that your promise enables; and (3) connecting the dots for the customer. Let all of your 4 Ps help you to do these three things.

PLUS IT

"The park means a lot to me in that it's something that will never be finished. Something that I can keep developing, keep plussing and adding to—it's alive. It will be a live, breathing thing that will need changes."

—WALT DISNEY

As you grow, always consider ways that you can increase the thing that customers love about you. As Disney used to tell his Imagineers, "plus it." You iterate and build and take the promise from awesome to mind-blowing. Disney plussed the earliest Mickey Mouse cartoons by adding sound to them. He plussed *Fantasia* by partnering with Leopold Stokowski of the Philadelphia Orchestra to create stereophonic sound. He plussed the movie *Bambi* by bringing live animals into the artists' studio so the Imagineers could observe and copy their natural movements.

Volvo is plussing right now as it crosses to the next era of automobiles: self-driving cars. The current technology still requires significant driver participation. So, when naming this generation's autonomous driving feature, Volvo plussed safety by naming the feature Pilot Assist. Not Auto Pilot, as competitor Lexus calls it. Sven Desmet, Volvo's head of brand, told me that when your brand equals safety, you don't want to exaggerate how passive the driver can be—you want to reference supporting the pilot (Pilot Assist), not taking over for the pilot (Auto Pilot). This is plussing.

Note that on-brand plusses are not arbitrary or braggadocian. They do not reinvent the brand promise or target a different customer. Plusses expand the promise so that it touches more target customers more deeply. Here are some more brand plussing examples:

- Zappos plussed fast service by building a distribution facility near the Las Vegas airport so that items could be shipped hours faster.
- Tesla plussed accessible environmentalism by creating an electric car available at a mid-tier price point so that they could touch more customers.
- JetBlue plussed service by creating a Customer Bill of Rights.
- Airbnb plussed travel joy by adding a blind feedback system so that guests would feel encouraged to leave comments without fear of hurting their hosts' feelings.

Brand is the meaning you stand for. So really *stand* for it! Let what you stand for invite in others that resonate with that meaning. And then make that meaning ever more resonant.

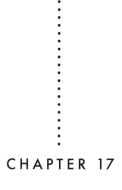

CHAPTER 17

TELL STORIES

Brand strategy is distilling the story of your business: What are you about? What are you here to do? How will you show up? Why should people care?

Whether we are sitting around a fire, reading a book, or watching an internet video, we humans *love* stories. They light us up. They make us feel part of something bigger, something more primal, and part of one another. They bind us. We instinctively want to hear them and tell them. Telling stories extends your reach beyond face-to-face communication, attracting customers and galvanizing employees from afar. Stories enable businesses to express what is distinctively theirs to tell.

In this chapter, we will explore the following ways stories make our business vibrant:

- Brand Is Story

- Story Is the Human Advantage
- Use Story to Command Attention from Tension
- Use Story to Persuade
- Show, Don't Tell
- Empathize

Throughout the chapter, you'll find that I've included a few of the most compelling brand stories out there, from both B2B and B2C worlds. Observe how these brands have leveraged story to captivate and inspire their target customers and internal teams.

BRAND IS STORY

"In good companies, the story and the strategy are the same thing. As a result, the proper output of all the strategic work is the story...The story of the company goes beyond quarterly or annual goals and gets to the hard-core question of why. Why should I join this company? Why should I be excited to work here? Why should I buy its product?"

—BEN HOROWITZ, ENTREPRENEUR, VENTURE CAPITALIST, AND AUTHOR OF *THE HARD THING ABOUT HARD THINGS*

Humans connect with each other through stories. Any leadership device meant to inspire and connect—whether a public speech, an investor pitch, a motto, or an advertising message—is effective when it tells a story.

This entire book has, in fact, been about storytelling. Discerning your own ironclad brand strategy is an act of defining your story. We note our audience (target customer). We observe the relevant context, worry or problem (frame of reference and customer need). We take stock of what we know, possess, or can do to solve the problem (Uncommon Denominator and promise). We channel our own voice (character, personality, and tonality). We customize the storytelling to the audience (stage). We share the resolution of the story (brand promise). These are the elements of a business's story.

In the Listen step (Chapter 8) of building your ironclad brand strategy, you strove to understand the latent problems your customer experiences. You wanted to hear the nuances so that even if your customers couldn't articulate the problem eloquently, you could discern it from what they were saying and not saying.

When you can articulate for your customers the problem they face, this articulation—this storytelling—provides value. It transforms blurry, chaotic, and anxious into lucid, sensible, and empowering. They feel both witnessed and relieved.

By defining your brand strategy, you have developed the transcendent story of why your business exists and deserves to exist. You identified the problem by listening, and you identified the solution through your brand promise. Armed with that, you now tell stories that help your customers understand your meaning and, in the process, grow your Uncommon Denominator.

Sometimes, you will tell a story of your business's promise itself, and that story will closely resemble your brand strategy. These are the major messaging touchpoints with customers, such as your website copy, a mass market advertisement, your elevator pitch, and your tagline (e.g., Nike—Just Do It). Other times, you will tell a subset of the story, such as when you are entering a new market, you lead with a functional benefit that makes you easy to understand (e.g., Netflix—No Late Fees).

Your audience will vary, too. Sometimes, your audience will be potential customers. Other times, it will be current customers, employees, investors, or the press. In all these scenarios, you are most effective when the audiences recognize themselves in what you say, feeling part of your story. As Daniel Coyle wrote in *The Culture Code*, "The deeper neurological truth is that stories do not cloak reality but create it, triggering cascades of perception and motivation."

REAL-WORLD BRAND STORY 1:
VOLVO'S ORIGIN STORY

TENSION

In 1920s Sweden, there was no domestic Swedish car manufacturer. All cars driven in Sweden were imported from manufacturers designing for more temperate climates. These imported cars could not reliably withstand the foreboding temperatures and road conditions of Sweden. Cars would break down from the cold while on the road, endangering drivers and passengers. Since non-working cars in frigid temperatures can be life-threatening, the Swedes had a problem: there was no car safe to drive in Sweden.

RESOLUTION

Volvo's head of brand Sven Desmet related to me, "We said, 'Let's build a car for us here, for our zero-degree temperatures.'" Volvo did just that, giving Swedes a car safe to drive on Swedish roads. Almost a hundred years later, Volvo has amplified that promise and delivery of safety, so that across the globe, we can drive these safe cars.

STORY IS THE HUMAN ADVANTAGE

Storytelling is what unites us as humans. It connects us to one another, and it distinguishes our species from other species. Historian Yuval Noah Harari wrote in *Sapiens* of how story itself contributes to our species' competitive advantage. Our capacity to tell stories enabled us to modify behavior and evolve more successfully than did our peers in the animal kingdom.

Through storytelling, we could collaborate, persuade, lead, and follow. Storytelling put the power into the collective, instead of into a single individual or family. This enabled us to cross barriers of time and geographical distance. We could band together to hunt big game more effectively. We could migrate in groups large enough to survive and colonize new continents that previously knew no humans. Our instinct to tell and be moved by stories enabled us to thrive despite inferior physical strength and brain size.

Harari illustrates that storytelling resulted in previously unseen large-scale cooperation between large numbers of strangers, and that cooperation included trade, group hunting, and migration. "No animal other than Sapiens engages in trade, and all the Sapiens trade networks about which we have detailed evidence were based on fictions," Harari writes. With stories, "Sapiens can cooperate in extremely flexible ways with countless numbers of strangers. That's why Sapiens rule the world."

Story facilitated cooperation through trade, and this is what businesses still utilize today. Trade is possible because of cooperation. Cooperation is possible because of storytelling. This is the heart of brand storytelling. The promise of your business is the story of why a person should trade with you. It's the reason you are allowed to ask them for this trade.

TENSION

A 1989 *Newsweek* article first reported a story you might well recognize now because it's been told so many times since. A man walked into an Anchorage Nordstrom store to return a set of tires. While Nordstrom has sold shoes since 1901 and upscale fashion since 1963, it has never sold tires.

RESOLUTION

The Nordstrom salesperson accepted the tires and gave the man cash equal to the price sticker on the tires—a full refund for something obviously not purchased at Nordstrom. That is how outrageously excellent Nordstrom's customer service is. Whether fiction or nonfiction, the tire story is plausible because it is consistent with a brand that always goes to great lengths to please customers.

USE STORY TO COMMAND ATTENTION WITH TENSION

We discussed in Chapters 2 and 13 how a major challenge of business is capturing the attention of an audience whose mental bandwidth is scarce and getting scarcer. This challenge mounts exponentially as more and more stimuli compete for that same mental bandwidth. The internet and social media escalate these stimuli and, consequently, deplete our attention bandwidth.

Herein lies the power of a deliberate brand strategy, which uses a central principle of story—tension—to capture and sustain the prized attention of our audience.

Stories relate a tension followed by a resolution. Loss followed by victory. Suffering followed by salvation. This pattern is a hallmark of the human condition. We continually encounter obstacles, overcome those obstacles, and then confront a new one. It is our Hero's Journey, our *Odyssey*.

Tension is what sustains people's attention as they listen to story. We recognize ourselves in the character. We recognize our problems in theirs. So, when a storyteller or a business leader sets up a character facing a tension, the audience cannot help but listen and be captivated. They, too, yearn to experience the resolution. And that satisfying resolution comes in the form of a redeeming event or person or epiphany or product.

Here are some famous story tensions and resolutions:

- Homer's *Iliad* is a story of the war between the Greeks and the Trojans of Troy. The Greeks needed to infiltrate Troy to fight their enemy, but the walls around this enemy kingdom blocked their attempts (tension). The Greek army secretly built a giant hollow wooden horse and filled it with hiding Greek warriors. When the rest of the Greek army sailed away, the Trojans interpreted this showy exodus as an admission of defeat. Believing the wooden horse a gift, they brought it inside Troy's walls. That night, the hidden Greeks emerged from the horse and opened the kingdom gates to let in their comrades who had surreptitiously returned to shore. The Greeks fought the Trojans inside Troy and won the war (resolution).
- When Harry Potter came face-to-face with Voldemort in the final book of J. K. Rowling's series, he realized with despair that since a part of him was inside Voldemort, defeating Voldemort would lead to his own death, too (tension). Harry took an inward journey and uncovered a love that enabled him

to save his world and, in the process, his own life (resolution).

- In the 1980s film *Can't Buy Me Love*, high school student Ronald Miller wants to shed his nerdy image and be cool. But in the process, he banishes his true friends, disgusts his girlfriend, and loses his own true nature (tension). At the movie's climax, Ronald stops a fight among his friends and recounts a story to remind them of their close friendship. As a result, Ronald regains his friends and girlfriend, as well as the respect of the cool kids (resolution).

Your business resolves a tension for your customer. The story frames this tension as conflict that the customer (protagonist) is trying to resolve. This resolution is why your business deserves to exist. By communicating that tension and your uncommon way to resolve it, your business will attract customers who need that problem solved. For example:

- My mother wants to read a book, but her aging eyes feel fatigue after ten minutes of reading (tension). Audible lets her enjoy those books by listening to them rather than reading them (resolution).
- Your colleague wants to participate in a meeting across the country, but it will take too much time and money to travel (tension). Zoom lets him participate without having to spend the time and money traveling to the distant meeting (resolution).
- Our team likes to collaborate and brainstorm at a whiteboard. But the constant erasing and rewriting as ideas are reconsidered, re-catalogued, and recontextualized impedes the creative flow (tension). 3M Post-its encourage collaboration

through the easily rearrangeable medium of sticky notes. They liberate us to move concepts around at will, unleashing the creative flow we had missed (resolution).

As you build your business, remain focused on the tension you're offering to resolve for your customers. While developing your offering, while delivering on your promise, and while messaging to customers, keep central on your mind the nature of the problem your customer is experiencing. This will set you up to resolve that tension in a way that satisfies and delights your customer.

REAL-WORLD BRAND STORY 3: SALESFORCE'S ORIGIN STORY

TENSION

While floating in the Pacific Ocean just off the Big Island of Hawaii during a sabbatical, the thought struck Marc Benioff, why can't enterprise software be as easy to use as a website like Amazon? When examining the market further, he has said, "It struck me as curious that although this [type of] software was so troublesome, it remained wildly popular. I attributed this to the fact that if the software could increase sales productivity by even 5 percent, it made a meaningful difference to a business."

RESOLUTION

He founded Salesforce in 1999 because, in his words: "What would happen, I wondered, if we offered a product that could increase productivity by the same amount, or more, *and* we made it easier to afford and use? Could you get a return on investment in six to twelve months rather than in three to five years?" The answer was a resounding yes, with Salesforce's market cap in 2018 landing over $100 billion.

USE STORY TO PERSUADE

Stories persuade. As Harari wrote, the persuasive power of stories distinguished Homo sapiens in the animal kingdom. "Much of history," he said, "revolves around this question: How does one persuade millions of people to believe particular stories about gods, or nations, or limited liability companies? Yet when it succeeds, it gives sapiens immense power, because it enables millions of strangers to cooperate and work toward common goals." Whether it was joining forces to fend off a predator or to sail across oceans, the early sapiens persuaded and flourished by telling stories.

We modern sapiens still persuade through storytelling. Stories succeed because they work in concert with the neural wiring of our audience. Facts and claims engage the prefrontal cortex, inviting debate and pushback. Stories circumvent that newer, slower, critical brain. They create an express lane to the brain stem, enabling you to persuade before their prefrontal cortex wakes to the conversation. It enables your Dorothy to skip the judgmental gatekeepers at the entrance to Oz and speak directly with the sympathetic Wizard himself.

In the last chapter, I shared a story about my experience with the Tully's restroom. I described the incongruously shabby restroom so that you might internalize my point that brand belongs to everyone, not just to marketing. I could have merely written, "brand is not just for marketing—it's for everyone." Even if you were open to that idea and found my statement reasonable, your prefrontal cortex would have activated and lobbed counter-arguments. It would have told Dorothy that the Wizard is busy so cannot see her.

Through story, I sought to bypass your prefrontal cortex so

that you might discover for yourself the truth my experience high-lighted. Your empathetic brain activated, and you might even have felt a kinship with me, as you too have felt the disappoint-ment of a neglected restroom or an unfulfilled promise. If my story worked, your prefrontal cortex remained outside the gates, outside the conversation. As a result, you grasped for yourself the underlying message that brand should be experienced through all customer interactions, including the less obvious ones.

There may even be a chemical basis for the persuasive power of story. Author, professor, and TED Talk celebrity Dr. Paul Zak has discovered that storytelling encourages oxytocin release which increases likelihood that listeners will trust the storyteller. You tell me a story, I relate to the tension that the character in your story faces, which releases oxytocin in my brain, which makes me like and trust you, the storyteller, more for having told me a story. You are now in a good place to persuade me.

Persuasion is the fundamental challenge of marketing. And storytelling is a powerful tool as you approach this challenge. When you tell stories, your customer is more likely to trust you, and to feel they can safely believe your promise. So, use story-telling to set these conditions so that you succeed in persuading your target customer.

REAL-WORLD BRAND STORY 4:
SLACK'S STORY OF ROCKS

TENSION

Gaming company Tiny Speck released a much-loved, browser-based game called Glitch in 2009. Players collaborated to collect rocks and other resources that they would then use to build homes and create personalized avatars. In 2012, Glitch was shut down after failing to make the leap from browsers to smartphones.

The remaining Tiny Speck team members realized they had unearthed an insight: the boredom and monotony many people experience during the workday resembles rock collecting. Developing Glitch had taught the team how to transform boring activities—like collecting rocks—into engaging and satisfying interactions.

RESOLUTION

Renamed as Slack, the company built a business team communication and file transfer platform that connects people in a useful and lighthearted way. The cheeky, cheerful voice of the system (borrowed from Glitch) lured work co-workers into exploring, laughing, and working online together. The now-ubiquitous software took off quickly, its customers are feverishly engaged, and its market cap in 2017 was over $5 billion.

SHOW, DON'T TELL

Effective storytelling invites the audience to participate. Persuasion is most potent when the audience reaches the conclusion themselves. They envision what comes next in the story, anticipating and co-creating the persuasion. They believe the conclusion because they helped generate it. The more participatory your story, the more the audience is moved by it.

The best storytelling invites that participation by leaving room for the audience to interpret. These stories show, rather than tell. Instead of telling the audience that "the girl is angry," the story shares that "her face is growing red and her breathing has become shallow." The audience constructs the conclusion "she is angry" themselves. They like their own conclusion more than one you could have given to them. They will embrace it, believe it, and remember it.

The highest form of show-don't-tell is imagery. Although sharp copywriting will be critical for building your brand, imagery enjoys an enormous advantage over words because images grab attention instantaneously. In the course of human development, language through words is wildly new to our brains, and therefore wildly slow. While words must go through the slow prefrontal cortex for processing, our brain stem processes images in a flash. The human brain processes images 60,000 times faster than it processes text. Even today, 93 percent of all human communication is visual. Storytelling through imagery is a brand's superhighway to persuasion. Here are a couple examples:

The Blendtec blender could have been just another blender in a sea of utilitarian kitchen gadgets. But its inventor, Tom Dickson, used imagery to capture attention and persuade. Blendtec's promise is "super-powerful blending," and Dickson showed, rather than told, that promise being delivered. Dressed as a mad scientist, Dickson filmed himself challenging his Blendtec to blend shockingly difficult objects, such as marbles and iPods. He did not need to say "super-powerful blending" because the viewer *sees* the power without words. The "Will It Blend" video so captured our attention that it went viral before "going viral" was a thing.

Etsy made use of storytelling through imagery when they ignited and mainstreamed a previously cottage industry. Etsy began in a Brooklyn, New York, apartment in 2005 as a community of makers selling their homemade goods. To bring makers and buyers together, Etsy created mini documentaries of the makers, telling the backstory of how they got into their craft. "Storytelling was definitely the word you heard the most," Jesse Hertzberg, an early leader at Etsy, shared with me. "Etsy was all about putting the makers front and center, and about sharing the makers' stories—either the stories behind the products or the stories behind why someone became a maker. And in elevating the makers, we would elevate the marketplace, and in elevating the marketplace, we would elevate the brand. All by storytelling." Hertzberg gave me an example: "If you go look at any of these old videos, you'll go visit some guy who makes guitars in the woods of Alabama and you'll get the whole story from the beginning of when he first picked up his first guitar, to why he started making them, to how he makes them. It's a very compelling story."

Use imagery to tell your story. Let photos, graphics, and drawings lead while words support. When you do use only words, let the words invite the audience into a story so that they picture an image of their own making. The audience then can participate in discovering and developing the message themselves. Since they co-created the message, they will like it, believe it, remember it, and share it.

EMPATHIZE

As you've done throughout brand building, continually orient yourself to the customer's perspective. Your customer—not your business—should be the hero of the story. Your business exists to help the hero, the customer, to resolve the tension and advance his story. It is not to show the world how great you are. It is to show the customer how his tension and resolution might look. When you do tell stories about your own business, let that be a device to show the audience themselves in your business story.

In Chapter 8, you placed yourself in your customer's shoes. You identified what it is like to be your customer so that your promise could resolve their problem. Keep channeling this customer empathy as you tell the story of your business.

Here is an example of how *not* to tell story—a missed opportunity for empathy. In late 2008, Seattle's adored Washington Mutual Bank (known locally as WaMu) failed and was subsumed in a shotgun wedding with Chase Bank. We Seattleites and the rest of the country were reeling in the early days of the Great

Recession, and WaMu going under was salt in that raw wound as we watched thousands laid off with the bank's failure. We did not particularly want the swaggering newcomer—we wanted our hometown pride, our venerated WaMu. Chase's greeting did little to change our minds and hearts. The company plastered this line on buses and billboards throughout the city: "Seattle: land of coffee, seafood, and now helpful banking."

Now helpful banking? We previously *did* have helpful banking. It was called WaMu. Who did this outsider think they were, coming in and telling us we needed them? How dare they? Understanding our response required empathy from Chase—stepping into our shoes and feeling the wound with us. Chase could have empathetically let us Seattlites be the hero and resolve the tension. Instead they positioned themselves as the hero and insulted us further.

Here's how another financial services brand successfully related to the Seattle market during the same era. PEMCO Insurance developed a bus ad campaign that featured humorous Pacific Northwest images that only insiders would relate to, sparking our sense of community, pride, and kinship. The caption for each ad was "We're a lot like you. A little different," featuring inside jokes like the "Supercharger Seahawks fan," "Green Lake Power Walker," "Recumbent Bike Commuter," "Oblivious Left Lane Occupant," and "Fremont 60s Holdout."

PEMCO did the opposite of what Chase did. Instead of presuming a superior place at the family table, they became one of us. They felt the zeitgeist and made the Seattleite the hero of the story. I still witness people grin when they encounter a PEMCO ad. Not surprisingly, PEMCO's revenue has flourished in recent years, growing 30 percent between 2003 and 2015.

As you bring your promise forward through storytelling, tap into your own empathy for your target customer. Tell your story in a way that allows your respect for the customer to shine. Before seeking to resonate with them, first seek to let them resonate with you. Before asking them to like you, make sure that you first like, understand, and empathize with them.

Stories give us meaning by helping us to parse all the stimuli we receive in our lives. As we address challenges, both existential and trivial, stories organize and elevate meaning. Journalist Emily Esfahani Smith wrote that "storytelling is how we make sense of [things]...We have a primal desire to impose order on disorder, to find the signal in the noise." Stories are our ancient and trusty tool for knowing what matters for surviving and thriving. They make sense of our lives, deeply satisfying both the storyteller and audience. For humans doing business, story connects. It persuades. It casts the customer as the hero moving through tension into resolution. It shows the customer your meaning, allowing them to be a part of that meaning, binding you together.

CONCLUSION

"The best time to plant a tree was 20 years ago. The second best time is now."

— CHINESE PROVERB

Brand is the largest driver of value creation. It is good for your customer. It is good for your business. In fact, it makes up the very fibers of the relationship between your customer and your business.

Creating your brand strategy is about declaring your stance and then aligning to it. Be the master of your business by defining your business's meaning proactively, so that you can position yourself, rather than be positioned. Doing this intentionally will fuel your business like a force multiplier.

As you build your brand strategy, remember to bring all of yourself to this exercise—your curiosity, honesty, logic, and inspiration. In brand, there is science, and there is also poetry, neurobiology, ancient storytelling, and transcendence. Let brand be this multidimensional, this profound, and it will faithfully guide you as only a North Star can.

Essayist Frederick Buechner said that a fulfilling vocation is located "where your deep gladness and the world's deep hunger meet." This is an apt description of brand. Brand is the thing you must bring the world, partly because your customers need it, and partly because you alone can give it. Brand makes for more value-creating businesses, more courageous leadership, more fulfilled employees and more delighted customers. Nurture your brand as you would nurture your most valuable asset.

And then it will be just that.

For Ironclad Method tools and materials that supplement this book, come visit www.ironcladbrandstrategy.com. *I also invite you to subscribe to our newsletter, in which each month we explore a provocative topic in brand and leadership.*

GLOSSARY

3 Ds: A framework introduced to me by Don Knauss while he was CEO of Clorox. The 3 Ds—desire, decide, and delight—are the three moments of the customer journey when you have a potent opportunity to influence customers on their journeys with your brand.

4 Ps: A framework to help you imbue all aspects of your customer experience with brand, from product to price to place to promotion.

addressable market: The full spectrum of customer opportunity for your business. While the target customer is the bullseye customer who brings disproportionate value, the addressable market represents any customer who might purchase from your business.

availability bias: A cognitive shortcut that privileges the data most readily *available* in a person's mind while making a decision, rather than the data that is the most relevant and useful for that decision.

behavioral economics: The study of how human psychology affects economic decision making.

brand: The crux of commerce itself—the value your business brings that gives it the right to exist. Defining and operationalizing your brand formulates the most direct route for your business to create, sustain, and scale value.

brand character: How your business shows up to deliver a promise to the customer. It is what your business would be like if it were a human being. When thoughtful and genuine, brand character forms another source of differentiation for your business.

brand character edges: A tool to give nuanced precision to your brand character. So that your brand has character but not caricature, you dimensional-ize the qualities of your brand's personality and tonality, making it real and, therefore, inviting for your customer to bond with it.

brand positioning: The place your business occupies in your customer's mind in the context of the customer's alternative options. When you define your brand positioning, you are identifying the doorway into the customer's world. This makes your offering compelling compared to the alternatives and easier for your customer to see you and choose you.

brand promise: The benefit you pledge to your customers and fulfill when your customers choose to engage with your offering. Your brand promise is also known as your value proposition. It forms the heart of your brand strategy.

brand strategy: The deliberate articulation of what your business will mean in the mind of the customer so that you can make decisions to render your meaning ever truer and more compelling.

category: The group of offerings adjacent to yours, which are often the frame of reference, or consideration set, for your customers as they are considering a purchase.

end reward: The ultimate benefit the customer enjoys because she experienced your brand promise. It's the "So what?" or the "Why should I care?" It is how the customer's life is better because of the promise you delivered.

force multiplier: A tool that amplifies the effectiveness of something else to produce more output. In physics, levers and fulcrums are force multipliers. In military science, air power and air superiority are force multipliers. In business, a cherished brand is a force multiplier.

frame of reference: The alternative your customer would be using if your offering did not exist. It is the true competitive set—the things your brand competes against for your customer's heart and mind. This might be a direct competitor, a substitute, or a workaround behavior.

Hawthorne effect: The phenomenon in which research findings are skewed as an inherent result of their being studied.

high-to-low-altitude interviewing: An approach to customer interviewing that starts with the big picture of your customer's life and ends at the level of your business's offering.

HOPE framework: A framework for evaluating creative that leverages intuition, analytical thinking, and detail projection. The steps in the HOPE framework are: Heart, On-Point, and Execution.

mental file folder: The way your customers organize your business in their minds. Providing an accessible mental file folder for your customers helps them to remember and like your offering, making your positioning efforts more useful for you and less work for your customers.

metacognition: Awareness of your own thinking processes and the capability of controlling those processes by organizing, monitoring, and adapting.

need state: The setting and context when the problem your offering solves is particularly relevant to the customer.

optimally distinct: Jonah Berger's phrase for when a proposition is the right blend of familiar and different. When it is similar enough to something customers already know, they trust it. When it is different enough from those things they already know, it stirs the customers' curiosity and desire to be different themselves. Berger and many others have taken inspiration from Marilynn Brewer, who wrote extensively about the theory of optimal distinctiveness throughout her career as a social psychologist.

P&L: A profit and loss statement is both figuratively and literally an encapsulation of a business's financial health. The P&L owner of a business is the person for whom the buck stops—the person responsible for creating business growth and value.

positioning: See brand positioning.

pricing power: Your ability to charge customers meaningfully more than the offering costs you to provide. Customers' willingness to pay gives you pricing power, and you establish willingness to pay by providing huge value through your offering.

reasons to believe: Your offering's attributes that enable you to deliver on your brand promise (also called proof points, pillars, and support).

scalability: The capacity for a business to grow and accommodate its own growth.

substitutes: An offering or behavior not in a business's category but that the business nonetheless competes with.

target customer: The person your business will optimize for throughout decision making.

workaround behaviors: The behaviors your customers engage in to work around a problem your offering would solve, rather than addressing that problem directly.

PHOTO CREDITS

Thank you to these creators for giving your permission to reprint your work.

CHAPTER 13: ACTIVATE CREATIVE

Figure 13.3 Miele Vacuum billboard by Jon Kubik, Art Director, and Renee Hwang, Copywriter. Courtesy of Jon Kubik.

CHAPTER 17: TELL STORIES

Figure 17.2 Chase bus ad photo. Courtesy of Carla Saulter

Figure 17.3 PEMCO bus ad. Courtesy of Kyle Parker-Robinson

NOTES

PART 1: THE WHAT AND WHY OF BRAND

CHAPTER 1: WHAT THE HECK IS BRAND?

Once, I heard Malcolm Gladwell share on Debbie Millman's Design Matters podcast that the word *brand* reminded him of the word *Africa*: Malcolm Gladwell, on "Malcolm Gladwell & Joyce Gladwell," *Design Matters with Debbie Millman*, February 7, 2013, https://soundcloud.com/designmatters/design-matters-with-debbie-42.

"A brand is your distinct meaning...": interview with Tim Calkins, August 17, 2017.

Dollar Shave Club produced its launch promo video on a shoestring ($4,500), posted it on YouTube, and created a business so valuable...: Lindsay Blakely, "How a $4,500 YouTube Video Turned into a $1 Billion Company," Inc., July 2017, https://www.inc.com/

magazine/201707/lindsay-blakely/how-i-did-it-michael-dubin-dollar-shave-club.html.

"A brand is a promise of performance...": interview with Don Knauss, January 8, 2018.

"If you are in commerce, you need a brand strategy": Knauss, 2018.

For example, the *availability bias* is a cognitive shortcut that leads people to make decisions based on the information most easily accessible...: "Swimming with Sharks," *Choiceology with Dan Heath* (podcast), April 9, 2018, https://itunes.apple.com/us/podcast/choiceology-with-dan-heath/id1337886873?mt=2.

Another cognitive shortcut we use as a filter is the *confirmation bias*, in which we seek and interpret new data that confirms our existing beliefs and theories: Shahram Heshmat, "What Is Confirmation Bias?" *Psychology Today*, April 23, 2015, https://www.psychologytoday.com/us/blog/science-choice/201504/what-is-confirmation-bias.

"Brand strategy is a tool...": interview with Tarang Amin, October 26, 2017.

"Our brand story reflects who we are at our core...": interview with Carolyn Feinstein, September 17, 2017.

Brand strategy "is how we tell employees and customers what we stand for...": interview with Sven Desmet, November 28, 2017.

Clorox Bleach still wins 65% market share of the bleach category:

The Clorox Company, "The Clorox Company Updates Investment Community on 2020 Strategy," *PR Newswire*, October 5, 2017, https://www.prnewswire.com/news-releases/the-clorox-company-updates-investment-community-on-2020-strategy-300531894.html.

CHAPTER 2: CREATE VALUE NOW

"The biggest driver of value creation is brand": interview with Tarang Amin, October 26, 2017.

A recent study found that 84 percent of business value…: "Annual Study of Intangible Asset Market Value from Ocean Tomo, LLC," March 4, 2015, http://www.oceantomo.com/2015/03/04/2015-intangible-asset-market-value-study/.

Another study valued S&P 500 companies' intangible assets…: Jonathan Knowles, "How Much of Enterprise Value Is Intangible?" LinkedIn, March 8, 2017, https://www.linkedin.com/pulse/how-much-enterprise-value-intangible-jonathan-knowles/.

Nestle's acquisition of Blue Bottle Coffee in 2017 reveals brand's sizable influence…: James Rufus Koren, "What Exactly a Giant Like Nestle Gets When It Buys an Upstart Like Blue Bottle," *Los Angeles Times*, September 16, 2017, http://www.latimes.com/business/la-fi-nestle-blue-bottle-20170916-story.html.

"The single most important decision in evaluating a business…": Warren Buffett, in Andrew Frye and Dakin Campbell, "Buffett Says Pricing Power More Important Than Good Management," Bloomberg, February 18, 2011, https://www.bloomberg.com/news/articles/2011-02-18/ buffett-says-pricing-power-more-important-than-good-management.

In a recent study, strong brands on average commanded a 13 percent price premium...: Nigel Hollis, "Command a Price Premium for Profitable Growth," Millward Brown, https://www.millwardbrown. com/Insights/Point-of-View/Command_Price_Premium/default. aspx.

"A unique and meaningful brand promise that you truly deliver on...": interview with Matt Oppenheimer, October 17, 2017.

"Go to an Apple store and then go to a Microsoft store...": interview with Jason Stoffer, November 14, 2017.

The UK's Aviva produced a £9 million aspirational TV ad in 2008...: Lucy Cockcroft, "Bruce Willis and Elle Macpherson Star in £9 million Norwich Union Advert," *The Telegraph*, December 22, 2008, https://www.telegraph.co.uk/news/celebritynews/3899637/ Bruce-Willis-and-Elle-Macpherson-star-in-9-million-Norwich-Union-advert.html.

"How do I understand what this thing is in the crazy world around me...": interview with Jeremy Korst, November 20, 2017.

This leads to more value for me, the customer, and more value for the dry shampoo category...: "Global Dry Shampoo Market to Witness 6.1% CAGR During 2017–2023," April 2017, https://www. psmarketresearch.com/press-release/global-dry-shampoo-market. According to a market intelligence firm, Transparency Market

Research, the global dry shampoo market is estimated to reach US$4.1 billion by 2022 with a CAGR growth rate of 6.1 percent from 2017 to 2023.

The iPhone has contributed to Apple becoming the most valuable brand on earth...: Sara Salinas, "Apple Hangs onto Its Historic $1 Trillion Market Cap," CNBC, August 2, 2018, https://www.cnbc.com/2018/08/02/apple-hits-1-trillion-in-market-value.html.

For a brand position to be compelling to customers, it should be similar enough to something a customer already knows...: Jonah Berger, *Invisible Influence: The Hidden Forces that Shape Behavior* (New York: Simon & Schuster, 2017). Also: Marilynn Brewer wrote extensively about the theory of optimal distinctiveness throughout her career as a social psychologist. Marilynn B. Brewer, "Optimal Distinctiveness Theory," *Encyclopedia of Social Psychology*, Roy F. Baumeister and Kathleen D. Vohs (Eds.), http://dx.doi.org/10.4135/9781412956253.n381.

"If you want to have a deep relationship with your customers...": interview with Rob Grady, October 27, 2017.

"A great brand is one where consumers are willing to pay...": interview with Clayton Lewis, November 13, 2017.

"Brand can be a way of defending what you have...": interview with Denise Lee Yohn, October 18, 2017.

"If you don't understand what you stand for, your customers will decide...": interview with Ethan Lowry, May 15, 2018.

"Brand strategy is how you safeguard and grow the value of your business...": interview with Pamela Dressler, September 1, 2017.

"In a crowded category, true differentiation is mandatory...": interview with Carolyn Feinstein, September 17, 2017.

"A brand is who you are...": Dressler, 2017.

CHAPTER 3: SCALE FOR ENDURING VALUE

"A lot of people do it backwards...": interview with Kirby Winfield, October 18, 2017.

"Brand is a really pragmatic tool...": interview with Don Knauss, January 8, 2018.

"It is possible or even likely that a $5 million budget behind a brilliant idea will be superior...": David Aaker, *Aaker on Branding: 20 Principles That Drive Success* (New York: Morgan James Publishing, 2014), 22.

"Brand is the principles you live by for your people...": interview with Kristen Hamilton, October 27, 2017.

"When you know your brand, you know your mission...": interview with Ethan Lowry, May 15, 2018.

"Unless you stand for something clearly articulated...": interview with Dan Levitan, December 1, 2017.

"We are trying to grow and scale our company...": interview with Andrew Sherrard, September 17, 2017.

At Patagonia in 2016, teammates were brainstorming ideas for a marketing splash for Black Friday...: "Culturati Summit 2018," *The Rework Podcast*, https://rework.fm/culturati-summit-2018/.

"Often founders have a brand idea in their heads...": interview with Tarang Amin, October 26, 2017.

"With Angie's, there was a brand strategy...": interview with Suzanne Senglemann, October 26, 2017.

"Where brand really gets powerful for me is as an internal prioritization tool...": interview with Jeremy Korst, November 20, 2017.

"Brand is all-encompassing for all of our stakeholders...": interview with Jonathan Zabusky, November 27, 2017.

"I don't think anything differentiated...": Levitan, 2017.

CHAPTER 4: KNOW YOUR PURPOSE

"Every business will have a brand...": interview with Dan Levitan, December 1, 2017.

"Brand is in this sense like your culture...": interview with Andrew Sherrard, September 17, 2017.

"Without a brand strategy, you're haphazard...": interview with Pamela Dressler, September 1, 2017.

"You could hope that people get what you want...": interview with Kirby Winfield, October 18, 2017.

"A lot of times entrepreneurs will wait too long...": interview with Erika Shaffer, October 25, 2017.

"People want to work on something big and important...": Rich Barton, in Nat Levy, "Expedia and Zillow Co-founder Rich Barton on Building Great Teams: Have a Purpose and No Scumbags," *GeekWire*, November 5, 2017, https://www.geekwire.com/2017/expedia-zillow-co-founder-rich-bartons-secrets-building-great-team-no-scumbags-purpose/.

"Great brands stand for something. ...": interview with Carolyn Feinstein, September 17, 2017.

"Having a higher-order purpose...": interview with Robert Neer, October 30, 2017.

A 2015 Gallup poll found...: Amy Adkins, "Majority of US Employees Not Engaged Despite Gains in 2014," Gallup, January 28, 2015, www.gallup.com/poll/181289/majority-employees-not-engaged-despite-gains-2014.aspx.

UC Berkeley Professor Morten Hansen surveyed...: Morten Hansen, *Great at Work: How Top Performers Work Less and Achieve More* (New York: Simon & Schuster, 2018).

Woven into your culture, "brand can even become a criterion...": interview with Jonathan Zabusky, November 27, 2017.

"If you like the brand...": interview with Sven Desmet, November 28, 2017.

"Ultimately, what a customer is buying is your promise...": interview with Denny Post, December 29, 2017.

"Strategy in general is about the choices...": interview with Tarang Amin, October 26, 2017.

"Focus is scary...": Clayton Christensen, in Clayton Christensen and Michael Raynor, *The Innovator's Solution: Creating and Sustaining Successful Growth* (Boston: Harvard Business Review Press, 2013), 87.

CHAPTER 5: DECONSTRUCTING BRAND

Brand positioning is the place your business occupies in your customer's mind...: Geoffrey Moore, *Crossing the Chasm: Marketing and Selling High-Tech Products to Mainstream Customers* (New York: HarperBusiness, 2006).

Said another way, "positioning is not what you do to a product...": Al Ries and Jack Trout, *Positioning: The Battle for Your Mind* (New York: McGraw-Hill, 1981).

"All the leadership decisions you make...": interview with Carter Cast, December 20, 2017.

"Equating brand strategy with advertising is like saying...": interview with Kirby Winfield, October 18, 2017.

"Most businesses want more media attention...": interview with Erika Shaffer, October 25, 2017.

"I used to think that brand was either a consumer packaged goods brand...": interview with Kristen Hamilton, October 27, 2017.

"Brand is not just a logo...": Marc Benioff, in Marc Benioff and Carlye Adler, *Behind the Cloud: How* Salesforce.com *Went from Idea to Billion-Dollar Company—And Revolutionized an Industry* (Hoboken, NJ: Wiley-Blackwell, 2009).

"I can't market my way out of a bad product...": interview with Aaron Woodman, October 30, 2017.

CHAPTER 6: THE NINE CRITERIA FOR AN IRONCLAD BRAND STRATEGY

"In the long run, the measure of our success will be how much value...": Stewart Butterfield, on "Stewart Butterfield, Co-Founder and CEO of Slack," *Office Hours with Spencer Rascoff*, August 8, 2018, https://www.podcastone.com/episode/ Stewart-Butterfield-Co-founder-and-CEO-of-Slack.

"Pick battles big enough to matter, small enough to win": Jonathan Kozol, *On Being a Teacher* (New York: Continuum Intl Pub Group, 1981).

Be the only player in a space by thinking vertically rather than horizontally...: Peter Thiel with Blake Masters, *Zero to One: Notes on Startups, or How to Build the Future* (New York: Currency, 2014).

How we can think of competitive advantage through a Greek parable about foxes and hedgehogs: James C. Collins, *Good to Great: Why Some Companies Make the Leap...And Others Don't.* (UK: William Collins, 2001).

"Make sure you are ten times better...": interview with Jason Stoffer, November 14, 2017.

The research findings of social psychologist Harry Reis...: Chip Heath and Dan Heath, *The Power of Moments: Why Certain Experiences Have Extraordinary Impact* (New York: Simon & Schuster, 2017).

Harvey-Davidson provides huge meaning to its customers: I learned a great deal about several companies from the following insightful book. Dev Patnaik, *Wired to Care: How Companies Prosper When They Create Widespread Empathy* (San Mateo, CA: Jump Associates LLC, 2009).

And consider OXO Good Grips: Patnaik, *Wired to Care*, 2009.

This concept of "optimally distinct...": Jonah Berger, *Invisible Influence: The Hidden Forces that Shape Behavior* (New York: Simon & Schuster, 2017). Marilynn Brewer wrote extensively about the theory of optimal distinctiveness throughout her career as a social psychologist. Marilynn B. Brewer, "Optimal Distinctiveness Theory,"

Encyclopedia of Social Psychology, Roy F. Baumeister and Kathleen D. Vohs (Eds.), http://dx.doi.org/10.4135/9781412956253.n381.

Gillian Fournier, "Mere Exposure Effect," *Psych Central*, 2016, https://psychcentral.com/encyclopedia/mere-exposure-effect/.

"Often when I work with startups and organizations, they say...": interview with Jonah Berger, January 9, 2018.

"Because Fage was very different...": Berger, 2018.

"During brand strategy creation...": interview with Clayton Lewis, November 13, 2017.

CEO Tony Hsieh says Zappos "proudly...": "What's Your Competitive Advantage? Zappos.com Edition," *The Startup of You*, May 10, 2012, http://www.thestartupofyou.com/2012/05/whats-your-competitive-advantage-zappos-com-edition/.

A University of Michigan study asked participants to estimate the battery life of two GPS devices...: Y. Charles Zhang and Norbert Schwarz, "How and Why 1 Year Differs from 365 Days: A Conversational Logic Analysis of Inferences from the Granularity of Quantitative Expressions," *Journal of Consumer Research* 39, iss. 2 (August 1, 2012): 248–59, https://doi.org/10.1086/662612.

"Brands are two things: promise and performance": Scott Galloway, *The Four: The Hidden DNA of Amazon, Apple, Facebook and Google* (New York: Random House, 2017).

"The better and more consistently you deliver on your unique promise...": interview with Andrew Sherrard, September 17, 2017.

"A delivery service that promises to meticulously care...": Marc Benioff, in Marc Benioff and Carlye Adler, *Behind the Cloud: How Salesforce.com Went from Idea to Billion-Dollar Company—And Revolutionized an Industry* (Hoboken, NJ: Wiley-Blackwell, 2009).

"Courage is in even shorter supply than genius," Thiel, in Thiel and Masters, 2014.

"Delight is the greatest form of virality...": Andy Rachleff, "The Unique Economics of Wealthfront," *Medium*, May 17, 2018, https://medium.com/work-ing-at-wealthfront/the-unique-economics-of-wealthfront-9761fab8da7a.

PART 2: THE HOW OF BRAND
CHAPTER 7: ORIENT

Roughly 10 percent of customers account for roughly 50 percent of profit: Eddie Yoon, "Tap into Your Super-Consumers," *Harvard Business Review*, November 25, 2009, https://hbr.org/2009/11/surprising-insights-from-super.

According to The NPD Group's Checkout Tracking Service, 95 percent of Americans shopped at Walmart in 2016: Krystina Gustafs, "Nearly Every American Spent Money at Wal-Mart Last Year," CNBC, April 12, 2017, https://www.cnbc.com/2017/04/12/nearly-every-american-spent-money-at-wal-mart-last-year.html.

Renowned social work researcher Brené Brown uses an inductive
research method called "grounded theory"...: Brené Brown, https://
brenebrown.com/the-research/. Brown credits Barney Glaser and
Anselm Strauss for developing the grounded theory methodology.

"Power leads individuals to anchor too heavily on their own
vantage point...": Adam D. Galinsky, Joe C. Magee, M. Ena Inesi,
and Deborah H. Gruenfeld, "Power and Perspectives Not Taken,"
Psychological Science 17 (December 2006): 1068–74.

"Each week I fly on JetBlue flights and talk to customers...": David
Neeleman, https://www.jetblue.com/about/ourcompany/flightlog/
index.html. Though Neeleman's blog post is no longer available,
reports of Neeleman flying commercial regularly for this purpose
do exist, for example, David Kohn, "Jet Blue: Flying Higher?"
CBS News, October 16, 2002, https://www.cbsnews.com/news/
jet-blue-flying-higher/.

Proctor & Gamble's Gillette razor team conducted ethnographies...:
Vijay Govindarajan, "P&G Innovates on Razor-Thin Margins,"
Harvard Business Review, April 16, 2012, https://hbr.org/2012/04/
how-pg-innovates-on-razor-thin.

Howard Schultz, CEO of Starbucks, hangs out in Starbucks cafés
almost every day: "Live Episode! Starbucks: Howard Schultz," *How
I Built This with Guy Raz*, September 28, 2017, https://www.npr.org/
templates/transcript/transcript.php?storyId=551874532.

"Forget being a comedian...": Chris Rock, in Frank Rich, "Chris Rock

Talks to Frank Rich About Ferguson and What 'Racial Progress' Really Means," *Vulture*, November 30, 2014, http://www.vulture.com/2014/11/chris-rock-frank-rich-in-conversation.html.

There is something about holding physical pen and paper that helps one listen with presence: Allison Eck, "For More Effective Studying, Take Notes with Pen and Paper," Nova Next, June 3, 2014, http://www.pbs.org/wgbh/nova/next/body/taking-notes-by-hand-could-improve-memory-wt/.

"Nature hath given men one tongue but two ears...": Epictetus, http://www.gutenberg.org/files/871/old/epict11.txt.

"The ability to move others hinges less on problem solving...": Daniel H. Pink, *To Sell Is Human: The Surprising Truth About Moving Others* (New York: Riverhead Books, 2013).

The Five Whys: Eric Ries, *The Lean Startup* (New York: Currency, 2014).

CHAPTER 9: EXAMINE

"What can you do really well that is also really hard?" Scott Galloway, *The Four: The Hidden DNA of Amazon, Apple, Facebook and Google* (New York: Random House, 2017).

"I attributed this to the fact that if the software could increase sales productivity...": Marc Benioff, in Marc Benioff and Carlye Adler, *Behind the Cloud: How* Salesforce.com *Went from Idea to Billion-Dollar Company—And Revolutionized an Industry* (Hoboken, NJ: Wiley-Blackwell, 2009).

CHAPTER 10: LADDER

The concept of brand benefit ladders is explored in the classic marketing textbook by Philip Kotler and Keven Lane Keller, *Marketing Management*, 15th edition (New York: Pearson, 2015).

"You're looking for space that emotionally gives permission...": interview with Aaron Woodman, October 30, 2017.

"The ladder helps you keep answering the question 'why?'...": interview with Robert Neer, October 30, 2017.

CHAPTER 11: CHARACTER

"Brand is what you want to be...": interview with Jonathan Zabusky, November 27, 2017.

We can learn about stories from the work of Swiss psychologist Carl Jung: Carl Jung, *Structure & Dynamics of the Psyche, Collected Works of C. G. Jung,* Volume 1 (Princeton, NJ: Princeton University Press, 1970).

On character archetypes in brand building: Margaret Mark and Carol S. Pearson, *The Hero and the Outlaw: Building Extraordinary Brands Through the Power of Archetypes* (New York: McGraw-Hill Education, 2001).

"Each archetype contains a wide emotional range...": interview with Catherine Carr, October 10, 2017.

"As soon as we learned about the twelve archetypes...": interview with Pamela Dressler, September 1, 2017.

CHAPTER 12: STAGE

You may be familiar with the notion of the sales funnel...:
"AIDA," Oxford Reference, last accessed November
2018, http://www.oxfordreference.com/view/10.1093/oi/
authority.20110803095432783.

"Brand is your chief way to fight for space...": interview with Paul
Tiffany, August 7, 2017.

"In the modern world, what do you think is the single most scarce
resource?...": interview with Andrew Sherrard, September 17, 2017.

"Having a strong brand just makes everything *easier*...": interview with
Leigh McMillan, October 18, 2017.

"Grasp the subject...": "Cato the Elder," Wikiquotes, last updated
October 26, 2016, https://en.wikiquote.org/wiki/Cato_the_Elder.

CHAPTER 13: ACTIVATE CREATIVE

"Brand is strategy...": interview with Denny Post, December 29, 2017.

And consider the Road Runner cartoons: Chuck Jones, Chuck
Amuck: The Life and Times of an Animated Cartoonist, 2nd edition
(New York: Farrar, Straus and Giroux, 1999).

And like Shakespeare and the adored Road Runner, Trader Joe's is
an unequivocal success...: Ashley Lutz, "How Trader Joes Sells Twice
as Much as Whole Foods," *Business Insider*, October 7, 2014, https://
www.businessinsider.com/trader-joes-sales-strategy-2014-10.

There are whole books on naming brands—my favorite is...: Alexandra Watkins, *Hello, My Name is Awesome: How to Create Brand Names That Stick* (San Francisco, CA: Berrett-Koehler Publishers, Inc., 2014).

CHAPTER 14: ZOOM OUT

"Leaders can get stuck...": interview with David Aaker, October 11, 2017.

"What's more...": Aaker, 2017.

The 4 Ps is a framework for marketing decision-making first proposed: E. J. McCarthy, *Basic Marketing: A Managerial Approach* (Homewood, IL: Irwin, 1960); S. A. Keelson, "The Evolution of the Marketing Concepts: Theoretically Different Roads Leading to Practically the Same Destination!" *Global Conference on Business and Finance Proceedings* 7, no. 1, 2012, ISSN 1941-9589.

Smirnoff Vodka successfully fought a price competitor, Wolfschmidt...: Joe Salvatori and Suzi Marigold, "Case Study Analysis of Smirnoff," *Bartleby Writing*, November 17, 2008, https://www.bartleby.com/essay/Case-Study-Analysis-of-Smirnoff-FKE9V2HKD6TA.

"Three moments of truth...": interview with Don Knauss, January 8, 2018.

"During the recession, on the Glad brand...": Knauss, 2018.

"With all 3 Ds...": Knauss, 2018.

PART 3: AMPLIFY YOUR BRAND

CHAPTER 15: EXTEND YOUR STRENGTHS

"Real strategy—in companies and in our lives—is created...": Clayton Christensen, in Clayton Christensen, James Allworth, and Karen Dillon, *How Will You Measure Your Life* (New York: Harper Business, 2012).

"Brand is not somebody's job...": interview with Denny Post, December 29, 2017.

"I used to think, oh, I'm not a marketing person...": interview with Kristen Hamilton, October 27, 2017.

"Once your rules of the road are in place...": interview with Matt Crum, October 12, 2017.

"Your brand strategy only means as much as...": interview with Tarang Amin, October 26, 2017.

Suggestions for building brand into the nuts and bolts of your business...: interview with Carter Cast, December 20, 2017.

"There are a handful of capabilities that really matter...": Cast, 2017.

"We have doubled down...": interview with Matt Oppenheimer, October 17, 2017.

"What you decide *not* to do is probably more important...": Tom Peters, in Thomas J. Peters and Robert H. Waterman, Jr., *In Search for Excellence*, HarperBusiness Essentials edition (New York: HarperCollins Publishers Inc., 2004).

"For us, the store is our brand...": Jon Basalone, on "The Store Is Our Brand," *Inside Trader Joe's*, episode 4, May 1, 2018, https://www. traderjoes.com/digin/post/inside-tjs-podcast.

"I came to believe that business...": interview with David Aaker, October 11, 2017.

Time Management Quadrants: Stephen Covey, *7 Habits of Highly Effective People* (New York: Free Press, 1989).

"I told the whole world...": interview with Tarang Amin, October 26, 2017.

"You can't neglect your brand...": Amin, 2017.

CHAPTER 16: DEEPEN LOVE

"Brand cannot come just from marketing...": interview with Sangita Woerner, October 27, 2017.

"It can't just be a surface thing...": interview with Pamela Dressler, September 1, 2017.

"We're taking time to perfect our espresso...": Howard Schultz, *Onward: How Starbucks Fought for Its Life without Losing Its Soul* (New York: Rodale Books, 2011), https://www.starbucks.com/onward/ excerpt.

"Your product can be absolutely great...": interview with Halle Hutchison, October 18, 2017.

Phil Knight described a scene of victory...: Phil Knight, *Shoe Dog* (New York: Simon & Schuster, 2016).

"The Park Means a Lot to Me...": "In Walt's Own Words: Plussing Disneyland," Walt Disney Family Museum Blog, July 17, 2014, https://www.waltdisney.org/blog/walts-own-words-plussing-disneyland.

CHAPTER 17: TELL STORIES

"In good companies, the story and the strategy...": Ben Horowitz, *The Hard Thing about Hard Things: Building a Business When There Are No Easy Answers* (New York: HarperBusiness, 2014).

"The deeper neurological truth...": Daniel Coyle, *The Culture Code: The Secrets of Highly Successful Groups* (New York: Random House, 2017).

"No animal other than Sapiens engages in trade...": Yuval Noah Harari, *Sapiens: A Brief History of Humankind* (New York: Harper, 2015).

A 1989 *Newsweek* article first reported a story...: David Mikkleson, "Nordstrom Tire Return," *Snopes*, April 30, 2011, https://www.snopes.com/fact-check/return-to-spender/.

"Much of history...": Harari, *Sapiens*, 2015.

There may even be a chemical basis for the persuasive power of story: Paul Zak, *The Moral Molecule: The Source of Love and Prosperity* (New York: Dutton, 2012).

"We said, 'Let's build a car for us here'...": interview with Sven Desmet, November 28, 2017.

On the human brain processing images: Rito Pant, "Visual Marketing: A Picture's Woth 60,000 Words," Business 2 Community, January 16, 2015, https://www.business2community.com/digital-marketing/visual-marketing-pictures-worth-60000-words-01126256.

The Blendtec blender could have been just another blender...: "'Will It Blend?' Company Embarks on New Influencer Marketing Program," Natalya Minkovsky, Content Marketing Institute, June 28, 2015, https://contentmarketinginstitute.com/2015/06/blendtec-influencer-marketing/.

"Storytelling was definitely the word...": interview with Jesse Hertzberg, August 2, 2017.

"It struck me as curious that although this [type of] software was so troublesome...": Marc Benioff, in Marc Benioff and Carlye Adler, *Behind the Cloud: How* Salesforce.com *Went from Idea to Billion-Dollar Company—And Revolutionized an Industry* (Hoboken, NJ: Wiley-Blackwell, 2009); Scott Carey, "A Brief History of Salesforce.com," May 31, 2018, https://www.computerworld.com.au/article/641778/brief-history-salesforce-com/.

"Salesforce Revenue 2006-2018 | CRM". www.macrotrends.net. Retrieved October 30, 2018, https://www.macrotrends.net/stocks/charts/CRM/salesforce/revenue.

Slack is a business team collaboration platform...: Drake Baer, "Inside the Video Game Roots of Slack, Everyone's Favorite Workplace Messaging App," *Business Insider*, March 17, 2016, https://www. businessinsider.com/inside-the-video-game-roots-of-slack-2016-3; Ryan Browne, "Slack Is Now Worth Over $5 Billion After $250 Million Cash Injection Led by Japan's SoftBank." CNBC, September 18, 2017, https://www.cnbc.com/2017/09/18/slack-worth-over-5-billion-after-250-million-investment-led-by-softbank.html.

"Storytelling is how we make sense...": Emily Esfahani Smith, *The Power of Meaning: Finding Fulfillment in a World Obsessed with Happiness* (New York: Broadway Books, 2017).

CONCLUSION

"Where your deep gladness...": "Vocation," Frederick Buechner Center blog, July 18, 2017, http://www.frederickbuechner.com/quote-of-the-day/2017/7/18/vocation (originally published in *Wishful Thinking: A Seeker's ABC*, 1973).

ACKNOWLEDGMENTS

Writing this book for the past three years has been both harder and more rewarding than I ever could have imagined. Without my family, colleagues, clients, friends, and editors, I would not have begun, and I would not have finished. To all of you: thank you.

To the editors and writing professionals who recognized the power of these ideas and this method, helped me to find my voice, and structure what was so clear in my head to something that is now clear on paper. In particular, Kristin Thiel, Genevieve Margherio, and the publishing team at Scribe Media. I'm indebted to each of you.

My sincere thanks to the business leaders, thought leaders, clients, professors, and authors who allowed me to interview them for this book. I thought I understood brand pretty well before I began interviewing you, but you showed me this topic is much larger and more worthy. In particular, I would like to thank David Aaker, Tarang Amin, Jonah Berger, Tim Calkins,

Carter Cast, Matt Crum, Sven Desmet, Heidi Dorosin, Pamela Dressler, Carolyn Feinstein, Rob Grady, Andrew Grauer, Kristen Hamilton, Jesse Hertzberg, Halle Hutcheson, Don Knauss, Jeremy Korst, Denise Lee Yohn, Dan Levitan, Clayton Lewis, Ethan Lowry, Leigh McMillan, Stewart Meyer, Debbie Milliman, Robert Neer, Jennifer Nuckles, Matt Oppenheimer, Denny Post, Grant Ries, Elyse Rowe, Suzanne Senglemann, Erika Shaffer, Andrew Sherrard, Matt Shobe, Jonathon Sposato, Jason Stoffer, Paul Tiffany, Kirby Winfield, Sangita Woerner, Aaron Woodman, Alison Worthington, Jonathon Zabusky, and Kyra Zeroll.

I have the best clients in the world. This book is a fan letter to each of you. Thank you for inviting me to build your brands with you, and for letting me guide you. This has allowed me to create and refine the Ironclad Method I use today and detail in this book. I feel privileged to have worked with you.

To my mentors and coaches: thank you for encouraging me to think big and listen to my instincts. Robbie Baxter Kellman, Jenny Blake, Lenora Edwards, Mark Levy, and Jac McNeil. Thank you to my team at Ironclad Brand Strategy who make our work ever better and more joyful: Genevieve Margherio, Deborah Lahti, Kerr deRainier, and Lisa Hauswirth.

Thank you to my friends, Nika Kabiri, Molly Kertzer, Jeremy Korst, and Leora Zabusky, for graciously reading my manuscript and giving me the feedback I needed to make this book sing. And to my friend Catherine Carr, who hugely expanded my understanding of brand through the character archetypes. You all made this infinitely better.

My late friend and client, Matt Bencke, encouraged me to write this book, insisted I rename my business (and book) "Ironclad," and gave me the push I needed to put pen to paper. Matt died before this book took shape, but his bravery and joie de vivre were with me the whole time. I'm grateful to have known you, my friend.

To my family: I am so lucky to be yours. To Steve Clarke, Kathy Clarke, Robb Clarke, and Chris and Jodie Clarke, who would have thought I was awesome no matter what I did. To my children, Luke and Kate Pedersen, who have heard enough about brand that they could enlighten many a business person. And to my husband, Alex, who when it's mattered most, has said, "Go for it."

ABOUT THE AUTHOR

LINDSAY PEDERSEN is the founder of Ironclad Brand Strategy, a Seattle, WA-based consulting firm that works with leaders to build value-creating brands using the Ironclad Method™. Ironclad Brand Strategy has advised companies from burgeoning, venture-backed startups to national corporations, including Zulily, Starbucks, T-Mobile, Coinstar, and IMDb.

Before starting Ironclad Brand Strategy, Lindsay worked in Brand Management at Clorox on businesses ranging from Hidden Valley Ranch to Armor All to Brita to Clorox Bleach. Lindsay credits her P&L ownership at Clorox with fostering a deep appreciation for the leader's charge: increasing the business's value. Whether a startup or a Fortune 500 corporation, leaders are charged with growing the value of their business. Lindsay believes that an intentional and precise brand forms the most durable source of that value creation.

As a brand strategist, executive coach, and public speaker,

Lindsay has presented to thousands of people in corporations, incubators, and universities. Lindsay taught the popular digital "Create a Brand Strategy" course through LinkedIn Learning.

Lindsay has a BA from Georgetown University and an MBA from UC Berkeley's Haas School of Business. Keep in touch with Lindsay through her website: www.ironcladbrandstrategy.com

INDEX

Page numbers with *italics* denote figures and photos.

categories
    familiar, connecting with, 47-48, 50-51, 103-6, 130-31, 168, 215
    new, expanding with, 48-51
    optimally distinct, 50-51, 103-6
    and selection of archetypes, 205-7
    see also frame of reference
characterizing brand (step 5), 191-209
    overview, 81-82, 191-93, 208-9
    archetypes for, 193-98, 204-5, 205-7
    for building trust, 207-9
    for differentiation, 82, 97, 98, 192, 205-7
    with edges, 97-98, 201-2, 203
    with personality and tonality, 198-202, 204, 205, 237, 238, 242, *278*
    for style guide and checklist, 202-3, 278-79
    on what, why, and how levels, 203-5
Chase Bank, 317-*18*
checklist for brand applications, 202-3
Chobani yogurt, 104
Christenson, Clayton, 74-75, 275
clarity of focus, 36-38, 45-47, 58-61, 109-10, 231
Clorox products, 38-39, 102, 103, 132-33, 145, 224-26, 278, 283-84
cognition, human
    and associations, old and new, 47-51, 103-6, 130-31, 215
    and shortcut filters, 33-34
Collins, Jim, 99-100
Commit mindset of customer journey, 213, *214,* 217-18, 220-21, 227
commodities vs. differentiation, 42, 164
Common Denominators, *159-160, 161-63,* 168
communication
    of brand to users in company, 156-58, 202-3, 208-9, 277-80, *278-279* (*see also* activating creative
      (step 7))
    of business's meaning, 35-38, 63-64, 79-80, 85-86, 321
    for promotion, 252-54, *256,* 258, 259, 260-61, 263-64
    with timing for customer stages, 217, 219, 222-29, *223,* 225-26
    with web platforms, 32
company-wide ownership of brand, 62-63, 64, 85-86, 202-3, 276, 280, 289, 293-96
competition
    for customers, 53-55, 84-85, 96-101, 127-34, 164, 176 (*see also* Uncommon Denominators)
    strengths of, *159-160, 161-63,* 197, *269, 272*
competitive advantages, 29, 108, 158-65, 167-68, 176, 268, *272*
components of brand, *see* brand strategy, components of
confirmation bias, 34
Considering to Purchase stage, 212, *214,* 216-17, *223,* 227
    see also decide as second "moment of truth"
consistency, need for, 207-9
consumer businesses (B2C), 91
copywriters, help for, 203, 219, 222, 278
courage in leadership, 74-76, 114-15
Covey, Stephen, 287-88
Coyle, Daniel, 306
creating value, *see* value creation, immediate; value creation, longterm

Y

Z